KAMIKAZE

President of the Institute of Nautical Archaeology, James Delgado is a marine archaeologist who has led and investigated shipwreck expeditions around the world. The author or editor of thirty books, when not travelling the world for the INA in a quest for lost ships, James Delgado lives on the waterfront in Vancouver.

JAMES DELGADO

Kamikaze

History's Greatest Naval Disaster

VINTAGE BOOKS
London

Published by Vintage 2010

2 4 6 8 10 9 7 5 3 1

Copyright © James Delgado 2009

James Delgado has asserted his right under the Copyright, Designs
and Patents Act 1988 to be identified as the author of this work

First published by Douglas & McIntyre,
201-2323 Quebec Street, Vancouver, BC V5t 4S7 Canada

First published in Great Britain in 2009 by
The Bodley Head

Vintage
Random House, 20 Vauxhall Bridge Road,
London SW1V 2SA

www.vintage-books.co.uk

Addresses for companies within The Random House Group Limited
can be found at: www.randomhouse.co.uk/offices.htm

The Random House Group Limited Reg. No. 954009

A CIP catalogue record for this book
is available from the British Library

ISBN 9780099532583

The Random House Group Limited supports The Forest
Stewardship Council (FSC), the leading international forest
certification organisation. All our titles that are printed on
Greenpeace approved FSC certified paper carry the FSC logo.
Our paper procurement policy can be found at:
www.rbooks.co.uk/environment

Printed and bound in Great Britain by
CPI Bookmarque, Croydon CR0 4TD

Contents

*Timeline of Chinese, Japanese
And Korean Dynasties and Periods*

CHINA

T'ang 618–907
Five Dynasties and Ten Kingdoms 902–979
Liao 916–1125
Jin 1115–1234
Xia 1038–1227
Northern Song 960–1127
Southern Song 1127–1279
Yüan 1279–1368
Ming 1368–1644
Qing 1644–1911
Republic of China 1911–1949
Japanese Occupation 1937–1945
People's Republic of China 1949–

JAPAN

Kofun 300–538
Asuka 538–710
Nara 710–784
Heian 794–1185
Kamakura 1192–1333
Muromachi 1338–1573
Azuchi-Momoyama 1573–1603
Edo (Tokugawa) 1603–1867
Meiji 1868–1912
Taisho 1912–1926
Showa 1926–1989
Heisei 1989–

KOREA

Three Kingdoms Period 313–688
United Silla Dynasty 688–935
Kōryo Dynasty 935–1392
Choson (Yı) Dynasty 1392–1910
Japanese Occupation 1910–1945
North and South Korea 1945–

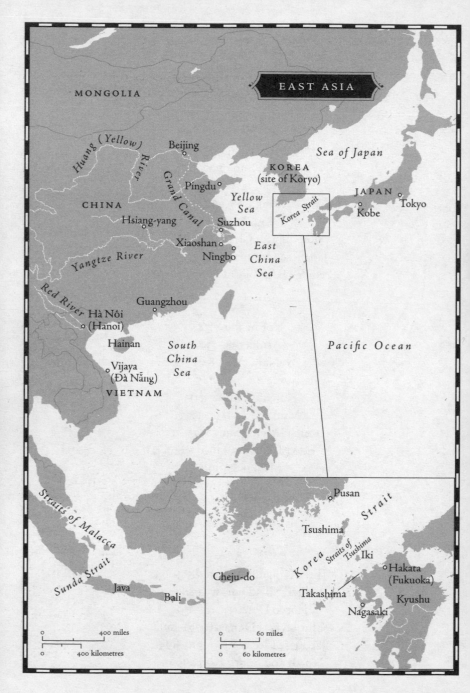

MONGOLIA

Huang (Yellow) River

Beijing

Grand Canal

Pingdu

KOREA
(site of Koryo)

Sea of Japan

JAPAN

Tokyo

Kobe

CHINA

Hsiang-yang

Suzhou

Yellow
Sea

Korea Strait

Xiaoshan

Yangtze River

Ningbo

East
China
Sea

Red River

Guangzhou

Hà Nôi
(Hanoi)

Hainan

South
China
Sea

Pacific Ocean

Vijaya
(Đà Nẵng)

VIETNAM

Straits of Malacca

Sunda Strait

Java

Bali

EAST ASIA

Pusan

Tsushima

Korea Strait

Straits of
Tsushima

Iki

Hakata
(Fukuoka)

Cheju-do

Takashima

Kyushu

Nagasaki

0   400 miles

0   400 kilometres

0   60 miles

0   60 kilometres

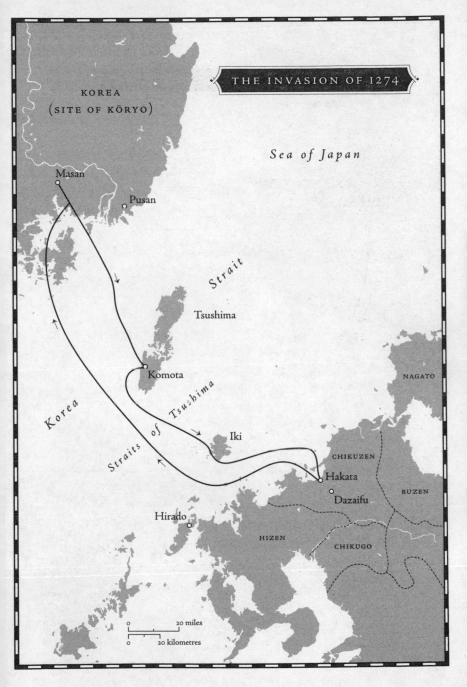

THE INVASION OF 1274

KOREA
(SITE OF KŌRYO)

Sea of Japan

Masan

Pusan

Strait

Tsushima

Komota

Korea

Straits of Tsushima

Iki

NAGATO

CHIKUZEN

Hakata
Dazaifu

BUZEN

Hirado

HIZEN

CHIKUGO

0   20 miles
0   20 kilometres

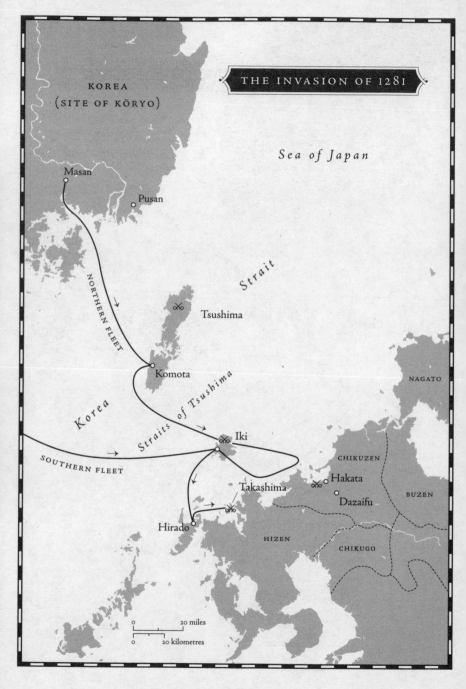

THE INVASION OF 1281

Sea of Japan

KOREA
(SITE OF KŌRYO)

Masan

Pusan

Strait

Tsushima

NORTHERN FLEET

Komota

NAGATO

Korea

Straits of Tsushima

SOUTHERN FLEET

Iki

CHIKUZEN

Takashima

Hakata

Dazaifu

BUZEN

Hirado

HIZEN

CHIKUGO

0   20 miles
0   20 kilometres

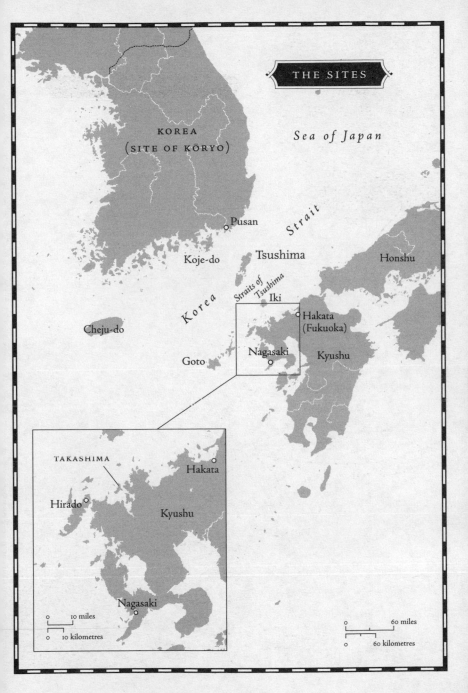

THE SITES

KOREA
(SITE OF KŌRYO)

Sea of Japan

Pusan

Koje-do

Tsushima

Honshu

Korea Strait

Straits of Tsushima

Iki

Cheju-do

Goto

Nagasaki

Hakata
(Fukuoka)

Kyushu

TAKASHIMA

Hakata

Hirado

Kyushu

Nagasaki

○ 10 miles

○ 10 kilometres

○ 60 miles

○ 60 kilometres

Introduction

AS I STAND on the concrete dock looking out over the murky, green-gray waters of Imari Bay, the modern landscape of Japan dominates my view. A concrete seawall curves away to the west, motorized fishing boats putter by, massive cargo ships bob on the horizon and the blue sky overhead is streaked with the contrails of passenger jets. I dress slowly, stepping into the wetsuit, strapping on the heavy tank, pulling on thick gloves, then slipping the face mask over my head. Wearing dive fins that make my feet seem like those of a duck, I waddle up to the edge of the dock, top heavy and awkward. I grasp my mask in one hand and the bottom of my tank in the other—to keep the mask from pulling off and the tank from coming up and hitting me in the head—and drop several feet in a giant stride. Plunging into the water, I go deep into the murk before surfacing in a froth of bubbles. I signal that I am okay and ready to start the dive.

I drop back down with my three companions and descend to find a heavy nylon line that disappears into the darkness. Tracing it with my fingertips, I continue to drop, following the bank of the submerged beach into a thick pea-soup cloud of algae and silt that hovers over the muddy seabed. The line ends at the corner of a heavy iron grid that stretches away into the gloom. Here and there, divers work with handheld dredges, carefully vacuuming up the mud to expose the remains of the past. These are ancient waters, and the mud holds their secrets.

Moving slowly, hovering silently over the grid, I look down and see scattered timbers, some smashed, others seemingly charred. There are thick masses of rust I recognize as concretion, the result of years of corrosion working on iron and steel lying at the bottom of the sea. Then my heart skips a beat, for below me, Mitsu Ogawa is pointing excitedly at a dark shape on one of the grids. A diver's light flicks across it and I see that it is a Mongol helmet, lying upright on the seabed. A startled fish swims out from beneath the rusted brim. Another rusted mass is a thick bundle of crossbow bolts, and everywhere, scattered in the mud, are small red rectangles that look like the scales of a huge fish. I realize that these are pieces from a suit of leather armor, and it dawns on me that this is where the team recovered the broken bones of a man the other day.

What may be lying beneath me is the grave of a drowned Mongol soldier, lying face down, surrounded by his arms and armor, buried in the thick mud for seven centuries. Then Mitsu swims up to an overturned bowl, and with the thumb of his glove gently wipes it free of silt to reveal writing. He writes me a message on his diver's slate, a translation: "Wang, Commander of 100." Is this the rice bowl of the drowned soldier? Was he not a Mongol, but Chinese? There are many questions that fill my head, but as I hover, I think of Wang, whoever he was. Did he ever think that he would end up here, sealed in cold, thick mud for centuries? Did his family ever wonder what actually happened to him, when he never came back from battle those centuries ago? Did his father and mother, or his wife and children, stand by the shore and look out, wondering if one day he might just come home? Floating in the water above what may well be Commander Wang's grave, I am reminded of how history is, at its most basic, the story of individuals caught up in it all.

MOST HISTORIES portray the story of humanity's progression through the millennia as the movement of peoples, empires, trade goods and warfare across the vast landscape of the world's continents. That is fair enough, for you cannot picture the past without thinking of the pyramids rising above the desert sands of Egypt, Roman chariots thundering around the Circus Maximus, Mongol hordes sweeping across the plains on horseback, castles rising above the feudal fields of Medieval Europe or soldiers huddled in trenches cut through those same fields, centuries later, as shells scream overhead and biplanes duel in the skies.

You also cannot picture the past without thinking of the ships that built these civilizations, defended them in war and expanded them through exploration, conquest and trade. George F. Bass, the father of underwater archaeology, sees the history of the world from a mariner's perspective. He reminds us that river craft built of cedar and papyrus carried the blocks of stone that built Egypt down the Nile, that the rowed warships of Greece defeated the Persians at Salamis in 480 BC, and that huge ships carrying grain from Egypt kept Rome's population fed. Bass is correct. You cannot conceive of a history without Viking longboats, Chinese junks, Mississippi River steamers, clipper ships, ironclads, battleships or submarines. Landlocked history would not include the voyages of Vasco da Gama, Columbus or Magellan, nor would it include the Atlantic slave trade or the immigrant steamers of the North Atlantic. The world would have been a different place without the battles of the Spanish Armada, Trafalgar and Midway, or the invasion of Normandy on D-Day. Likewise, as this book reveals, the history of the world would be very different if Khubilai Khan's invasions of Japan in 1274 and 1281 had been successful.

Khubilai is famous, and has been ever since the fifteenth century, when Marco Polo published memoirs of his travels and time in the court of the Khan. Samuel Taylor Coleridge's poem, penned in 1797, added to the Great Khan's fame and helped fuel the Western world's fascination with this distant potentate, all powerful, mysterious, someone to be admired as well as feared:

> In Xanadu did Kubla Khan
> A stately pleasure-dome decree:
> Where Alph, the sacred river, ran
> Through caverns measureless to man
> Down to a sunless sea.

Just as famous as this Mongol leader is the name of the storm that many Japanese believe stopped his invasion of their islands: kamikaze. That "divine wind"—as it is translated—inspires even more awe and fear than the name of Khubilai Khan.

But for all the fame of these iconic words, very few Westerners have any understanding of how the forces of nature and history brought Khubilai Khan and kamikaze together off the shores of Japan's southern coast in the late thirteenth century. Even today in China and Japan, where Khubilai once reigned and where the battles and shipwrecks that marked his failed invasions played out, most do not have more than a cursory understanding of what really happened. Dimmed by the centuries, the details seemingly lost forever, the saga of Khubilai's fleet has become a legend, a mythical tale of how two massive armadas, the greatest the world had ever seen, met their doom through the intervention of Japan's ancestral gods, or a typhoon, depending on your beliefs. The legend, oft repeated in countless history books, speaks of gigantic ships, numbering into the thousands, crewed by indomitable Mongol warriors, and of casualties on a massive scale, with more than 100,000 lives lost in the final invasion attempt of 1281.

Determining the truth about these events is in the hands of historians and archaeologists who sift through the surviving archives and the broken, discarded or once-lost detritus of the past in search of answers. This task has fallen, for the most part, to scholars in Japan and China, although a handful of Western scholars, writing in English, have worked to bring the recent scholarship to a Western world eager to learn more about Asia. The work of Morris Rossabi, John Man, Thomas Conlan, Stephen Turnbull and others has resulted in a better understanding of Khubilai and of the Mongol invasion of Japan in the thirteenth century. There is much more to be learned, though, and it comes to us still dripping after centuries of immersion at the bottom of the sea.

For the past two decades, Japanese archaeologists seeking the traces of Khubilai Khan's lost fleets—and by extension, from the submerged battlefields of 1274 and 1281, a better understanding of just what happened to them, and why—have searched the waters of Kyushu, Japan, for those ships. Their success, particularly in recent years with the excavation of an underwater site off Takashima Island in Imari Bay, south of the great port city of Fukuoka, has revealed the remains of at least one Mongol vessel. However, their work, published in exquisite scholarly detail in Japanese, has scarcely reached the English-speaking world. It deserves to, as does appreciation of what these scholars have done, digging into the thick mud of Imari Bay to recover more than the traces of the past, but to challenge a legend and rewrite history.

It is now possible to access the history of Commander Wang—as well as the history of Khubilai Khan, the man who sent him off to fight and die—because of the work of archaeologists in the depths. They practice a unique form of science, stripping away the mud and mapping with care the well-preserved but shattered remains of ships that are surrounded by scattered provisions, weapons and more intimate finds like the bones and shredded leather armor of a drowned soldier. These scientists then bring their finds to the surface to begin years of treatment in laboratories to ensure the relics and remains do not disintegrate after their long burial. The work in the labs will also unlock more of the secrets the artifacts can tell. That work has been going on for years now, and will continue for many more. It has already revealed a few surprises, including the anatomy of Khubilai's ships and some of the technological marvels and deadly weapons they carried. It also suggests, and compellingly so, what happened to the Great Khan's fleets and why his two bids to conquer Japan failed.

The story of Khubilai Khan's navy, as it unfolds in the pages that follow, is not an isolated saga just of those two battles, or of just those ships and men. Rather, it is one drama in the centuries-long progression of Japan's complex interrelationship with China and its close neighbor Korea. It is also part of the millennia-old saga of China's ties to the sea. Born of the great rivers that dominate its history, economy and culture, China also has a maritime history of deep-sea trade, exploration and war that long predates the famous voyages of Zheng He in 1421 and beyond. This book sets out to trace how the ships of Khubilai Khan fit into the progression of China's seafaring endeavors of the preceding dynasties, and how the events of 1274 and 1281 relate to the longer story of Japan's links to mainland Asia.

This story is not, and should not be, confined to the distant past. The other consequences of the invasions, in particular the rise of the myth of the kamikaze and its ultimate and tragic role in the Second World War, also bear scrutiny. Political use and misuse of history is a common theme that cuts across cultures and the ages. Archaeology, too, can be appropriated for various agendas, because it has the power of physically connecting modern generations to the "reality" of the past.

The art and the science of archaeology underwater, and the ongoing forensic analysis of the lost fleet's remains, are also shared, as are the stories of dedicated scholars such as Torao Mozai, Kenzo Hayashida and Randall Sasaki. Without their groundbreaking work, the full tale of the Mongol invasions and the destruction of Khubilai Khan's navy could not be told. Why, you might ask, is that so? Is it just because they have added details, or challenged ancient stories? It is because these scholars have brought the stories to life. Swim through the remains of a lost ship or over a recently unearthed naval battlefield like the one described in this book, and you are confronted by the confluence of the past with the present.

Tour the ancient shrines of Japan, walk through timeless hills and beaches shrouded with fog or rain, and your mind can wander back through the centuries. Listen intently to the words of the priests, watch the worshippers praying or spend hours of intense conversation with an octogenarian veteran of a global conflict in which he pledged to die in a suicide attack in the name of a legendary storm, and you can feel how the past and present are separated by precious little. The events of yesterday continue through time, like the ripples from a stone tossed into a pond.

JAMES P. DELGADO
Steveston, British Columbia
April 2007

A Divine Wind

Soaring into the sky of the southern seas,
it is our glorious mission to die as the shields of His Majesty.
Cherry blossoms glisten as they open and fall.

FLYING PETTY OFFICER FIRST CLASS ISAO MATSUO,
701st Air Group, October 28, 1944

KAMIKAZE IS a word that elicits instant recognition throughout the world. It is a famous word, a notorious word to some—a reminder of acts of desperation in the final months of a fierce war. It is a name that history will never forget, even long after those who witnessed those acts have passed. Images spring to mind of grainy black-and-white footage of tiny aircraft falling from the sky toward the decks of ships. Flack fills the sky, climbing toward the planes, some of which blossom into flames, break apart, or splash into the sea. Other planes hit, exploding into fireballs that sweep over decks or through superstructures as men scatter or vanish in a rain of burning fuel and torn metal. Many of America's children who grew up in the decades after the Second World War relived the war on the televisions and movie screens of their childhood, wondering what led to such brave, at times fanatical, heart-rending, frightening acts.

At just twenty-one years of age, Ensign Teruo Yamaguchi knew, with absolute certainty, that he was about to die. He had volunteered for a suicide mission, one of many acts of extreme sacrifice that he and others of his generation were performing to save their nation from defeat. As he prepared for his last mission, Teruo wrote a final letter to his father to explain his decision:

> The Japanese way of life is indeed beautiful, and I am proud of it, as I am of Japanese history and mythology which reflect the purity of our ancestors and their belief in the past—whether or not those beliefs are true. That way of life is the product of all the best things which our ancestors have handed down to us. And the living embodiment of all the wonderful things out of our past is the Imperial Family which, too, is the crystallization of the splendor and beauty of Japan and its people. It is an honor to give my life in defense of these beautiful and lofty things.

The history that Teruo Yamaguchi wrote of dated back seven hundred years, to an almost mythical period, to the only other time when the Japanese had been at the brink of defeat at the hands of an invader on their shores.

In 1281, Khubilai Khan, the Mongol emperor of a recently conquered China, sent a massive armada of warships and troops to subjugate Japan. Seven years earlier, another invading force had been turned back, and so this new fleet was even larger—according to legend, as many as 4,400 ships and more than 100,000 troops set out to do the Khan's bidding. Two fleets, one from Mongol-controlled Kōryo (today's Korea) and the other from China, sailed with orders to rendezvous off the coast of Japan and then hit the Japanese with their combined might. With them sailed shock-trained troops, veterans of the Khan's wars, skilled in the tactics that had carried the swift Mongol conquerors from the steppes of Asia across the Middle East and as far as the gates of Europe.

The juggernaut of Mongol expansion might have overwhelmed Japan, but the Khan's plans began to unravel soon after the two fleets set sail. Separated by distance and by rivalry, the two fleets never met. The ships and troops from Kōryo landed at Hakata Bay, today's port city of Fukuoka. There they were met with fierce resistance from Japanese defenders who pushed the invaders off the beaches, back onto their ships and finally back out to sea. The bulk of Khubilai Khan's forces, however, were still coming. They landed south of Hakata, anchoring off the small island of Takashima in Imari Bay.

There, in a running two-week battle, the Khan's soldiers and Japanese samurai fought their away across the island's rugged countryside. Some samurai took to the sea, piloting small boats into the massive fleet. There, on crowded decks, warriors hacked and slashed at each other. Others filled their boats with dry straw and set them ablaze, driving them into the Khan's fleet. It was a time of incredible bravery as the samurai pitted themselves, David-like, against the Mongolian Goliath.

But despite the valour and sacrifice of the Japanese defenders, the battle was slowly, inevitably, being lost to the superior numbers and brute force of the Mongols and their vessels. Japan was doomed, and so the emperor appealed, in devout prayer, to his ancestors, the gods, who had created Japan and ruled it for centuries with his highness as their representative on Earth. The gods listened and answered those prayers.

According to the legend, a divine wind rose that whipped the ocean into a frenzy and sent massive waves into the Mongol fleet. Ships dragged their anchors, crashed into each other and broke apart. Waves swept men from decks, and the weight of their armor pulled them beneath the water while others were pummeled by debris. When the wind and waves had subsided, the Mongol fleet was gone, and over 100,000 men had drowned.

The exultant Japanese dragged exhausted Mongol survivors out of the water and killed them on the shoreline. Troops abandoned by their comrades and left stranded on the beach, demoralized and cut off from escape, were rounded up and executed by the victorious samurai. The gods had saved Japan. Khubilai Khan abandoned his dreams of conquest, and Japan's shores were not threatened again by an invader for the next seven centuries. Japan, it was now clear, was a divinely protected land, ruled by a living god who had called on heavenly intervention in the form of a "kamikaze," a divine wind.

The story of the Mongol invasion and the kamikaze became one of Japan's best-known stories, a tale that helped build the nation's pride and belief in its divine status in the decades of industrialization, modernization and militarization that preceded the Second World War. That belief was not challenged in the period of conquest and expansion that brought the Japanese empire new lands overseas, with victories on land and at sea against neighboring China and Russia in the late nineteenth and early twentieth centuries. And this belief was not challenged while Japan renewed its advances through China in the 1930s, or during the heady days of victory that accompanied the country's rapid expansion across the Pacific following victorious attacks at Pearl Harbor, Singapore, Manila and in other locations throughout Southeast Asia.

The flush of victory did not subside until mid-1942, with Japan's disastrous losses at Midway. Defeats in other battles, the losses of critical island bases, the steady war of attrition with American submarines that sank ships filled with supplies and troops, and the combat losses of ships, airplanes and men—especially skilled men, veterans of combat and the art of war—pushed Japan against the wall. Defeat was imminent as the battle moved closer and closer to the shores of Japan itself.

Desperate times called for desperate measures. Those measures were a call to *tokkō*, or suicide attacks. The concept, inspired by earlier tales of samurai sacrifice and wartime exploits of *taiatari* (body-crashing), was born in October 1944 at Mabalacat, a Japanese airfield on Luzon. There, Admiral Takijiro Ōnishi, the newly appointed commander of all Japanese naval air forces in the beleaguered Philippines, met with his commanders and broached the idea of "special attack units." Formed with squadrons of Zero fighters laden with 250-kilogram bombs, these suicide attackers would crash into enemy carriers.

The hope was that these acts, driven by loyalty, duty and love of country, would turn the tide of the war and save Japan. Perhaps the blood sacrifice of Japan's warriors would lead the gods to send another divine wind and smash the enemy. Ōnishi named the new corps the "*Shinpū* Special Attack Unit." *Shinpū* is ancient Japanese for a "god wind," otherwise translated as kamikaze. With this formal designation, the admiral was essentially naming the *tokkō* unit as descendants of the storm that had destroyed Khubilai Khan's fleet in 1281.

Others throughout the ranks carried the point forward. Naval Ensign Toshiharu Konada, who had volunteered for submarine service, joined the *kaiten* ("shake heaven") corps, the undersea version of the aerial kamikaze, in 1944. Standing at attention with his fellow *tokkō* warriors, Konada listened intently as his commanding officer told the assembled men, "You know the story of the kamikaze. This time, the kamikaze will not blow. Instead, the kamikaze will be you." With those sentiments—as Teruo Yamaguchi wrote, "whether or not those beliefs are true"—young men like Yamaguchi went into battle to "shake heaven" through their sacrifice. Their actions remain one of the indelible memories of a long and terrible war.

The tales of the kamikaze are many, replete with stories of bravery, horror and carnage. For the Americans and their allies, who pushed closer to the inevitable victory promised by President Franklin D. Roosevelt with his call to Congress to declare war against Japan following the devastating surprise attack on Pearl Harbor, the arrival of the kamikaze in October 1944 was a strange and terrible thing. With emotions that ranged from rage and bewilderment to pity and begrudging respect, the men on the carriers, destroyers, tankers and troop ships that faced the kamikaze pilots underwent a trial by fire.

By the end of the war, *tokkō* tactics had claimed a terrible toll. Japan sacrificed over 1,228 planes and their crews to sink thirty-four Allied ships and damage 288 others. They killed and maimed thousands of Allied sailors. The human torpedoes of the *kaiten* corps had claimed another two ships and damaged several others at a cost of over one hundred young Japanese submariners. The scope of the horror of the kamikaze attacks, in a war already distinguished by savagery and excess, is still felt six decades after the war's end. The kamikaze remain the subject of admiration in some quarters, condemnation in others and intense curiosity among generations born after the war.

Neal Nunnelly, a sailor on the carrier USS *Anzio*, watched as kamikaze aircraft sank the carrier USS *Bismarck Sea* and mauled the carrier USS *Saratoga* off Iwo Jima in February 1945. He probably speaks for many of his generation when he said, "We didn't know or care that the word kamikaze meant a divine wind and came from ancient Japanese history... In my time the word only told us we were dealing with a bunch of psychopaths." There is more to the story—far more. But Nunnelly is right about one thing. The events of the ancient past sometimes do reach into the future, at times with terrible consequences.

ONE

Hakozaki

To the waters of Tsukushi
We advance through flood and wave;
We with bodies stout and vigorous,
If we die, and find a grave,
Dying, we become the guardian
Gods of home, for which we fell,
To Hakozaki's God I swore it,
And he knows the pure heart well

GHENKŌ-NO-UTA (*Song of the Mongol Invasion*),
translated by Nakaba Yamada (1916)

THE MORNING sun's rays strike the paving stones at the entrance to Hakozaki Shrine. The roar of traffic on the way into downtown Fukuoka fills the air as rush hour begins in this crowded urban center of 1.4 million. A bustling, modern port city, Fukuoka is Japan's eighth largest metropolis. Just a few steps from the road, stone barriers mark the transition from busy road to pedestrian path and from the twenty-first century to the past. Hakozaki is a venerable place. The curved stone gate, or *torii*, halfway up the entrance path is said to be four hundred years old. The gate also marks the original shoreline from the days when this was the medieval port of Hakata, Kyushu's ocean gateway to mainland Asia, which lies just over 120 miles across the strait that separates Japan from the Korean Peninsula. The strait is an

14

ancient highway for trade and conquest, and Hakozaki itself is a reminder of war.

According to old texts, Hakozaki was founded over a thousand years ago, in 923, and is the site where the legendary Empress Jingu returned to Japan after sailing with her husband Emperor Chuai to Korea to conquer the Empire of Silla. The conquest was successful, but Chuai fell in battle. His triumphant widow, pregnant with his child, returned to Japan and landed at Hakata. There she gave birth to a son who would later ascend the throne as the Emperor Oujin. The fifteenth emperor of Japan, in death he was enshrined as the Shintō *kami* or ancestral God of War, Commerce, Travel and Safe Childbirth, Hachiman. To mark this significant event, Jingu placed her *hako* (placenta) in a box and buried it here at this *zaki* (a place where the land meets the water).

Thus, the placenta that nourished an emperor and a god also gave birth to a shrine that today is one of Japan's most sacred places. Along with the Usa Shrine in Ohita and the Iwashimizu Shrine in Kyoto, Hakozaki is one of three great Hachiman shrines dedicated to prayers for the national security of Japan. I have come here in search of truth, or, to be more precise, to inquire into the faith that underlies the story of Japan's divine salvation through the kamikaze.

From the entrance path, with its rough paving stones surrounded on both sides by tall trees, the graceful and ornate wooden tower gate of the shrine rises before me. Its sixteenth-century curved roof reaches toward the sky. The first stop is a stone anchor said to have come from a wrecked Mongol ship, placed here as an ironic trophy because Hakozaki was destroyed in the first Mongol invasion of 1274. Rebuilt the following year, it is now a monument to those invasions and their dramatic end said to be brought on by the ancestral gods of Japan, notably Hachiman, who answered the prayers of the emperor and sent the divine wind, the kamikaze, to destroy the invaders. Inside the shrine is a placard with the kanji script of the emperor's prayer, "May the Enemy Prostrate Themselves in Defeat."

Off to the side, a platform filled with strips of colored paper and wooden tablets known as *ema*, or painted votive offerings, catches my attention. A small stand next to it sells more *ema*, incense and souvenirs. A handful of worshipers and visitors cluster around the stand, some of them affixing their offerings to the platform while others walk to the open front of the shrine. There, before a small fence, they stop, clap three times and bow deeply. Above them flutter brightly decorated banners emblazoned with the chrysanthemum emblem of the emperor of Japan. I stand silently and think of the story of how another, more distant emperor prayed before another shrine seven centuries earlier, then I turn and head through a small door to be greeted by the chief priest of the Hakozaki Shrine.

"The precincts of this shrine resonate with a profound sense of both history and the divine," the priest tells me. Sitting in his office, he talks about the *Ghenkō* (the Japanese term for the Mongol invasions) and explains how his Shintō faith guides him today as it protected Japan in those long-ago days. The priest also mentions his hero, Admiral Heihachiro Togo, whose victory over a Russian fleet in these waters a century ago electrified the world and set Japan on a path to military greatness—and eventual defeat. Revered as Japan's version of Admiral Nelson and one of the world's greatest strategists, Togo is important to the priest for another reason. He was a devout worshipper at this shrine, and the priest shows me a prayer, personally inscribed by the admiral, which he keeps in his office close to a bronze bust of Togo. When he was a young man, the priest adds, many people, including the nation's influential and powerful leaders, came to worship at Hakozaki. But all that has changed. Visitors still come, but they are the very old, the curious or schoolchildren on a tour. Not all of them pray.

As I leave, nodding to the attendants sweeping the path and the monks who walk quietly around the grounds, I stop in the small garden close to the shrine's gate. There, beautifully displayed on a base of stone, is a rectangular cut piece of granite. The small placard close to it explains, in Japanese and English, that this is the stone anchor that was found in Hakata Bay, just off the city's shores. It is designated as a "tangible cultural asset of Fukuoka Prefecture," an assertion that this relic is from the invasions, a reminder to the credulous that, despite the passage of centuries and the blurring of time, the events of 1274 and 1281 were real. A stone marker stands close by, its kanji characters cut crisply into the bright stone. There is no English placard to explain what it is, but my interpreter is happy to translate. These are the words to a famous Japanese song.

It is a song about the legend of the *Ghenkō*, and how Hachiman and the other ancestral gods extended their divine protection over Japan to end the Mongol Invasions. The song was brought to the West via a small book written by Nakaba Yamada and published in London in 1916. In it, Yamada tells the story of the Mongol invasions. In the introduction, Yamada explains that he has included the song "Ghenkō-no-Uta," or "Song of the Mongol Invasion," otherwise known as *"Shihyaku-Yoshu,"* or "Four Hundred States."

"The song is so renowned and never-fading in Japan that generation after generation sing it in praise of the country's honour," Yamada writes. "It is so instructive that even one who has no other knowledge of the national event is instinctively made aware by it of his ancestors' exploit and of *Tenyū*, the Grace of Heaven. The Japanese find in the song something of a very impressive character—a conception of pride, justice, and self-sacrifice."

I ask my aged interpreter if he knows the song, and he answers by standing at attention, his reedy voice cracking as he belts out the verses. Amazingly, a group of adolescent schoolgirls, on a tour of the shrine, also know the words. They stand in their blue blazers, skirts and white knee socks and join in with the interpreter at a higher pitch, singing:

> *From four hundred states and more*
> *Hundreds of the foe appear,*
> *Looms a peril to the nation*
> *In the fourth the Koan year.*

What should be our fear? Among us
Kamakura men will go,
Martial discipline and justice
To the world with shout we'll show.

From the Tartar shores barbarians,
What are they, The Mongol Band,
Fellows insolent and haughty,
'Neath their heaven we will not stand.
Onward now our arms were practiced
For our native country's sake,
For our country now a trial
Of these Nippon swords we'll make,

To the waters of Tsukushi
We advance through flood and wave;
We with bodies stout and vigorous,
If we die, and find a grave,
Dying, we become the guardian
Gods of home, for which we fell,
To Hakozaki's God I swore it,
And he knows the pure heart well.

Heaven grew angry, and the ocean's
Billows were in tempest tossed;
They who came to work us evil,
Thousands of the Mongol host,
Sank and perished in the sea-weed,
Of that horde survived but three,
Swift the sky was clear, and moon beams
Shone upon the Ghenkai Sea.

Seven centuries after the "insolent and haughty" Mongols appeared on these shores, the legend of how the gods of Japan saved the nation by wrecking the invading ships in a tempest lives on in song. It also lives in other modern forms. Booksellers in Fukuoka sell two small, bound volumes of manga—Japan's famous illustrated novels—that depict the story of the Mongol invasions, fierce battles and climactic storms that swept the invaders from the seas. Old stories die hard, especially in a city built over the remains of what is said to be that ancient battlefield.

MONUMENTS, MEMORIALS AND THE *Ghenkō Borui*

The remains of that battlefield are not to be found in Fukuoka's Higashi Park, a half hour's drive across town from the shrine. Described in the guidebooks as the site of the battlefield from the first invasion, it is now a beautifully landscaped oasis of paths, shrubs, trees and lawn. There are no traces of the battle, but there are two magnificent monuments. The first, atop a low hill, is an impressive bronze statue of Kameyama, Japan's emperor at the time of the invasions and the author of the appeal to the gods for Japan's salvation. Rising fifteen feet from his tall stone pedestal, the emperor stands proud, facing the sea. A bronze plaque on the pedestal states: "The Enemy Surrendered, and Was Subdued."

This second monument, completed in 1904 like Kameyama's, is a massive, thirty-foot bronze statue of the priest Nichiren. Nichiren advocated a strong, independent nation and warned of foreign influences, railed against a weak country, and warned that the Mongols would invade Japan to punish it for its weakness. Mocked and threatened for his beliefs, he was the prophet to whom no one listened. When the Mongol invasions came, Nichiren was at last heard. Centuries later, Meiji-era rulers venerated him as a holy man whose forecasts were matched by his belief in Japan's unique, if not divine, nature. Banners bearing the priest's tenets surround the Nichiren monument, waving in the breeze.

On the monument's pedestal, large cast bronze plaques depict scenes from Nichiren's life and lurid images of the Mongol invasion, including one of a vanquished samurai with a Mongol's foot pressed to his body, and another of a woman screaming as soldiers hold her and a Mongol cuts a hole in her palm to lash her hands together. These are powerful images in more ways than one. On every panel depicting Nichiren, the hands of the devout have over the years worn down the sharp edges of the bronze, blurring his features and polishing him so that he brightly and yet obscurely dominates each scene in an almost otherworldly way. The worn bronze is a reminder of a once fervent faith in a monument now empty except for a few foreign tourists and a solitary worshiper—a bent, old man who silently prays in one corner.

So where are the relics of the thirteenth century? Those traces exist in seven scattered locations throughout town. They are sections of a stone and clay wall excavated by Japanese archaeologists between 1913–1927, in 1957, 1968, 1970, 1979, and in 1998–1999. The *Ghenkō Borui*, or "Mongol invasion wall," was built in 1276 after the first attack, to try and thwart a second. It appears in an illustrated scene painted around 1293 showing samurai waiting to repel the invaders, some on horseback, others seated cross-legged atop it. Once on the shoreline, much of the wall now lies in the urban core, surrounded by buildings. At one place, Ikinomatsubara, the wall lies along the beach, looking much as it did centuries ago thanks to a reconstruction by the Fukuoka Board of Education.

Standing on that beach, I feel like I am at last getting closer to the actual invasion. But where is the archaeological evidence of the battle? Where are the fallen soldiers' graves, the lost ships, the scattered weapons? Where did that stone anchor at Hakozaki come from? Many have asked these questions. Japanese scholars have sought the answers by searching the nearby waters for shipwrecks. They have found the occasional stone anchor and some pottery, but nothing else. Excavations for high-rises on the former waterfront, now predominantly landfill, have unearthed other anchors, but it is impossible to determine whether they came from the *Ghenkō* or from Hakata's centuries as a trade port.

If you ask locals about graves of the fallen Mongols or the Japanese defenders, you will be pointed to a few sites. There are two mounds that cover "Mongol graves" at Moko-zuka near Imazu. On Shikanoshima Island, at the entrance to Hakata Bay just outside the city, is another mound with a monument requesting eternal rest for the souls of the soldiers who are buried there. But are these monuments old? The latter monument was built in 1927. What, then, if anything, in Fukuoka dates back to that time, to those battles?

Fukuoka is a modern town because it was devastated during the Second World War by American firebombings. Very little survived, and the monuments and shrines speak more to faith and memory than to physical links to the reality of 1274 and 1281. There is a museum of the Mongol invasions in Higashi Park next to Nichiren's monument, with displays of weapons, armor and helmets said to have been captured after the battle. Were they? I have only the curator's word for it, and while I want to trust him, my archaeologist's soul cries out for a glimpse of these relics or others like them lying exactly where they fell, untouched for centuries until revealed by excavation, not sitting orphaned in a dusty case.

For that I must leave modern Fukuoka and journey south to the rural island of Takashima. There, in the waters of Imari Bay, fishermen have for centuries plucked weapons and other relics of the *Ghenkō* from the sea. In 1980, Torao Mozai, the father of underwater archaeology in Japan, made headlines worldwide when he discovered traces of the Mongol fleet in those same waters. Archaeologists with the Kyushu Okinawa Society for Underwater Archaeology (KOSUWA), working two decades later, finally unearthed the broken remains of several of the Khan's ships. In doing so, they came face to face with the reality behind the story of the kamikaze.

Riding the fast train south out of Fukuoka and into the countryside, I have time to sit back and think about what the waters of Imari Bay have sheltered for seven centuries. They are part of a longstanding tradition, dating back thousands of years, to the very beginnings of Asian seafaring. Those millennia of maritime activity and wars should have left thousands of shipwrecks in the waters of Japan, Korea, China, Vietnam and their neighbors. A few dozen wrecks have been found, but amazingly few given that this region, like the Mediterranean, was an ancient center of maritime activity. Nautical archaeology—the study of the past through shipwrecks—is a relatively new development in Asia, although the finds of the last decades have added a great deal to our understanding of the development of Asian ships and maritime trade. It is a fascinating story that the West is only beginning to appreciate. The story is made all the more appealing by the discovery of wrecks associated with the Mongol invasions and the fabled Emperor of Xanadu, the Great Khan of the Mongols, Khubilai Khan. The archaeology of Asian ships, however, shows that Khubilai's ships were relative latecomers, inheritors of a tradition of boat- and shipbuilding that stretches millennia into the past, a tradition that began on the banks of China's great rivers. Indeed, it all begins with China.

TWO

Asian Mariners

Hatō no utsu Tokoro wa Bummei no okoru Tokoro nari—
Where roll the waves, there arises civilization.

TAKENOKOSHI YOSABURO

A T THE DAWN of the twenty-first century, stories about China fill the news. The world is fascinated with this gigantic, rapidly industrializing nation. But we must not forget that interest in China, or more specifically, the desire to tap into the great market that China represents, has gripped the Western world for centuries. So, too, has the desire to acquire Chinese commodities, such as porcelain, silk and large-cast bronzes, and innovations and inventions such as paper, gunpowder and compasses. All of these products originated in China and spread to the rest of the world. At a time when Europe was gripped by the Dark Ages, when the great capitals of the West were sprawling cesspits of squalor and disease and men of learning were few and far between, China was the world's greatest civilization. Its cities were vast and clean, its ports filled with merchants from around the world, and knowledge of astronomy, chemistry, engineering and classics was diverse and honored. Song China far outstripped medieval Europe.

Dominating the Asian landmass, China spreads west from the shores of the China Sea to the Mongolian Steppes in the north and the mountains of Tibet in the south. Ask your average Westerner about China's greatest achievement, and he will probably answer, the Great Wall. This massive stone and mud brick barrier stretches across 1,400 miles and dominates the former inland frontiers of China as much as it does the world's consciousness. Like the pyramids of Egypt, the Wall is visible from great altitude, cutting a wide swath across the desert and into the mountains. It is even more impressive up close. Standing on it and looking into the distance, first in one direction, then the other, the Wall continues on over the horizon, a stunning reminder of the incredible determination, expertise and insularity of the people who built it. That insularity, that innately Chinese need to pull into the nation's own frontiers, was occasionally challenged, however, by another great contribution: the oceangoing ship—arguably China's greatest creation. The progenitors of Khubilai Khan's massive fleet of warships were born out of China's long ties to the great rivers that bisect the land. The craft that plied those rivers, the coastline and the distant oceans beyond were the technological marvels of the eleventh through fifteenth centuries, surpassing anything that Europe put into the water.

Chinese ships of this period were nearly two hundred feet long. By way of comparison, the typical European vessel of the eleventh century was an open-decked Viking ship less than a hundred feet long. The ships that Europeans used to explore, conquer and colonize in the fifteenth and sixteenth centuries ranged from Columbus's flagship *Santa Maria*, which measured around eighty-six feet, to Francis Drake's famous *Golden Hinde*, which was about seventy feet long. The Vikings steered their vessels with long oars attached to the sides of their hulls; Chinese ships of the period had rudders attached to their sterns—an Eastern innovation that took centuries to reach Europe.

Viking ships, and Columbus's *Niña*, as well, were open-decked craft that sank easily. Chinese ships were shaped like ducks to ensure that they shed water, and watertight bulkheads reinforced their decked-over hulls, an innovation that even the builders of the *Titanic* did not quite get right. In many ways, it took Europe and America until the eighteenth and nineteenth centuries to build ships as big and as sophisticated as the ones the Chinese were sailing nearly a thousand years ago. HMS *Victory*, Nelson's flagship at the Battle of Trafalgar, was 225 feet long, and USS *Constitution*, "Old Ironsides," was a stocky and short 175 feet. The famous American clipper *Glory of Seas*, built in 1869, was no larger than a Chinese seagoing ship of the thirteenth century.

For the best part of two millennia, the technology of Chinese watercraft and oceangoing ships made China the dominant maritime influence in much of the Eastern world. That legacy, abandoned in the fifteenth century, would not be revived until the twentieth century, and even today the West is only just beginning to appreciate the incredible technological achievements and navigational feats of ancient and medieval Asian mariners. Without them, Khubilai Khan's navy would have never existed.

Korean, Japanese and Vietnamese ships of antiquity all owed their basic form to Chinese predecessors. China dominated Asia's maritime technology, which is not surprising given how pervasive and influential a role other aspects of Chinese civilization played in Asia, especially in those lands and cultures connected to China by the South China Sea, a sort of Asian Mediterranean, a closed sea on which the various cultures traded and fought. Archaeologist Gina Barnes argues that in ancient times, all Eastern Asian civilizations were linked together by the centrally located Yellow Sea that hugs the shores of northern China, Korea and Japan. In many ways, that oceanic link dominated the rise of the various civilizations in what are now Japan, Korea and China, with people, goods and ideas moving constantly in all directions. Barnes understands what any experienced mariner will tell you: the ocean is not a boundary or a border, it is a highway for exchange.

What were the first boats? Like those of the ancient Middle East and Egypt, they were probably simple river craft. When civilization first emerged in China several thousand years ago, it took shape on the banks of the two great rivers that continue to dominate the land to this day. Falling out of the steppes, cutting through rocky gorges and then meandering across the muddy alluvial plains before reaching the sea, the Yangtze and Huang (Yellow) rivers have defined China's landscape and life since civilization first took root there. The two great rivers are the cradles of Chinese culture, flooding the rich plains to give birth to the rice farms and connecting cities and markets more effectively than any paved road.

The Yellow River, thick with the yellowish silt that gives it a name, flows out of the plateaus south of the Gobi Desert, cutting a 3,400-mile swath through the land. It is not a particularly navigable river for large craft and since antiquity it has flooded, its waters spreading out across the marshy plains to create vast lakes. The Yangtze, the world's third largest river (after the Amazon and the Nile), is fed by melting snow from the Tibetan Alps, falling dramatically from 16,000 feet on a serpentine, 3,900-mile course before reaching the East China Sea. Three spectacular river gorges, numerous cities and an expansive network of tributaries that drain 650,000 square miles of land define the Yangtze as much as its fast, muddy brown waters.

ANCIENT ASIAN WATERCRAFT

These water links—rivers, streams and lakes, along with an intricate system of canals—dominate China. While the Chinese, like the Egyptians, developed a variety of river craft early in their history, Chinese endeavors on the high seas took thousands of years to unfold.

The earliest ancient Chinese craft doubtless derived from more than one tradition, perhaps simultaneously, as skin and bamboo rafts and floats continued in use for thousands of years alongside canoes and planked craft. The earliest boats discovered so far are 7,500- and 5,000-year-old dugouts and paddles excavated by archaeologists at Suzhou in Jiangsu province and Xiaoshan in

Zhejiang province, where the Yellow River meets the East China Sea. The obvious antiquity of the Xiaoshan boat, a six-foot long, shallow and narrow craft, excited Chinese archaeologists when it was found in 2002.

Dugouts like the Xiaoshan boat gave way to planked vessels and rafts about four thousand years ago. Inscriptions on bone and shell fragments from the Shang Dynasty (1766–1122 BC) depict raft-like craft suited to rivers and sheltered coastal waters. Some historians suggest the Chinese first used skin or bamboo rafts, and from these beginnings, plank boats gradually came into use. Others argue that plank boats derived from dugout canoes.

The classic plank boat is the sampan, whose name comes from combining the Chinese words *"san,"* meaning "three," and *"bǎn,"* meaning "planks." It was these craft, not bamboo or skin rafts, that gradually evolved into larger boats and ships, although scholar Joseph Needham suggests that the internal structure of bamboo probably gave early Chinese boatbuilders the idea of using bulkheads and watertight compartments in their wooden ships. It is a fascinating concept, and when you split open a piece of bamboo and throw it on the water, you can see how a simple intuitive leap could be made—build a boat like this, and not only is it larger than a dugout, it is next to impossible to sink.

Archaeologists seeking ancient Asian watercraft outside of China have also found evidence of dugouts dating back thousands of years. Excavations of ancient shell mounds from the Jōmon period (10,000 to 2,400 years ago) show that these ancient Japanese people took to the open sea to hunt sea mammals and dolphins. They may have journeyed a hundred or more miles from shore, and in their travels—and we know this because archaeologists have found their campsites and settlements—they also crossed the Korea Strait that separates Japan and Korea.

In the 1920s, Japanese naval architect Shinji Nishimura published a series of detailed books on ancient Japanese watercraft. He believed that log rafts were used to populate Japan in the Jōmon period. Nishimura based his work on Japanese rafts of the late nineteenth and early twentieth centuries that he believed were "throwbacks" to antiquity—a "don't fix it if it isn't broke" theory that makes sense. He also based his belief regarding rafts on Japan's creation story, wherein two gods descended from the skies and created Japan in the midst of the primeval sea by dipping a spear into the water and stirring up mud that congealed to form land. The gods did their work from the *amé kihashiamé-no-uki-hashi*, the "floating bridge of heaven," which, to Nishimura, could only be a log raft. Perhaps, in ancient rafts of bundled logs or dug-out canoes, the Jōmon reached Japan from the Asian mainland in distant prehistory, populated the empty countryside, then lived off the bounty of the land and the sea.

Archaeologists compare these people, whose culture spanned nine thousand years of human history until around 300 BC, to the indigenous peoples of the North American Pacific Northwest. The Jōmon must have been prodigious canoe builders like the Haida, Tlingit, Coast Salish and other people who lived along the shores of Alaska, British Columbia and Washington State. However, Japanese archaeologists have not found much evidence to prove this.

Why have archaeologists not found other, more direct evidence of ancient Japanese seafarers? It may be, as Nishimura writes, because the Jōmon also used *ashi-buné*, craft made of bundled reeds. These craft were still in use after the Jōmon period, but none have survived archaeologically. The fragile reeds would rot and be lost forever. But there are some archaeological traces. Nishimura wrote about a bronze bell, dating to around 300 BC, that depicts what he firmly believed was a reed boat—long and narrow with a high raised bow and stern, with a "striking resemblance" to ancient Egyptian papyrus boats.

At around 300 BC the Jōmon gave way to the Yayoi, a culture that seems to have come from an intermingling of the Jōmon with settlers—or invaders—who crossed the sea from Korea and China. These new arrivals traversed the same narrow straits that Khubilai Khan would use to attack Japan 1,500 years later. The

Yayoi were farmers, not hunters, but they apparently had better sea craft than the Jōmon. This period of Japanese history coincides with a rise in the maritime trade that linked the Chinese mainland with Korea, Japan and Okinawa—a trade made possible only if large, oceangoing craft—the type of boats built with planks—were in use. Chinese accounts of the first century AD note that Korean ships traveled to China, which means that Koreans were using larger craft built for open water voyages by then, and had probably been doing so for some time.

If the Yayoi were mainland Chinese and Koreans with planked boats, this technological advance—along with others, such as rice paddy agriculture, that they also brought with them to Japan—may have helped them displace the Jōmon or assimilate these ancient people into a new culture that was more sedentary. This shift gave rise to a more unified Japan. Japanese archaeologists have methodically excavated a large number of Jōmon and Yayoi sites, but what have they found in the sea? As with the Jōmon's dugouts, only fragments remain, dating to around AD 500. A paddle, a curved rib and a piece of plank are all that have been found of what must have been incredible seagoing craft.

CHINA'S MARINERS

The earliest references to watercraft and marine warfare in Chinese literature relate to the fifth century BC Kingdom of Yue. Finds from excavated tombs show the Yue were receiving rhinoceros horns, ivory and jewels from as far away as India. Their southern trading port, established by the second century BC, survives to this day as Guangzhou, still one of China's great ports. Chinese archaeologists have excavated one of Yue's ancient shipyards in Guangzhou. Dating from 221 to 207 BC, the slips where ships were built show that the yard was building vessels with a beam or width of some twenty-seven feet and more than a hundred feet in length, and capable of carrying as much as fifty tons of cargo.

While these coastal trade ships were not huge, their counterparts on China's inland waters were. A fifth-century BC bronze shows what some scholars believe are large, decked canoes engaged in battle. The bronze dates to the Warring States Period, a time when various Chinese states engaged in a war that culminated in the rise of the state of Qin and the unification of China under its first emperor. This artifact shows men paddling below decks while fighters armed with halberds and swords face off on deck. Two figures at the bow grapple, with one man grabbing the other's head and thrusting his neck down onto his sword. Behind the figure being stabbed, another warrior wields a long-hafted dagger-axe, hacking at the stabbing swordsman. Three figures bob in the water beneath the boats. They may be swimmers—or the dead.

The account of a king of Wu who reigned from 514 to 496 BC explained naval tactics. "Nowadays in training we use the tactics of land forces for the best effect. Thus great-wing ships correspond to the army's heavy chariots, little-wing ships to light chariots, stomach-strikers to battering rams, castled ships to mobile assault towers and bridge ships to the light cavalry." The "great" and "light" wings probably referred to sails, while the "stomach-strikers" were probably rams, as were the "colliding swoopers" mentioned in later accounts.

Scholars debate whether the Chinese warships of this period were as diverse in design and use as this account suggests, and believe that the text, which is referred to in later histories, might describe ships of a more recent vintage. This is one of the fundamental problems archaeologists in this field face. Brief descriptions of boats and battles, colourful and wonderful to imagine as they are, do not provide details of construction, types of ships or maneuvers and tactics. The best way to reconstruct the past is to excavate an actual ship or the remains of a battle. Without such concrete evidence, we have to make do with a very vague and foggy picture, which new discoveries and excavations can help fill in or clarify.

Other archaeological evidence, however, does document more sophisticated ships and extensive naval forces. Clay models from tombs that date to the Han period (210 BC–AD 220) show that side oars were replaced by a new invention for steering ships: the stern rudder. Unknown in the Mediterranean world until the thirteenth century AD, the stern rudder was yet another Chinese innovation—like the compass, invented several centuries earlier—that aided overseas travel. During the Han period, shipbuilders were also launching larger ships, both on the open water and on the rivers, including some very sophisticated craft. A first century AD wooden model of a riverine patrol boat, recovered from a Han tomb, shows that it was a sleek, fast and deadly member of a large fleet. Propelled by oars, these craft carried a substantial deck structure with a sterncastle and an elevated rampart amidships. Contemporary accounts from the Han period mention naval forces with thousands of ships and boats like these, as well as larger craft, engaged in battle.

Chinese river craft also advanced in size and complexity during this period. Chinese archaeologists have studied an amazing wreck dating from AD 581 to 618, excavated at Pingdu in Shandong province, which borders the Yellow Sea and is also bisected by the Yellow River. The Pingdu ship is a 105-foot long catamaran capable of carrying a large number of men or heavy cargoes. It was a harbinger of even larger ships yet to come, built to trade and fight on the rivers.

An AD 759 text, *T'ai Pai Yin Ching*, lists six types of warships for use on inland rivers or lakes. They are not that different from those of the Kingdom of Wu more than a thousand years earlier. The largest were "tower ships," with three-storied superstructures supporting catapults and trebuchets for throwing projectiles of molten-iron, stone and fire. These ships were sheathed in felt or leather armor to protect the wood from burning arrows. Next were "covered swoopers," swift fighting craft armored with rhinoceros hide: "Enemy parties cannot board, nor can arrows or stones injure them." Then came "combat junks," sail- and oar-powered vessels with an elevated fighting castle amidships. "Flying barques" were lightly armed, multi-oared fast ships with elite troops, while "sea hawks" were rugged craft, possibly built for combat on the open sea or in rough weather. Finally there were small patrol boats with elevated sides or ramparts to protect the crew.

Some of these war craft were large, including the multileveled tower ships. The *T'ai Pai Yin Ching* describes them thus: "These ships have three decks, equipped with bulwarks for the fighting-lines, and flags and pennants flying from the masts. There are ports and openings for crossbows and lances... while (on the topmost deck) there are trebuchets for throwing stones... (the whole broadside) gives the appearance of a city wall." The account goes on to describe one such ship that was one thousand feet wide, "and on it set... hanging galleries on which chariots and horses could go." However, while these massive floating fortresses dominated the rivers, no large warships or ocean traders matched them on open water. Despite its 3,100 mile-long coastline, China never faced an enemy from the sea in antiquity. Invaders came from the interior, over land, and the opposing armies used rivers and lakes as defensive barriers and battlegrounds as well as highways.

To control the rivers was to control trade, and to augment economic growth, the ancient Chinese also created and then expanded a network of man-made canals. In the fifth century BC, workers from the Kingdom of Wu began excavating a canal from the Yangtze to the city of Huai'an. That canal, expanded and extended by later kingdoms and their rulers, still survives. Standing on its muddy banks, one realizes this two-hundred-foot-wide body of water known in China as the *Yunliang-ho*, meaning "Grain Transport River," known in the West as the Grand Canal, is one of the world's great engineering wonders, a veritable rival to the Great Wall. The world's oldest and still longest manmade waterway, it stretches across 2,100 miles of Chinese landscape, from just outside Beijing to the Hangzhou, connecting four rivers and countless cities.

From its circa 500 BC beginnings, the canal was extended by Emperor Shi Huangdi, the first ruler of unified China, during his reign from 221 to 206 BC. Extended again in the sixth century AD, the Grand Canal was, by the seventh century, China's lifeline, with tributary canals and rivers connecting to create 30,000 miles of linked waterways. The canals and the barges that moved along this network formed the world's largest and most heavily populated trading area. The Grand Canal remained the lifeline of empire over the next five centuries, reaching its ultimate configuration when it was once again expanded and modernized in 1293 during the reign of Khubilai Khan.

The craft on the rivers and canals were many, and they were large. An account from the eighth century AD, during the T'ang Dynasty, talks about huge river craft: "the crews of the ships lived on board, they were born, married and died there. The ships had... even gardens on board. Each one had several hundred sailors. South to Chiangsi, and north to Huai'an, they made one journey in each direction every year, with great profit."

The Chinese had been trading with their neighbors since as early as the Han period, a time of extended commerce with Southeast Asia, India, and even with Rome via Arab, Indian, Indonesian and other Southeast Asian middlemen. The Yellow Sea Basin also opened to merchants, with oceanic trade between Japan and Korea and between China and Japan's southern island of Kyushu. China's huge fleets of the Han period did not take to the open sea, however. Voyagers from the west and the south conducted most of the trade. "The sea-going junks are foreign ships," the T'ang account of the eighth century bluntly notes. "Every year they come... everywhere the various kinds of merchandise are stacked up. Whenever these ships arrive, crowds come forth into the streets, and the whole city is full of noise."

By the ninth century, Chinese trade goods had reached the Indian Ocean, the Gulf of Oman and the Persian Gulf, as well as the east coast of Africa thanks to Indian and Arab seafarers and merchants. Goods flowed back and forth, and China's products were highly prized. In AD 903, Arab geographer Ibn al-Faqih commented that China was renowned for its exports of silk, porcelain and lamps. His account is verified not only by trade goods from both Arab and Chinese cultures found in tombs and in city dumps, but also by a ninth-century shipwreck.

Discovered off Belitung Island, between Sumatra and Kalimantan, the so-called "Belitung Wreck" was full of Chinese ceramics and other trade goods. The ship was apparently sailing from China, but it was not Chinese. Rather, it appears to have been owned by either Arab, Persian or Indian merchants; the archaeologists who excavated it are still not sure. The Belitung Wreck is solid archaeological evidence of direct sea trade with the Islamic and Chinese worlds, and of an important time in Chinese history in which the Chinese gradually came to realize that they should start to shift control of their trade from foreigners and their ships—cut out the middlemen—and build a fleet of Chinese vessels, manned by Chinese crews.

This shift began with a new dynasty, the Song. The rise of the Song was occasioned by what historian Jung-Pang Lo describes as an even greater shift, as China's cultural, economic and demographic center moved from the Yellow River, "once the heart of Chinese civilization," to the Yangtze Delta. By 1080, over half of China's population had settled around the mouth of Asia's longest river, producing as much as two-thirds to three-quarters of the empire's revenue. Ironically, these changes were propelled by conflicting forces—increased trade opportunities with neighboring states, such as Japan, as well as pressure from inland neighbors, especially the Mongols. They would lead to the rise and fall of the Song Dynasty and pave the way for Khubilai Khan's navy and its invasion of Japan.

THREE

Enter the Mongols

In a hundred battles I have been at the forefront and
within seven years I have performed a great work, for in the
six directions of space all things are subject to one ruler.

GENGHIS KHAN

T HE TIDES OF history brought the Mongols to the shores
of Hakata as surely as the currents of the Yellow Sea. The
attacks on Japan were part of a decades-long war to conquer
China. That war was part of an even longer quest begun by a legendary warrior, Temüjin, to push beyond the confines of Mongolia
and the limitations imposed by greater powers. Temüjin's quest
would change the world. Under his more famous name, Genghis
Khan, Temüjin led his people out of the Asian steppes and to the
gates of Europe even as he waged war against China's ruling dynasties, under whose thumb the Mongols had chafed for many years.

The origins of the Mongols are lost in the shadows of history.
They may be the descendants of ancient nomads, the Meng-wu,
who migrated out of Manchuria's forests and on to the grasslands
of the Asian steppe between the ninth and eleventh centuries.
We know for sure that the Mongols were among many tribes of
Turkic-speaking people who roamed the steppes east of the Altai

Mountains, north of the Gobi Desert and south of Lake Baikal, hunting, fishing and warring on the plains. Historian Frederick Mote lists several nomadic peoples who inhabited the steppes, notably the Uighurs, the Kyrgyz, the Tatars, the Merkits, the Keraits, the Naimans, the Ongüts and the Ongirats. In the late twelfth and early thirteenth centuries, Genghis Khan conquered these people one by one and united them as a new entity: the Mongol nation.

Always on the move, the Mongols' key to success was the Mongolian horse. Close relatives of the ancient horses first domesticated in Asia more than four millennia ago, these animals are stocky with a reputation for toughness, endurance, speed and an undemanding nature. The steppes molded these horses, which, like the people to whom they bonded, lived out in the open, exposed to the storms, dust, sun and cold of this harsh environment. In a single day, say the Mongols, a man can experience all four seasons. Temperatures can range across as much as 100 degrees Fahrenheit. The Mongol horse is an unusually calm animal capable of carrying up to a third of its own body weight for extended distances. It is also prized for its bursts of speed, its ability to gallop non-stop for half a day, and because it can subsist on little food.

For the Mongols, these horses were more than a source of transport. They were partners in the hunt and the warriors' closest allies in battle. They were even a source of nourishment. Mongolian mares produce a lean, nutrient-rich milk that, to this day, the Mongols ferment to make *airag*, a traditional drink that is the staple of Mongolian diets from August to December. *Airag* contains five times more Vitamin C than cow's milk as well as six other vitamins and a small percentage of ethyl alcohol. When you consider that the modern population of Mongolian horses still stands at 2.7 million, it is easy to see how in a vegetable-deficient diet, these horses not only fed the Mongols but also kept them healthy. Horses and people depend on each other in Mongolia. This is true today; so too was it nearly a millennia ago. Historian Morris Rossabi sums it up: the Mongols could not have "conquered and ruled the largest land empire in world history without their diminutive but extremely hardy steeds."

On his horse, a Mongol warrior was practically self-sufficient. A string of animals, up to five per warrior, allowed him to ride for days without stopping. One account tells of a Mongol horseman covering six hundred miles in nine days. Another talks of how Genghis Khan's army moved, *en masse* on horseback, over 130 miles in two days. A warrior would perch on a wood and leather saddle that kept him anchored to the horse's strong back, balancing, even at full gallop, with his feet planted in stirrups attached to short straps hanging from the saddle. The Mongol adoption of the stirrup, invented in the third century AD, gave Genghis's warriors mobility to ride and fight at the same time. The saddle also helped distribute the weight of heavy saddlebags loaded down with cooking pots, water bottles, *airag*, dried meat and weapons.

The warrior's principal weapon was a composite bow made of horn and wood and bound with sinew. The Mongolian bow was stronger and offered greater punch and distance coverage than any European bow of its time—even the vaunted English longbow. A Mongolian bow could loose a shaft that flew for 350 yards—a hundred yards farther than an arrow launched from an English bow. Combined with the stirrup, the bow made the Mongol warrior a formidable enemy, riding fast and hitting hard and accurately.

GENGHIS KHAN AND THE RISE OF THE MONGOLS

The man who united the Mongols and led them to greatness was born as Temüjin in 1162, the Year of the Horse in the Asian calendar. Son of a kidnapped mother, Hoelun, and the man who kidnapped her, a warrior named Yesugai, Temüjin would overcome great hardships in his rise to power. As historian Jack Weatherford notes, he was a man who made his own destiny, rising out of humiliation, hunger, capture and slavery to become the Grand Khan of the Mongols. As Genghis Khan, their supreme ruler, he would conquer twice as much territory as any other man in history, ruling over an empire that stretched across nearly twelve million square miles, all of it based on his desire to right wrongs and to institute a global order based on free trade.

Persian historian, Minhaj al-Siraj Juzjani described him as "a man of tall stature, of vigorous build, robust in body, the hair on his face scanty and turned white, with cat's eyes, possessed of dedicated energy, discernment, genius and understanding, awe-striking, a butcher, just, resolute, an over-thrower of enemies, intrepid, sanguinary, and cruel." When Temüjin emerged from his mother's womb, according to the legends, he clutched a solid clot of blood in his fist, a portent of his determination and his legacy of war.

Born into a small clan, Temüjin was one of many who answered to a chief, or khan. The khan, in turn, owed fealty to a greater khan. The Mongols were still a disparate group of clans who traded with and raided one another. In one such raid, Yesugai had stolen Hoelun, wife of another man. When Temüjin was eight, Tatar enemies poisoned Yesugai. Abandoned by Yesugai's clan, Temüjin, his mother and his half brothers Begter and Belgutei wandered as outcasts, eking out a miserable existence. Said to have been a frightened child, Temüjin grew into a tough young man. When Begter threatened to take control of the family and, in accordance with Mongol law, take Temüjin's mother, his father's widow, as his own wife, Temüjin murdered him. That act led to Temüjin's capture and enslavement by rival Mongols for as long as ten years, until he finally escaped.

Temüjin regained control of his family, married, and allied himself with an older, more powerful chief, Ong Khan. Temüjin's other ally, a friend named Jamuka, joined him when in 1197 he moved against his neighbors, the Jurchens. Absorbing them, he then moved against the Tayichuds—close relatives, with whom he had lived when his father was still alive—defeating them in 1201. Temüjin's growing power also brought conflict with Jamuka. As rival heirs to the older Khan, the two became blood enemies, forcing Temüjin to wage war against his friend. In 1202, he defeated the Tatars. All of his former foes were absorbed into his growing army, which, in 1203, he organized into a mobile fighting force divided by a decimal system into squads of ten, known as *arben*. Ten squads made a company, or *zagun*, and ten companies made a battalion, or *mingan*. Ten battalions made a *tumen*, an army of ten thousand.

After two decades of struggle, Temüjin finally controlled most of the Mongols, but he still faced his one-time protector, Ong Khan, and Jamuka. They offered to form an alliance with Temüjin, but it was a trap. Ambushed by Ong Khan, Temüjin's forces scattered, with some, including family members, deserting him. Reaching the muddy shores of Lake Baljuna, Temüjin regrouped. By now his fighting force consisted of only nineteen survivors— one of them his brother Khasar. At one point, the starving warriors were surprised by the arrival of a wild horse, which they killed and ate. Taking the horse's appearance as a sign of divine approval and eventual success, the nineteen reaffirmed their allegiance to Temüjin. Temüjin toasted them with the muddy waters of the lake, and the pact sworn that day, known to the Mongols as the Baljuna Covenant, became the seminal event in the ultimate rise of the Mongols to world power.

Jack Weatherford, Genghis's biographer, comments that the covenant spoke to more than the devotion to Temüjin's followers. It became a symbol of the diversity of the Mongols, "based on mutual commitment and loyalty that transcended kinship, ethnicity and religion." The nineteen men came from nine different tribes and four different religions, and their mutual oath of allegiance, theirs to Temüjin and his to them, became "a type of modern civic citizenship based upon personal choice and commitment," the beginning of the community sense that would form the basis of unity in the Mongol empire.

From Lake Baljuna, Temüjin rode on, regrouped his forces, and began his final battle for the control of Mongolia in 1204. First he defeated Ong Khan and took his throne, then struck at Jamuka and his "diehard collection of Mongol holdouts." Jamuka, betrayed by his last followers, was captured and executed in 1205. Temüjin was now the undisputed ruler of Mongolia. In 1206 he assembled a *khuriltai*, or grand assembly of the clans. There, he was elected Chinggis or, in the better known Persian spelling, Genghis Khan. At that *khuriltai*, the new Great Khan proclaimed the birth of *Yeke Mongol Ulus*, the "Great Mongol Nation," and passed a series of universal laws to bind the new entity together. Genghis brought in a rule of law, abolished kidnapping and torture and instituted a policy of diplomatic immunity for envoys from other rulers. He noted that no one was above the law, something that applied to rulers as much as it did to the ruled. Genghis also extended free trade and religious freedom, and he ordered a writing system for the previously illiterate Mongols.

At the age of forty-nine, a lifetime of struggle and strife behind him, Genghis launched a war of conquest that would lead south and then west, a campaign that Weatherford calls the "Mongol World War" of 1211–1261. While fighting just one war at a time, Genghis led campaigns that saw the horse-borne Mongol army he had created sweep out of its Asian homelands and "overrun everything from the Indus River to the Danube, from the Pacific Ocean to the Mediterranean Sea." German knights, Indian warriors, Islamic fighters, Chinese soldiers and Japanese samurai who had never met each other in combat would all come to fight the same enemy.

Genghis's first campaign was against the Jurchens, a former nomadic people who had conquered the Chinese states that bordered the heartland of the Song. Ostensible vassals to the Jurchens, the Mongols, particularly Genghis, were no longer willing to kowtow. In 1211 he refused to swear fealty to the Jurchens and called a *khuriltai* to decide whether to go to war. Backed by his people, he crossed the Gobi Desert and attacked. In his campaign against the Jurchen, Genghis fought with two principles. One was the Mongol tradition that there was no honor in fighting, only in winning. And victory, whether achieved through force of arms, clever deception or "cruel trickery," was victory, regardless. "There is no good in anything unless it is finished," Genghis reportedly said.

The other principle was Genghis's own: that anyone who yielded and submitted to him was safe. By waging a battle of wits as well as weapons, Genghis brought disaffected Jurchens into his camp and spared cities that surrendered. By 1214 he and his warriors were at the gates of the Jurchen capital of Zhongdu (modern Beijing). The Jurchen ruler surrendered and swore allegiance to Genghis, only to renege on the deal once the Khan had turned back toward Mongolia. Genghis returned, joined by even more Jurchen defectors, and in 1215, Zhongdu fell again.

A campaign against Siberian tribes that did not swear fealty, and another war against the Black Khitans, solidified Genghis's power and brought the Mongols control of the overland Silk Road into China. Here Genghis might have halted, content to trade with the rich Muslim states of the interior, particularly the new and thriving kingdom of Khwarizm, ruled by Shah 'Ala' al-Din Mohammed. But arrogant men governed the Shah's empire, which stretched from the mountains of Afghanistan to the Black Sea. When Genghis sent a caravan to inaugurate trade, the governor of the province of Otrar (today's southern Kazakhstan) seized it and killed the 450 merchants sent by the Khan. It was a deadly mistake. Infuriated, Genghis invaded Khwarizm in 1219, splitting his army into three forces to take the cities of Jend, Otrar and Khujand. After they were overwhelmed, he marched on Bukhara and killed its defenders to the last man. Samarkand fell, as did city after city. Within a year, the kingdom had fallen and the Shah was a fugitive, harried to his death on a small island in the Caspian Sea.

Fierce, bloody battles marked this and other campaigns. Mongols brought terror to the cities that defied Genghis. According to Persian historian Ata al-Mulk Juvayni, when the city of Merv defied Genghis and finally fell in 1221, "the Mongols ordered that, apart from four hundred artisans whom they specified and selected from among the men and some children, girls and boys, whom they bore off into captivity, the whole population, including the women and children, should be killed, and no one… be spared. The people of Merv were then distributed among the soldiers… to each man was allotted the execution of three or four hundred persons." Arab historian Ibn al-Athir would later write in the thirteenth century that the Mongols "have done things utterly unparalleled in ancient or modern times... May God send a defender to the Muslims for never since the Prophet have they suffered such disasters."

Genghis's advance into the heart of Islam continued through 1222. Thwarted by the humidity and jungles, he pulled back from an invasion of India that year. His top general, Subodei, and another general, Jebe, joined Genghis's oldest son, Jochi, and rode north against the Russians in 1221–1223, easily defeating a Russian army at the Kalka River before holding fast and creating a permanent garrison. In 1225 Genghis returned home. His final campaign brought him into the field in his sixties against the Hsi-Hsia (Tangut) in 1226–1227. In the summer of 1227, following a fall from his horse, Genghis died, leaving his heirs an incredible army and a vast kingdom full of riches.

CONTESTED SUCCESSION

Genghis's son Ögödei inherited the empire and the title of Grand Khan. Instead of continuing his father's legacy of conquest, however, he stalled, and simply lived off the wealth he had been handed. It wasn't until 1235, with his fortune squandered, that Ögödei assembled a *khuriltai* to decide which direction the army should march to renew its conquering efforts. Subodei called for a new campaign against the Slavs, remembering his own successful thrusts against the Russians in 1223. Other generals argued for a renewed push south, against the Song in China. What followed was a compromise—a decision to split the army and strike in both directions. This two-front war would stretch the Mongol forces over eight thousand miles, a feat that no other Army would achieve until the Second World War.

The invasion of Europe began in 1236. Over the next five years Ögödei's armies spread Mongol power to its greatest ever extent, sweeping through Russia and into the heart of Eastern Europe as far as the gates of Vienna. A force of fifty thousand Mongols and one hundred thousand allies crossed the Volga in an assault against the Bulgars and established a base for the ongoing invasion. From there, an army under Subodei moved into Russia, while another under Möngke, one of Genghis's grandsons, struck at the Kipchak Turks. The war that followed was as brutal and decisive as the last Mongol invasion. While some cities surrendered, others fell after defying the Mongols. In the city of Ryazan, where resistance had been offered, a chronicler wrote that after the Mongols withdrew "no eye remained open to cry for the dead." Moscow, then a small trading settlement, was sacked before a spring thaw halted the Mongol advance until the next winter. Kiev fell on December 6, 1240, and after sacking the city, the Mongols burned it to the ground, completing their conquest of Eastern Europe.

From Russia, Subodei turned west. A German and Polish force fell at the Battle of Liegnitz in April 1241, stunning Christian Europeans, who were now convinced that the Mongols were a plague sent by God to punish them. Liegnitz was a feint, though, as the main detachment of the Mongol army headed south to the Balkans and into Hungary. In a great battle on the plains of Mohi, the Mongols once again slaughtered the defenders of Europe. The "dead fell to the right and left; like leaves in the winter, the slain bodies of those miserable men were strewn along the whole route; blood flowed like torrents of rain." There would be no savior of Hungary, it seemed, and there was no one to stop the Mongols from continuing up the Danube to the walls of Vienna. Then, on December 11, 1241, Ögödei died. Within six weeks, his armies received the news and the Mongols began their retreat, called back to another *khuriltai* to choose the next Grand Khan.

The struggle for control among the lineages of Genghis Khan's four sons would keep the Mongols occupied for the next decade. In 1242, as Mongol troops withdrew from Europe, the empire was held by several queens regnant, all of whom vied for power for their sons. Ögödei's widow, Töregene, held the upper hand for a time, but her son, Güyük, finally swept her aside. After a year and a half as Great Khan, Güyük died. It is possible he was poisoned by his aunt, Sorghaghtani, the widow of Genghis's youngest son, Tolui. Sorghaghtani was a remarkable woman. Survivor of what was essentially a civil war, she would emerge victorious over her rival queens, and her four sons would all play major roles in building upon Genghis Khan's legacy. All four would eventually become Khan, and among them they would expand the empire to its greatest extent.

With her ally, Batu Khan, ruler of conquered Russia, Sorghaghtani maneuvered to have her eldest son, Möngke, elected Khan at a *khuriltai* in 1251. Among his first actions was a purge of his relatives, whereby he killed seventy-seven of Ögödei's family and advisors. Nominally united under Möngke's rule, the Mongols called another *khuriltai* in the spring of 1253. The decision before them was where to continue their conquests. Ruling out another thrust against Europe, the Mongols voted instead for a double push against the Muslims and the Song, whom Ögödei had failed to subdue. This time Möngke granted responsibility for the war against the Song to his brother Khubilai who, despite being the least experienced warrior in the family, knew the Chinese well and spoke their language.

Another brother, Hülegü, pushed west to take the rich cities of Baghdad, Damascus and Cairo. But first he had to deal with a deadly cult of murderers, the Assassins, who were blocking trade and whose mountain fortress at Alamūt in Northern Persia had never fallen. Hülegü took Alamūt in November 1256, stamping out the Assassins in their other strongholds over the next year before continuing his march to Baghdad in November 1257. On February 10, 1258, Baghdad fell, and with it the Abbasid empire, founded in 750. The Abbasid Caliph, titular ruler of the Islamic world, surrendered with his sons. Hülegü sentenced them to death and, in keeping with Mongol tradition to never allow royal blood to spill on the ground, had them sewed into sacks and wrapped in carpets. Soldiers then kicked and pummeled them to death. In Baghdad, victorious troops "swept through the city like hungry falcons attacking a flight of doves, or like raging wolves attacking sheep, with loose reins and shameless faces, murdering and spreading fear." As many as one hundred thousand people (some exaggerated accounts say two million) died in the looting of what had once been the richest city in the world.

Damascus was the next target as Christian Crusaders united with the Mongols to defeat their Islamic enemies. Rather than suffer the fate of Baghdad, Damascus surrendered in 1259. The push west had now brought the Mongols to the shores of the Mediterranean. Hülegü continued to march for Egypt, but stopped when news of Möngke's death reached him in the last months of 1259. He returned to Afghanistan to see what would transpire, leaving one of his generals, Kitbuqa, in command of Mongol forces in the Middle East. Without Hülegü, the Mongols were finally defeated in battle. On September 3, 1260, as Kitbuqa marched south into the Jordan Valley, a Mamluk force from Egypt struck his army at Ayn al-Jalut, near the shores of the Sea of Galilee. Not only did this defeat mark the end to Mongol domination of Syria and the Middle East, it forever demolished the myth of Mongol invincibility.

That myth was also dying in China. Khubilai's war had stalled. His campaign began with a series of victories against bordering kingdoms, but the Song remained unmolested. Called before the court by Möngke, Khubilai faced possible execution. Instead, Möngke decided to lead the campaign against the Song himself. In May 1258, he led his army across the Yellow River to strike at Sichuan and Yunnan and envelop the Song. Disease struck the Mongol army, however, and men began to die of dysentery and fever. On August 11, 1259, Möngke himself succumbed to disease. Once again, the position of Great Khan was open. But this time there would be no retreat of armies in the field for the sake of a *khuriltai*. Hülegü remained in the east and held his own ground, while Batu and his people, the Golden Horde, abided on the Russian steppes. Khubilai remained with the army in China. Back in Mongolia, his brother Arigh Böke took advantage of the situation and called a *khuriltai* that elected him as Great Khan.

This Khubilai could not accept. Calling his own *khuriltai*, he had himself proclaimed Great Khan. The civil war that followed, brother against brother, raged for the next four years. Khubilai came into his own as a warrior and pressed back against Arigh Böke until his power weakened and he finally surrendered in 1264. Khubilai kept his brother alive, but even after Arigh Böke's convenient death in 1266, speculation over who was truly the Great Khan continued.

Khubilai, grandson of Genghis, was now the Great Khan of the Mongols. He ruled one of the world's greatest empires but his ascension had come at a steep price. Questions over Khubilai's legitimate right to rule followed him throughout his life. The Mongol royal family was divided on the issue as some members refused to acknowledge Khubilai's status. The empire effectively split in four. In the west, Hülegü ruled the Ilkhanate, the lands from Afghanistan to Turkey; while nominally loyal to Khubilai, he remained a force on its own. Batu's Golden Horde held its Slavic lands and never acknowledged or supported Khubilai, while in the Mongolian heartland, the most traditional Mongols, disdainful of Khubilai's "civilized" Chinese ways, retained their own sovereignty and never accepted Khubilai as Great Khan.

That left Khubilai, with dreams and ambitions of his own, with an empire in Eastern Mongolia, Manchuria, Tibet and portions of China. To expand that empire, and perhaps to demonstrate his moral authority to rule, Khubilai then launched a campaign to topple the Song and take all of China. That imperative would make him one of the greatest of the Mongols, on a par with his grandfather. It would also make him one of the most famous men in the world.

FOUR

Khubilai Khan

*Everyone should know that this Great Khan is the
mightiest man, whether in respects of subjects or of territory
or of treasure, who is in the world today or who has ever been,
from our first parent down to the present moment.*
MARCO POLO, *Description of the World*

NEARLY A century has passed since the departure of the
last emperor, but the Forbidden City and the Imperial
Palace still dominate Beijing, as they have for hundreds
of years. Walking through these magnificent precincts of imperial
power, one can't help but notice an odd aura, as if something is
missing. Of course, the courtiers have been replaced by thousands
of tourists, who come to marvel at the sumptuous architecture of
the halls and courtyards, to hear the tales of this enclave of a living
god and see the few treasures that remain after years of looting,
civil war and cultural revolution. The other thing that is missing, however, is the court's treasures. The best reside far away, in
the shadow of a mountain, the latest stop in a series of moves for
China's greatest treasures, the furnishings, goods and tribute that
once filled these halls. Some of them date as far back as the time
of the palace's founding by Khubilai Khan, the first and greatest
Mongol emperor of China.

Kept in the halls after the 1912 abdication of Pu-Yi, the last emperor, the treasures of the Imperial Palace remained mostly intact until the turbulent 1930s. Packed up and shipped away to keep them safe from the invading Japanese, the treasures remained in crates during the civil war while the forces of the Republic, the Guomindang, fought their death struggle with the Communists of Mao Zedong. In 1949, when the Guomindang's leader Chiang Kai-shek realized that he would lose the Chinese mainland to the victorious forces of Mao, he gave orders to ship the treasures to the island of Taiwan, where the Guomindang established a government in exile.

The treasures now all reside in the National Palace Museum, an opulent and spacious structure whose golden walls and brilliant blue tile roofs dominate a green-shrouded hilltop just outside the bustle and skyscrapers of modern Taipei. As one approaches the museum, the greenery of the mountain gives way to the terraced setting of the museum. Hanging in the shadow of the mountain, the buildings are impressive, but it is not until you step inside the multiple levels of the recently renovated building that the true impact of the museum hits you, for here are the missing riches from the emptied halls and palaces of the Forbidden City. The halls of the museum, filled with objects of silk, gold, porcelain, jade, bronze and ivory, hint at the splendors of a court so sumptuous that it stunned visitors.

One of those visitors was Marco Polo, whose account of the court of Khubilai Khan, with its "huge palace of marble and other ornamental stones... halls and chambers... all gilded, and the whole building... marvelously embellished and richly adorned" would inspire disbelief, hope, avarice and curiosity. Polo described Khubilai's palace at Khanbalik (now Beijing) as a massive complex, four miles square, with fortified palaces, military storehouses and gates leading to an inner enclosure. There were more palaces, including the Khan's own, reached by marble staircases, surrounded by huge columns and fitted "with gold and silver and decorated with pictures of dragons and birds and horsemen and various breeds of beasts and scenes of battle. The ceiling is similarly adorned, so there is nothing to be seen anywhere but gold and pictures."

In this palace, with a main hall that would seat and feed six thousand men, said Polo, were "extensive apartments, both chambers and halls, in which are kept the private possessions of the Khan. Here is stored his treasure: gold, and silver, precious stones and pearls, and his gold and silver vessels." It is hard to imagine, walking through the dazzling splendor of the National Palace Museum, that all this treasure, all these amazing and beautiful items, could all belong to one man alone. No wonder Marco Polo was stunned. One's eyes glaze over, overwhelmed by the ornate and intricate filigree, the smooth flow of jade, the rich embroidery on silk as a snarling dragon raises its five-clawed foot in a symbol of imperial might and privilege. Such artworks were but part of the splendor: "The roof of the palace, ablaze with scarlet and green and blue and yellow and all the colors that are, so brilliantly varnished that it glitters like crystal and the sparkle of it can be seen from far away." And the grounds, manicured and filled with greenery and paths, were parks filled with animals roaming free, with huge ponds fed by streams and filled with all sorts of fish.

Polo also describes huge banquets where more than forty thousand guests sat down to dine together. Massive vessels of jade and gold, filled with milk, wine and other beverages, were ladled into cups of gold, "for I can assure you that the Great Khan has such a store of vessels of gold and silver that no one who did not see it with his own eyes could well believe it... of the food I say nothing, because everyone will believe there is no lack of it." Every time Khubilai's cup was emptied, the cupbearer refilled it, retreated three paces and then knelt. As he drank, all those assembled dropped to their knees and prostrated themselves as musicians played every instrument in the hall. When the banquet ended, acrobats, jugglers and other entertainers performed "remarkable feats... and the guests show their amusement by peals of laughter." The Venetian visitor also described huge hunts with a retinue of ten thousand nobles, various festivals, including one where the Khan's lords presented him with one hundred thousand white horses, and thirteen feasts, one each lunar month, where Khubilai rewarded his lords—twelve thousand of them, claimed Polo—with thirteen robes "splendidly adorned with pearls and gems and other ornaments," silver embroidered leather shoes, and belts of gold. "The cost of these robes, to the number of 156,000 in all, amounts to a quantity of treasure that is almost past computation, to say nothing of the belts and shoes, which also cost a goodly sum. And all this the Khan does for the embellishment or enhancement of his feasts."

Through western eyes, Khubilai is the original oriental potentate, Great Khan, emperor of a vast land, warrior and patron, and for all that a dreaded "Tartar," inheritor of the Mongol throne of Genghis Khan.

But how reliable was Marco Polo? And who, really, was Khubilai Khan?

WHO WAS KHUBILAI KHAN?

The man who emerges from Polo's account, and from court records and other sources, is a capable if not brilliant ruler. A conqueror in his own right, Khubilai compares well to his rivals in Genghis's lineage, notably for his greatest achievement, the completion of the longstanding goal of the conquest of China. He is a compelling figure, not just for his achievements but also for his failures, especially the two attacks on Japan.

Morris Rossabi, Khubilai's most recent scholarly biographer, also points out that the Great Khan was a unique figure: the first Mongol to make the transition from nomadic conqueror to ruler of a sedentary society. That society, China, was forever changed by Khubilai and his court. His achievements in China included the construction of a capital, today's Beijing; the introduction of a new legal code; the development of a written script, not just for Chinese but for all the languages under Khubilai's rule; and court patronage of the arts and crafts, science and medicine, and the theater. These are not the actions of a "barbarian."

What also emerges is the story of a ruler who balanced his Mongol heritage with his acquired Chinese sensitivities; in some ways he was a man who never quite fit in with either group. In time, as his Mongol disparagers would assert, he became more Chinese than Mongol, addicted to the pleasures and luxuries of the sedentary court, not to the harsh, freewheeling life of a nomadic warrior. In this lies a hint of why his Mongol countrymen never fully accepted him as Great Khan, and may also lie the seeds of his insecurity and need to constantly assert his rule and role. Here may also lie the principal reason for the attacks on Japan. The surviving records and Marco Polo's account also talk about a careful planner, a master of detail, a leader with exceptional advisors that he freely consulted and used wisely.

There is also the story of a man very much in love with his wife Chabi, a husband who benefited from his wife's comfort and counsel and who lost his way in the years following her death—a period that includes his failed overseas invasions. And what was Khubilai Khan, the man, like in the flesh? Eight centuries after his death, the clues are few and tantalizing. The story begins, appropriately, with a portrait atop a mountain.

FACE TO FACE WITH THE KHAN

One of the treasures sealed in a wooden crate and secreted to Taiwan by the Guomindang was Khubilai Khan's official portrait, a painting on silk completed around 1260. It is one of only two known surviving images of Khubilai painted during his lifetime. The portrait is formal and stylized, and yet it shows a ruler that Rossabi describes as robust and determined, dressed in a simple white robe, unadorned with furs, and "certainly not gaunt, neither was he obese." He stares ahead, confident and yet distant, not yet ruler of all of China, but resolute in his determination to become so, in the prime of his life and locked in a struggle that would ultimately make his reputation. The portrait fits with Marco Polo's description of Khubilai as "a man of good stature, neither short nor tall but of moderate height. His limbs are well fleshed out and modeled in due proportion. His complexion is fair and ruddy like a rose, his eyes black and handsome, his nose shapely and set in place."

The second portrait—executed two decades later, circa 1280, a year away from his final, disastrous invasion of Japan—paints an altogether different picture. It is also one of the great treasures of the National Palace Museum in Taipei. In it the Great Khan sits astride a stocky horse, on a hunt, the traditional Mongol endeavor—and yet he is a very different man from the calm, confident warrior of the earlier portrait, and it is more than age that has changed him. He is fat, sitting draped in ermine robes on an unmoving horse, not galloping forth, firing his arrows. The Khan we see here has given way to the pleasures of the court and a sedentary, hedonistic existence—a man who may have, as Rossabi asserts, begun to lose touch with political affairs, if not control of his empire.

What transpired between those two decades? What blunted the instincts and shrewdness of a skilled warrior and politician who overcame his relations and his people's divided loyalties to become the Great Khan? The answers lie in Khubilai's strategies of conquest, his approach to governing the Chinese, and his personal life. To better understand Khubilai Khan, we must examine him as a warrior, a ruler and a man, particularly as a husband, and his relationship with his favored wife, Chabi.

THE RISE TO POWER

Not much is known of Khubilai's early life. Born in 1215, he was a minor member of the Mongol royal lineage, and not even one potentially in line for Genghis's throne. The rising fortunes of his family, brought about by his mother Sorghaghtani's adroit maneuvering, finally put him into that position, but as previously discussed, the future Khan was not the same type of Mongol as his cousins. Raised to be a literate, educated man, he clearly bore the stamp of Sorghaghtani, who Persian historian Rashid al-Din described as "extremely intelligent and able," a woman "who towered above all the women in the world." A Nestorian Christian, she did not persist in teaching her son her own faith, but encouraged him to take a more worldly, ecumenical view, a wise decision for a Mongol now living in an empire carved out by his grandfather and uncles from a wide range of lands and faiths.

Those lands included several regions bordering China as well as parts of China itself. As a minor prince, Khubilai received his own appanage, or region to rule, in 1236. A section of northern China occupied by farmers, this was a challenge. Khubilai ruled from a distance, never visiting his new land and leaving control of its affairs to officials who heavily taxed and extorted his new vassals. Only when many of the vassals had fled and his lands were in disarray did Khubilai learn what had happened. The actions he took are noteworthy. He dismissed his officials, many of them fellow Mongols, and installed local advisors and Chinese officials, reversed the taxes, and actively worked to have his former vassals return. Within a decade, the new approach had succeeded, and Khubilai had learned a valuable lesson.

From that time forward Khubilai surrounded himself with a wide number of advisors—Chinese, Uigher Turks, Mongols, Christians and Muslims. He also married Chabi, second of his four wives, in or around 1240. Not much is known of her, but as Rossabi asserts, her ardent Buddhism had an effect on Khubilai, for he learned the faith and their first son was given a Buddhist name. Chabi seems to have been a strong influence on Khubilai, taking over where his mother had left off, encouraging him to be worldly, compassionate and ambitious. She, herself, was full of ambition and interest in life and history, a student of early T'ang China and its customs. Perhaps in this woman, alone among his four wives, he found someone like his mother. Chabi is the only one of the four to be mentioned in any accounts of Khubilai's life, other than simply by name, and her portrait alone survives and is often displayed next to his at the National Palace Museum.

In addition to his early education in compassionate and pragmatic rule, Khubilai also learned the art of war. Marco Polo claimed that Khubilai ultimately won his crown "by his own valor and prowess and good sense; his kinsfolk and brothers tried to debar him from it, but by his great prowess he won it." He demonstrated that prowess as a warrior. Polo says that before he became Khan, Khubilai regularly went out into the field of battle, where "he showed himself a valiant soldier and a good commander." His approach here was one of careful planning. In his first military assignment, sent by his brother against the Kingdom of Ta-li, Khubilai made what Rossabi calls characteristically "minute, even exhaustive preparations... leaving nothing to chance." This included plenty of supplies and arms for his men, because Khubilai believed "his troops must be ready for any obstacle they encountered." He also trusted his advisors to guide him, relying on one military commander, Bayan, to spearhead a daring assault across a river. The ploy worked, and Bayan in time rose to become one of Khubilai's most trusted generals.

Khubilai's reliance on his advisors, especially the Chinese, paved the way for his successes but also nearly led to his downfall, as his connections to the ways, values and institutions of the Mongols weakened. Suspicion over just how Mongol he really was plagued him, led his brothers to mistrust him, and nearly denied him the throne. When he finally won, his victory came with what Rossabi calls "an aura of illegitimacy" that "would continue to haunt Khubilai through his reign" and "may indeed have motivated some of his later military campaigns."

Nonetheless, Khubilai stayed carefully focused on his Chinese subjects, turning his sights on the Song Dynasty, long a target of the Mongols, but waging a campaign that also stressed his desire to unite all of China's disparate states into a mighty empire, the likes of which had not been seen since the collapse of the T'ang Dynasty more than four centuries earlier. Here, too, was evidence of Chabi's influence, as well as his own ambition to rule a vast land, a goal denied even his famous conqueror grandfather, Genghis.

Khubilai sought to achieve these goals without resorting to brute force. In drafting a formal appeal to his ostensible Chinese subjects, he proclaimed a reign entitled *Zhong Tong*, literally "moderate rule," promising lower taxes, succor for the poor, reverence for the ancestral gods and respect for tradition, all lessons learned in his first attempt to govern Chinese subjects. He did not have to add that his appeal to rule all of China was backed by the fierce reputation of the Mongols, though it also came backed by a reputation for mercy in the face of submission, something Genghis had instilled from the start of the Mongol world wars.

Khubilai's demands for submission always came first in the form of envoys, not troops, offering benevolence and rewards for those who capitulated. When he finally vanquished the Song, in 1276, he granted titles to the conquered nobility and cared for the deposed royal family, and in the aftermath of victory, made sure his rule was established through respect. He kept the promises he had made when he had first proclaimed his divine right to rule the Chinese. He left Chinese officials in office, introduced tax relief, and actively solicited proposals from his new vassals on how to govern them, issuing an edict that reminded all his new vassals that, even if their proposals were not practical, "there will be no punishment. But if the proposals are useful, the Court will liberally promote and reward the persons who make the proposals in order to encourage the loyal and sincere ones."

A PRAGMATIC, UNIVERSAL RULER

Khubilai's reign of China demonstrated his commitment to governing a sedentary, urban and rural society as an enlightened ruler. In 1261, he created an Office for the Stimulation of Agriculture to bolster the economy in China's rural areas, especially in the north where years of warfare had devastated the farms. He also protected peasant farms from being used as pastures by conquering Mongols, a pragmatic move that may not have endeared him to his own people but which protected the backbone of China, the land that fed the empire. The new Emperor of China also introduced protections for artisans and craftsmen and incentives for merchants. Ever the pragmatist, Khubilai realized that a thriving Chinese economy would not only keep the government's and his own coffers filled, it would also keep the population content. Traditional Confucian ideals denigrated merchants and commerce, but under their new Mongol ruler, Chinese merchants enjoyed the highest status they ever would under an emperor.

To facilitate trade and encourage the economy, Khubilai introduced universal paper currency in his realm. This practice, now universal across the globe, was revolutionary in the thirteenth century. In his memoirs, Marco Polo waxed eloquent on the novelty and efficiency of the Khan's paper money, manufactured from the bark of mulberry trees. The Khan's mint organized the process so efficiently that "you might well say that he has mastered the art of alchemy." The government then distributed the final product with seals, stamps and signatures of key officials in a controlled procedure that greatly impressed the Venetian. "The... issue is as formal and as authoritative as if they were made of pure gold and silver... of this money the Khan has such a quantity made that with it he could buy all the treasure in the world. With this currency he orders all payments to be made throughout every province and kingdom and region of his empire... And I can assure you that all the peoples and populations... are perfectly willing to accept these papers in payment... With these pieces of paper they can buy anything and pay for anything."

As Emperor of China, Khubilai built roads, extended the Grand Canal, created the country's first postal service, built more than 1,400 postal stations, and revised China's legal system. His support of science included the construction of an astronomical observatory that still stands to this day in Beijing. Here his pragmatism is also evident; he did all he could to facilitate trade and clearly saw that the health, worldview and comfort of his subjects was beneficial to both the empire and himself as its ruler. His legal revisions introduced greater leniency, reducing the number of capital offenses to half the number under the previous government. He kept executions to an absolute minimum; Chinese sources show that during the years 1263, 1265 and 1269, Khubilai ordered ninety-one executions, "rather miniscule for the size of the population, the nature of the opposition, and the level of violence at the time." The Khan's leniency was also pragmatic— he introduced the Mongol system of "blood money," or financial compensation for crimes. In one case he reduced the death sentence of a number of prisoners, explaining, "Prisoners are not a mere flock of sheep. How can they be suddenly executed? It is proper that they instead be enslaved and assigned to pan gold with a sieve."

While establishing these tenets for his rule of China, Khubilai did not follow Mongol traditions. He chose instead to fashion an image of himself as a traditional Chinese ruler. He had to balance the perceptions of the Chinese, however, with those of his own people. He retained key Mongol traditions and ceremonies, such as an annual event in which a horse and some sheep were sacrificed, while bowing attendants scattered mare's milk from specially bred horses and called out Genghis Khan's name, a ritual overseen by shamans to insure good luck through the year. The Khan kept Mongolian shamans close by and made regular sacrifices to the native spirits of the land and, as Marco Polo attests, held lavish feasts and hunts, in which he and his retainers kept their Mongol heritage alive by riding under the open sky.

The Khan's policies for his Mongol subjects forbade fraternization or intermarriage with the Chinese. His edict applied to his own bedroom as well; he kept only Mongol women in his own harem. This is not to say that the Khan suffered from a lack of diversity. Marco Polo claimed that every other year Khubilai's ambassadors sent word to the Mongol provinces to find "the most beautiful girls according to the standard of beauty," and in this fashion "a hundred maidens, the most beautiful... are chosen and are brought to the Great Kaan [sic]." Ranked by older women of the harem—who spent an evening with the new arrivals to see if they had "good breath," were clean, slept "quietly without snoring," had "no unpleasant scent anywhere," and finally, were virgins—the successful candidates were welcomed into the harem and finally into Khubilai's bed. None of this stopped Khubilai from always retaining a special place, in his heart and by his side, for his second wife and consort, Chabi.

Caught between two worlds, Khubilai did not simply adopt a balanced view, nor was he simply a publicly Chinese but privately Mongol ruler. His pragmatism was paramount, but there was another element, a certain caginess, a wary approach that saw Khubilai, much like a chameleon, present a face that was ideally suited to whomever his audience might be. Commenting on Khubilai's religious views, Marco Polo quoted the Khan as telling him that there were four basic faiths: Christianity, Islam, Judaism and Buddhism, "and I do honor and reverence to all four, so that I may be sure of doing it to him who is greatest in heaven and truest; and to him I pray for aid." However, Polo also came away convinced that Khubilai was secretly a Christian, while visitors of other faiths felt affirmed in their own beliefs by the Khan. Despite his own native Mongol belief in the spirits of the earth, sky and water, Khubilai was ruler of a diverse, universal empire, and so in faith as well as all aspects of his rule, "he presented himself in different guises to the different audiences he faced."

KHUBILAI IN RETROSPECT

Khubilai Khan was a wary, pragmatic ruler, a man filled with ambition, perhaps driven by the demons of insecurity arising both from his status as the least likely member of the Mongolian royal family to assume the mantle of Genghis Khan as much as from his contested succession. He was also a man of insatiable desires: a driving curiosity, evident in his receipt of foreign envoys and ambassadors, including the Polos; a ravenous need for land, tribute and wealth; a lust for pleasure; but perhaps greatest of all, a never fully satisfied need for acknowledgement of his power and status. These desires all drove Khubilai to seek the throne of Genghis. They also impelled his relentless quest to conquer China and become ruler of the greatest empire the world had known since his grandfather had blazed a path out of the steppes and into the Middle East and Europe. They would also lead to his ill-fated campaigns abroad, against Japan, Vietnam and Java. As we will see, his first invasion of Japan, in 1274, was more a tactical move against an economic ally of the Song Dynasty that he sought to topple in China. While the failure of that invasion can be attributed to bad luck, the later attacks were even more costly in terms of money, effort and lives, and were ultimately disastrous for both his empire and his reputation. How did this happen? Because something had shifted in Khubilai's life after 1281.

In all people, our strengths are also our weaknesses, and in powerful rulers this is especially magnified. After 1279, Khubilai's hold over China began to falter. His health took a turn for the worse, his decline hastened by gluttony and alcoholism. In a way this too was part of his inheritance. His father, Tolui, had been passed over for Genghis's throne because he was a drunk. While the son avoided the pitfalls of his parent's alcoholism as a young man, once in control of China, and as host to the massive Mongol banquets reported by Marco Polo, the many glasses of wine and fermented *airag* bloated Khubilai and dulled his common sense. Traditional Mongol meals of wild game and birds also fattened the Khan, and combined with the alcohol to give him gout, a disease not unlike arthritis caused by a build-up of crystals in the joints. Gout strikes toes, ankles, knees, wrists, and attacks are intensely painful. The flesh over the effected bone swells into red, puffy masses of flesh with peeling skin and incredible tenderness. On average attacks last eight days, days that patients describe as the worst pain they have every experienced, or simply as "hell." A description written in 1683 by gout sufferer and physician Thomas Sydenham gives a sense of what Khubilai faced as the year 1281 was marked on his calendar:

The victim goes to bed and sleeps in good health. About two o'clock in the morning, he is awakened by a severe pain in the great toe; more rarely in the heel, ankle or instep. This pain is like that of a dislocation, and yet the parts feel as if cold water were poured over them. Then follows chills and shiver and a little fever.

The pain which at first moderate becomes more intense. After a time this comes to full height, accommodating itself to the bones and ligaments of the tarsus and metatarsus. Now it is a violent stretching and tearing of the ligaments—now it is a gnawing pain and now a pressure and tightening. So exquisite and lively meanwhile is the feeling of the part affected, that it cannot bear the weight of bedclothes nor the jar of a person walking in the room.

Addled by drink and tortured by gout, Khubilai had lost his edge. By 1281 he was also denied, by their deaths of old age, the counsel of many of his most talented advisors, men who had worked with him since he assumed the throne. Once a skilled politician and careful planner, a leader known for meticulous preparations and cunning execution, Khubilai now was ruled by pain and anger. Chabi, his most trusted advisor, had also died. The former strengths of a relentless drive and insatiable desire now were forged into weaknesses by age, food and drink. It was not a winning combination, and the Khubilai who now assembled the world's greatest naval force to smite Japan was a shadow of the old Khan. The Japanese campaign would be a shocking contrast to Khubilai's greatest triumph, the conquest of Song China. To better understand this contrast, we must now turn back to the story of the Song.

FIVE

The Song

Our strength lies in cavalry which is unbeatable,
but we are inferior to the Sung in naval warfare.
We can nullify their superiority by constructing
warships and training men in naval warfare.

LIU CHENG (1268)

QUANZHOU IS a bustling, densely packed Chinese city and seaport. The "Old City" at its center is home to nearly 200,000 residents. Around them in an urban sprawl, live six million more Chinese, including hundreds of thousands of "temporary" residents, workers drawn by the economic boom brought by the city's ongoing ties to other shores. For centuries intrepid men and women have ventured out from Quanzhou to other Asian ports, to North America and more recently to Taiwan. Many of them now send their money back to Quanzhou for investment. The result has been a massive campaign of urban renewal and construction. Wider roads cut through old neighborhoods, and the Quanzhou of old has steadily disappeared, replaced by highrises and smoggy boulevards.

Despite these changes, the city retains proud ties to its ancient past. Located on the coast of Fujian facing the Yellow Sea and Taiwan, Quanzhou sits at the mouth of the Jin River, whose tributaries penetrate some fifty miles into the interior of China. Here, at this confluence of river and sea, traders and merchants established themselves at the turn of the eighth century AD. By the mid ninth century, during the T'ang Dynasty, Quanzhou was trading with nearby ports and had grown in size, but government regulation kept it relegated to the status of a second-class port. All of that changed with the fall of the T'ang at the beginning of the tenth century.

The disruptions and shifting power bases of the intervening century saw Quanzhou, no longer shackled by a central government's restrictions, expand into a key port for trade with neighboring lands, especially the Nanhai trade, the Chinese term for the lucrative maritime commerce with the ports of the South China Sea. It flourished as an entrepôt, a place where goods arriving from Indonesia or points even farther west were offloaded and transshipped, either to the interior to centers such as Liangzhu and Jiangxi, or directly into the holds of Quanzhou-owned ships for trade with Manchuria, Korea and Japan.

The Nanhai trade expanded under the Song after they unified China into their larger empire between AD 960 and 978. Like its rival Guangzhou, Quanzhou was one of the major entrepôts of the empire, pumping large amounts of tax revenues into the government's coffers and sustaining the Song. It soon became one of China's most vital ports, part of an economic boom in a period of "unmatched economic expansion," in the words of one historian. The city's population grew with the prosperity brought in by trade between 978 and 1080 it increased by 125 percent, to an overall size of some 300,000.

In 1160, a scholar named Lin Zhigi explained, "there are three prefectures that carry on trade relationships with the lands of the South Seas, among which Quanzhou is number one. The long-distance trade ships of Quanzhou carry on trade with numerous lands across the seas, among which Śrīvijaya [Sumatra] is number one." Maritime trade routes out of Quanzhou and its neighboring rivals now surpassed the fabled Silk Road, China's overland tie to the West since before Roman times. Historian Hugh Clark describes these sea links as China's major channel for international exchange, and contemporary observers were well aware of their importance. "Among the inhabitants of China there are those who own numerous ships, on which they send their agents to foreign places," Arab traveler Ibn Battuta wrote in 1347. "For nowhere in the world are there to be found people richer than the Chinese."

Quanzhou's waterfront, the hub of all these riches, was crowded daily with ships just in from Champa, Śrīvijaya or Hakata, discharging their goods, while others laden with China's products weighed anchor and set sail from the docks. Unlike Asian craft of previous ages, these Chinese traders of the Song Dynasty were large, sturdy seagoing craft that have left few traces. Modern scholars who seek to learn more about the ships that built China's prosperity under the Song have relied on artistic representations and brief descriptions from the period. An engraving at the Bayon temple at Angkor Thom in Cambodia dated to around AD 1185, for example, shows a large two-masted Song ship that dwarfs the Cham canoes alongside it.

THE QUANZHOU SHIP

All of that changed in the summer of 1974, when Chinese archaeologists excavated a wreck from beneath six to ten feet of mud on a beach six miles out of Quanzhou, in a spot that had once been a channel along the shores of Quanzhou Bay. The ship's structure only survived below the original waterline, but the hull contained a number of artifacts, including 504 copper coins, seventy of which were minted during the Song dynasty, the latest dated 1272. No later coins were discovered onboard, leading archaeologists to surmise that the ship had foundered not too long after the last coin had been minted.

The remains of the hull revealed that the Quanzhou Ship was 113 feet long, with a breadth or beam of 32 feet. It drew only 10 feet of water and displaced 374.4 tons, "as large as any merchant vessel known from the same period in the West," notes archaeologist

Donald Keith. However, it was unlike any western vessel of the period, and it did not conform to what scholars expected a Chinese oceangoing ship of the period should look like. With its pointed bow, V-shaped bottom and twelve bulkheads separating the hull into distinct compartments, the ship was clearly built with a strong hull for rough seas.

The rugged construction included a double-planked hull that became triple-planked at the turn of the bilge. The planks were fastened with iron clamps and spikes. Like ancient Mediterranean shipwrights, the Chinese built this ship shell first, fitting the planks together to make a strong, flexible hull. Only then did the shipwrights add the frames (ribs) inside the hull. Another surprise was revealed when the shipwreck was lifted out of the beach. Most scholars of Chinese shipbuilding agreed before the excavation that early Chinese ships did not have a keel, or backbone. The Quanzhou ship did; its keel is made out of three separate pieces of timber. The rudder was fitted into the flat stern, suspended and angling down along that watertight transom but not attached to a sternpost. The interior of the hull contained the tabernacles, or mounts, for two masts, and their spacing indicated that a small third mast had probably been fitted at the stern.

Today the Quanzhou Ship is proudly displayed in the city's Museum of Overseas Relations, which sits on the shores of East Lake, an artificial body of water that dates to the T'ang Dynasty. Built in 1990, the museum's three halls include some three hundred ceramics and other relics, displayed in galleries that are also filled with models and images of China's maritime history and the story of the port. The Quanzhou ship takes pride of place, standing all by itself in the "Quanzhou Bay Ancient Ships Exhibition," a structure purpose-built in the late 1970s to house it. Nestled in a gray steel cradle and visible from below, the ship's knife-like hull dominates the space.

An elevated platform along one side of the ship allows the curious to look down into the weathered, gray timbers. The overlapping planks of the lower hull, stapled together by thick iron nails,

curve to form the lines of a once-large sea carrier. To the discern-
ing eye of a naval architect or scholar, the thick wooden bulkheads
that kept the ship watertight are striking material evidence of just
how advanced this craft was, centuries before Europeans made
ships that came anywhere near this level of sophistication. The
city's—the nation's—pride in this battered wreck is justifiable.

Donald Keith explains that the Quanzhou ship was "the product of an evolutionary development of considerable antiquity." It
was also vastly ahead of European ships of the same period, which
would not enjoy the benefits of the transom stern, the axial rudder, multiple masts or such large carrying capacity until the mid-
fifteenth century. Western shipbuilders did not adopt watertight
bulkheads until iron ships were invented in the nineteenth century,
and then not always satisfactorily, as the sinking of the *Titanic*
shows. Another maritime archaeologist who has analyzed the
Quanzhou ship, Jeremy Green, sees strong similarities between
it and Southeast Asian craft. Perhaps, he reasons, the Quanzhou
ship is a hybrid, representing Chinese adoption of external shipbuilding influences. That makes sense, for adaptation and links to
the sea characterized the rise and the fall of the Song Dynasty.

THE SOUTHERN SONG

The history of China is one of many wars and the rise and fall
of kingdoms and empires. Even as China began to build larger,
oceangoing ships and spread its reach far beyond its shores, internal problems and strife were altering the political landscape. The
fall of the T'ang Dynasty in 906 once again divided China into
warring entities, a situation that continued until 960, when the
victors of the struggle established the Song Dynasty, which would
unite the country for the next three hundred years. The Song were
the first Chinese political power to pay substantial attention to the
southern coast.

Under previous rulers, Chinese shipping had largely revolved
around inland, river-based fleets. Foreign ships from the Indian
Ocean carried on most of China's oceangoing maritime trade,

while Chinese ships crossed northern waters to trade with Korea and Japan. This began to change after the eighth century. Around that time China experienced a boom in shipbuilding, with Chinese shipbuilders learning from innovations brought to their lands by Arab, Singhalese and Persian traders. Influenced by the vessels of these foreigners, the Chinese built improved craft that merged Indian and Arab traditions with Chinese designs. The result was a significant merchant fleet that grew larger in both the number and size of ships from the eighth to the twelfth centuries. The Quanzhou ship, even in its broken and wrecked state, is a striking and tangible reminder of that fleet.

By the time they came to power, the Song were well positioned to use this new fleet of larger, oceangoing junks and sampans to encourage overseas trade, expanding routes that linked China with Indochina, Malaya, Korea and Japan. They generally did not use their naval power to force trade or subjugate other lands. They introduced Chinese porcelain to an expanding regional market, and used copper coins in exchange for a wide variety of goods. The peaceful expansion of trade into distant waters did encourage the development of a naval force, but the major factor that led to the rise of the Song navy was the arrival of invaders.

Two "barbarian" enemies, the Ruzhen Jin and the Mongols, warred against the northern border of the empire. The Ruzhen Jin occupied northern China after 1127, weakening the Song, who reacted by retreating south of the Yangtze to a new capital at Hangzhou. With its northern border cut off, Song China turned even more to the sea, continuing to expand trade and building up naval forces to meet their enemies on the sea as well as on land.

The threat from the north led to an energetic campaign of warship construction and the creation of China's first permanent navy. As Song official Chang I wrote in 1131, "China must now regard the Sea and River as her Great Wall and substitute warships for watchtowers."

The Song built up a fleet to patrol the Yangtze and the Huai rivers, as well as a coastal defense fleet. By 1170, a traveler on the

Yangtze described naval maneuvers by some seven hundred vessels, while the principal naval base on the coast, Hsu-p'u, which protected the mouth of the Yangtze (and is now known as Shanghai), had a detachment of 7,500 men manning a fleet of ships. Other naval bases and naval stations, manned by thousands of sailors and hundreds of ships, appeared on the coast in a program of expansion that saw the navy grow from eleven squadrons and three thousand men in 1130 to fifteen squadrons with fifteen thousand men in 1174, and then to an all-time high of twenty squadrons of ships manned by fifty-two thousand sailors in 1237.

The Song commanders kept their fleet well drilled and trained, ready to keep both the Ruzhen Jin and the neighboring state of Chin at bay, and to protect the coast from pirates and foreign raiders, with an effective range of control that stretched to Korea and Japan. The Song also relied on new weapons such as gunpowder, catapults and incendiary devices that had just been introduced to naval combat. In 1129, trebuchets throwing gunpowder bombs were adopted, and between 1132 and 1189 the Song navy pioneered paddle-wheeled warships. By 1203, the navy had added iron armor to its warships. The Song were particularly adept in the use of Byzantine Greek fire, imported from the west. As early as the tenth century, Song ships used piston-engine flamethrowers loaded with Greek fire (a chemical developed in the Mediterranean that burned when combined with seawater) to set enemy ships ablaze.

With eleven squadrons, three thousand sailors and control of the Yangtze, the Song were able to thwart a Ruzhen Jin naval invasion in 1160. The two fleets met in battle off the Shandong Peninsula, where the three-hundred-ship strong Song fleet apparently used either rockets or gunpowder-filled fragmentation bombs to set their enemies on fire. A Ruzhen Jin account describes how their admiral, Cheng Chia, was surprised by the approach of the Song fleet: "All of a sudden they appeared, and finding us quite unready they hurled incendiary gunpowder projectiles on to our ships. So seeing all of his ships going up in flames, and having no means to escape, Cheng Chia jumped into the sea and was drowned." With this victory, the Song gained control of the Yellow Sea.

Another battle in 1161 on the Yangtze thwarted a Ruzhen Jin invasion force trying to cross the river. Using armored paddle-wheel warships powered by human muscle (probably via treadmills), the Song met the Ruzhen near Chi-Pao island. Their fleet lay hidden behind the island, watching as the Ruzhen army loaded into boats and began to cross the river. When the Ruzhen reached mid-stream, the Song ships "rushed forth from behind [the island] on both sides." The defenders fired lime and sulphur bombs from catapults that exploded when they hit the water, filling the air with burning fumes and blinding the invaders in the boats. "Our ships then went forward to attack theirs, and their men and horses were all drowned, so that they were utterly defeated."

But the empire of the Song was still under siege despite these naval victories. Pressure from the hostile interior peoples began to disrupt the ancient overland caravan route, the fabled Silk Road, after the fall of the north in 1127. Under continued assault from the Ruzhen and, beginning in 1211, from the Mongols, the Song turned increasingly to the sea. They built fortified trade bases in the Philippines and their naval forces began to roam the South China Sea, patrolling the coast to guard against pirates and to protect several ports that had opened to foreign ships and expanded in response to the new policy of encouraging trade.

Before the changes brought about by the Song, the port of Guangzhou, established in the third century BC, had been China's greatest port, dominating the South China Sea and attracting overseas trade. Guangzhou flourished under the Song, but a new port, Quanzhou, as well as Ningbo and several smaller ports challenged its dominance. Guangzhou and Quanzhou were the hubs and centers of China's maritime trade, with Quanzhou finally surpassing Guangzhou in the twelfth century. On the crowded waterfront, ships lined the piers as longshoremen jostled and unloaded cargoes from some and sent baskets full of pottery and other commodities into the holds of others. A rich cacophony of voices, speaking Indian, Sinhalese and Arabic languages as well as those of the South China Sea, rose above the din of the workers.

Marco Polo visited Quanzhou in 1291. He knew it as Zaiton (Zaytun), the Arabic name of the city favored by Middle Eastern traders. He described it as the port,

> to which all the ships from India come with many goods and dear, and namely with many precious stones of great value and with many pearls both large and good. And it is the port from which the merchants of Manzi, that is, all the surrounding territory. So that thus as this port comes and goes so great abundance of goods and of stones and of pearls that it is a wonderful thing to see. And from this city of this harbor they go through all the province of Manzi and elsewhere. Moreover I tell you that for one ship load of pepper which may go to Alexandra or to other place to be carried into Christian lands, there come more than hundred of them to this port if Zaiton. And it would be almost impossible to believe the great gathering of merchants and merchandise at this city, for you may know that this is one of the two ports in the world where most merchandise comes, for its greatness and convenience.

At Guangzhou, the same scene was repeated daily. From the pier at Huangpu, in front of the five-hundred-year-old Nanhaishenmiao, the venerable temple to the god of the South Sea, ships raised sail and moved out to catch the wind, heading south for Indonesia or the Straits of Malacca, or north to cross the South China Sea.

The Song captains journeyed far and wide, not content to replace the foreign ships that had once carried the bulk of China's overseas trades in their holds, but also journeying to distant oceans and lands. In 1154, a Moroccan geographer, Muhammad Al-Idrisi, wrote how Chinese merchant ships were sailing to Aden and on up to the Tigris and Euphrates rivers with cargoes of silk, leather, iron, velvet and swords. While the western fleet sailed to the

Persian Gulf, the Red Sea and India, others maintained regular trade with Japan and Korea to the north. It was a rich and varied trade of all sorts of commodities, as suggested by another Chinese wreck. Now known as the Nanhai-1 wreck, this Song Dynasty merchant ship sank sometime between AD 960 and 1279 in the Yangjiang River in Guangdong Province with a cargo of sixty to eighty thousand valuable ceramics and a gold belt, all bound for the Middle East. Its treasures can be viewed near the Quanzhou ship in the galleries of the Museum of Overseas Relations.

The prosperity brought by maritime trade created a large middle class and increased the population of the coastal region as poor peasants moved to the ports in search of work—so much so that many of the coastal cities overflowed their walls and spread into the surrounding countryside. In the ports, one Chinese official observed, most urban dwellers were either merchants or artisans. The people were not the only ones to benefit from the profits to be made. Hungry for cash to maintain its military forces and to pay for the country's urban expansion, the Song government came to rely heavily on duties imposed on maritime trade. In the ports, maritime commissioners working for the *Shih-po ssu*, the Trade Commission, levied a 10 percent duty on all goods flowing in by sea. As Song Emperor Gao Zong put it, "profits from maritime commerce are very great. If properly managed, they can amount to millions. Is this not better than taxing the people?"

The promotion of maritime trade paid off for the Song. In the eleventh century, China's overseas imports doubled in volume, filling the government's coffers as well as enriching the growing merchant and artisan classes. By 1131, 20 percent of the government's revenue came in the form of duties from ship-borne goods. But the riches of the Song attracted the attention of their neighbors. Chin Tartar ambassador Fang Hsin-ju wrote how wealth filled the Chinese countryside, with "unending vistas of tea-shrubs and mulberry trees" that looked like "a sea on land." He was not the only rival to look jealously upon the Song's thriving seaports. The Mongols had also turned their attentions back to China.

Ancient enemy and oppressor of the Mongols, China had been the subject of both Genghis's and Möngke's last campaigns. It was not an easy task. The Mongol conquest of China took nearly a century, and under Genghis's grandson, Khubilai, the final battles to subjugate the last bastion of resistance, the Southern Song, took nearly twenty years. The principal obstacle was the Song navy, which as noted earlier, by 1232 the navy stood at twenty squadrons of ships and 52,000 men.

However, like much of the Song Empire, the navy had been weakened by internal dissension. Many of its sailors were discontented peasants who had not profited from the trade, and the government that sent it into battle was now so stretched for cash that it could not pay all of its bills. Corruption, waste, sloth and greed had sapped the strength of the Song. For example, an official report written during a naval inspection in 1239, found that at one base that was home to five thousand men, only five hundred were fit to fight; "the rest of the men were weary, dispirited, deaf, moronic, emaciated, short and frail. Look at them and one can see what the men [in other naval bases] are like. They cannot ride the waves and thrust with their spears. This is the result of thirty years of neglect. They cannot be used for combat and yet they cannot be demobilized." Another report, written in 1256, reported how a lack of ships and men left one naval base so short-handed that "the defense of this gateway to the country is now left in a state of impotence."

Knowing that he faced a demoralized and weakened enemy, Khubilai Khan used his usual opening gambit and demanded that the Song accept him as their ruler in exchange for annual tribute. The Song could then continue in power as vassals, and enjoy the benefits of being part of the much larger Mongol Empire. But after the Song emperor refused two delegations, one in 1260 and another in 1261, Khubilai set out to take China by force. Despite several skirmishes and one major battle, in Sichuan in 1265, the conquest did not begin in earnest until 1268. The Mongol victory would take a further eleven years to complete. It came thanks in part to Khubilai's encouragement of disaffected Song to join his army, in particular to create what would become Khubilai Khan's navy.

The critical battle was the five-year siege of Hsiang-yang, a nearly impregnable fortress on the Han River. To capture it, Khubilai's forces needed to wrest control of the river from the Song navy to cut off supplies and reinforcements. The Mongols had captured many boats and ships from the Song during the previous years of steady attrition. Liu Cheng, a former Song commander become Mongol general, suggested a switch in tactics, arguing that while Mongol cavalry were unbeatable, the Song had superiority in their control of the river. He suggested that the Mongols "nullify their superiority" by building their own fleet of ships and training their own navy.

Khubilai listened, and between April 1269 and 1270, the Mongols massed a force of about one hundred thousand men and five thousand boats to take the river and besiege Hsiang-yang by water. Cut off from reinforcements, with the Mongols now controlling the Han, Hsiang-yang was on its own. In 1272, the siege intensified when Persian engineers sent by Khubilai's nephew, the Mongol ruler of Persia, arrived to aid the Khan's cause. Constructing a mangonel (a traction-powered stone thrower) and a catapult, they fired rocks and bombs into the city with a noise that "shook heaven and earth." The addition of skilled mariners and tacticians, as well as the ships, gave the Mongol navy the advantage. Hsiang-yang fell in March 1273. The door was now open for the Mongols to pour into the Song heartland and down the Yangtze toward the capital, Hangzhou.

The Khan's army, a force of Mongols, Uighurs, Persians and Chinese under the command of Khubilai's general Bayan, crossed the Yangtze to meet the Song head-on at the river port of Ting-chia-chou. The two forces were equally matched in numbers, but again Bayan turned to the Persians. This time, the stones and bombs rained down on troops and ships, not buildings, and the Song lines broke. With the Song in retreat, the road to the capital was open. Throughout 1275, Bayan's troops took town after town, some of which capitulated easily, opening their gates and accepting Khubilai as their ruler in exchange for mercy, which the Mongols readily granted. Khubilai wanted the lands, ports and trade of the Song intact.

By the end of the year it was clear to the Song court that they were finished. The Song emperor Tu-Tsung had died in 1274, leaving his mother to rule as regent. In January 1276, Dowager Empress Hsieh surrendered the capital and acknowledged Khubilai Khan's sovereignty over her young grandson, the six-year old child emperor. This subjugation should have meant the end of the Song. But some members of the court and loyal naval commanders resisted, taking the emperor's two half-brothers south to fight on for another three years. The Mongols pursued the holdouts from coastal settlement to coastal settlement, taking the ports to cut off the Song navy's avenues of support as they retreated south to Quanzhou.

Quanzhou itself fell in 1277, surrendered by Song officials who saw in Khubilai's government an opportunity to continue to trade and reap their fortunes. The remnants of the Song navy retreated farther south to Guangzhou, with the Mongols hot on their trail. The Song again put to sea with Emperor Ping, an eight year old they had crowned in 1278 to replace his brothers, the eldest of which was a prisoner of Khubilai and the second, himself a boy of ten, now dead after years of fleeing and fighting. The Mongol fleet met them off Yai-Shan Island on March 1279.

The battle went badly for the Song. Of nine hundred ships, all but nine were either sunk or captured. The Imperial Flagship, a huge vessel unable to escape the surrounding Mongol vessels, surrendered. Sensing imminent defeat, Admiral Lu-Hsiu-Fu flung his family into the sea, then grabbed the young emperor and leapt into the ocean after them, drowning himself and the boy. The nine ships that escaped continued down the coast, fighting a typhoon that ravaged them further. A handful of survivors limped into Champa, on the coast of modern Vietnam. The Song were finished. The Mongols now ruled all of China, and commanded the world's largest navy. A new Mongol dynasty, which Khublai christened the Yüan Dynasty, had begun.

Now that he had control of the seas and ports as well as the farms and cities, Khubilai felt compelled to take to the sea. He had learned this lesson, not only from naval combat, but also through his understanding of the role of commerce in his new empire. Like Genghis, Khubilai believed in a Mongol world empire linked and made strong by trade. Control of commerce was key, and in his dealings with and conquest of the Song, Khubilai had learned the importance of maritime trade. Indeed, back in 1274, this new knowledge had inspired Khubilai to strike offshore with his developing navy against a Song trading partner, the Japanese, whose rich maritime dealings from the shores of Tsukushi were helping to prop up the Song. Tsukushi would become the arena in which Khubilai Khan's navy would flex its muscles. A centuries-old trade route would become a highway for war.

SIX

Tsukushi

Tsukushi, land of the white sun
Is a distant outpost of the realm,
A secure fortress to protect us from our foe…

May you who set off rowing
To the boatman's chant,
Thread your way between the waves
And safely reach your port…

YAKAMOCHI ŌTOMO,
the Man'yōshū poetry anthology, AD 755

FUKUOKA HAS few traces of its ancient past. A manmade firestorm immolated the city when it swept through its streets in the closing months of the Second World War. Fukuoka was not alone in its destruction. It was one of sixty-seven Japanese cities devastated by air raids in a campaign to destroy Japan's capacity to continue to wage war. The US Army Air Force, flying in from the sea, brought death from the skies in the spring of 1945 as American and Allied forces tightened the noose around Japan. Despite the intense fighting of the beleaguered defenders and the horrifying heroism of the young pilots who fell from the air in fuel- and bomb-laden planes to crash into Allied ships, Japan's outer defenses fell, island after island.

Nightly raids by fleets of B-29s now rained thousands of tons of high explosives and napalm into Japan's cities. On the night of June 19, 1945, it was Fukuoka's turn. Flying low above the city at nine thousand feet, a fleet of thirty-seven planes from the 9th Bomb Group unleashed 215 tons of incendiary bombs and 186 tons of high explosives. Fukuoka blossomed into clusters of fires. As civil defense teams sprang to work, the high explosives blasted into neighborhoods, killing fire fighters and demolishing their fire engines.

Stoked by the winds blowing in from Hakata Bay and fuelled by Fukuoka's wooden homes, a sea of fire engulfed the city and its people. Tens of thousands died, and more than half of Fukuoka—homes, shops, temples, ancient landmarks and modern buildings—vanished in that holocaust. It was all part of a savage war, wherein entire cities were incinerated, while the Japanese executed American pilots in Fukuoka's hospital through unanesthetized dissection.

One landmark, already fire-scarred, survived the flames of 1945. Fukuoka Castle's stone walls and moat, surrounded by a park and the barracks and headquarters of the 24th Infantry Regiment of the Imperial Japanese Army, remained unscathed. Built from 1601 to 1607 by Nagamasa Kuroda, the *daimyo* or feudal lord of Chikuzen, the castle had dominated the shores of Hakata Bay for nearly two centuries as a symbol of samurai rule in a Japan closed to foreigners, a Japan sealed off from the world. The mid-nineteenth century opening of Japan, forced by the arrival of American gunboats, brought sweeping changes. Among them was a shift in power from the samurai to a new bureaucracy that returned Japan's Emperor, for centuries an isolated figurehead, to the role of head of state.

The rise of Emperor Meiji and his courtiers triggered a bloody civil war between those who wanted to keep Japan as it was, splendid in its isolation, and those who saw an opportunity for the country to spread its power and take a place on the global stage. In those conflicts, known in Japan as the Bunjin wars, Fukuoka Castle was taken by rebels angry at the changes; its towers were set ablaze. The castle's fiery destruction was but one act in the rise of a new Japan, and a harbinger of Fukuoka's fate eight decades later, when the push for expansion resulted in the ruin of its cities and the fall of the nation just two months after Fukuoka burned to the ground.

But there is a deeper significance buried here—the reason why Khubilai Khan sent his navy to attack Japan. Fukuoka was the target of the Khan's wrath because of its ties to China and the Song, an ancient maritime saga that began centuries earlier. Its castle stands on the shores of what had once been medieval Japan's oceanic link to other lands, where traders, priests, diplomats and emissaries landed several hundred years before the Mongol invasion. Close to the walls of Kuroda's castle, forgotten and buried, lay the remains of a guesthouse built for those visitors and traders from afar, a place known as the Kōrokan. The invasions and wars of the thirteenth century had their origins in Japan's trade with the Asian mainland, especially its ties with China, and this small guesthouse was the first step in Japan's opening its waters to foreign trade, creating a port that in time would become the target of Khubilai Khan's navy.

THE KŌROKAN

After the Second World War, Fukuoka's citizens rebuilt their city. The army barracks that had stood next to Fukuoka Castle were torn down and in their place, a baseball stadium rose. Heiwadai (Peace Hill) Stadium—a symbol of Japan's adoption of the venerable American game and an arena for more peaceful competition— remained an important part of Fukuoka's daily life until October 1997, when its doors were locked for good. The stadium closed not for lack of baseball fans, but because beneath its diamond was a site of historical significance.

Chance discoveries, made when workers were digging irrigation lines in the stadium grounds, suggested that remains of the Kōrokan, remembered as a vague legend, lay beneath the ballpark. Archaeologists first thought that repeated construction at the site had destroyed all but a few traces, but work to repair the outfield spectator's seats in 1987 revealed substantial remains. Those finds sparked an archaeological project that began the following year and continues to this day. The project was seized upon by government officials eager to demonstrate that the city, once again a center for Japan's international trade, had ancient and venerable claims to their status as the nation's gateway. Despite Japan's almost fanatical devotion to baseball, the old stadium had to go.

Today, visitors to Fukuoka can visit a partially excavated Kōrokan and tour a covered building that protects the unearthed relics of the original. Exhibits tell the story of the ancient center of trade and display the fragile finds of the archaeologists who have spent the last two decades wresting the story of Japan's ties to the outside world from the soil. One enters the site by way of Ohori-koen, one of the largest urban parks in Japan and Fukuoka's pride. The gardens and waterways connect to the partially reconstructed remains of Fukuoka Castle. Beyond, on a site overlooking the highrises of modern, downtown Fukuoka, stands the Kōrokan Ruins Exhibition Hall.

A thousand years ago, this was an inlet of Hakata Bay known as Kusagae. It was the port of Dazaifu, then the provincial capital of western Japan. Overlooking the port, not far from the now-landfilled shoreline, standing on a low hill and facing the beach, a series of structures rose over the centuries. The first dates to around AD 688, when Japanese accounts mention foreign envoys at the Tsukushikan, the original name for the guesthouse for visitors that also served as the port of entry for Japan's foreign diplomats and a gateway to the Asian mainland. Envoys from T'ang China and Korea's Silla Kingdom were among the first to land and stay here, bringing goods, ideas and culture to exchange with the Japanese. From here, as well, Japanese monks and traders known as *kentoshi* sailed to China as part of those exchanges.

Successive structures stood at the Kōrokan site for nearly four centuries until a fire razed the entire complex in AD 1047. Ongoing excavations have revealed the stone foundations of these buildings, as well as the remains of walls and large numbers of artifacts, including plentiful Chinese and Korean pottery. Among the more amazing discoveries are a series of wooden tags with bearing traces of writing that detail the origins of the ancient goods that once landed upon these shores.

Sealed from air and light by their burial in wet mud, the tags are evocative evidence, among the more sturdy ceramics and glass, of how the Kōrokan, with its gates facing east, connected Japan with China, Korea, the kingdoms of Southeast Asia, India and even the Islamic world. They are also a potent reminder of how this bay, situated on the shores of narrow Tsushima Strait, was linked to vast networks of trade supported by ships that roamed the seas.

A HIGHWAY FOR TRADE AND WAR

The Fukuoka City Museum is an imposing modern structure that sits near the consulates of the Republic of Korea and the People's Republic of China. It is only a few subway stops away from Ohori-koen and the Kōrokan Ruins Exhibition Hall, but unlike the Kōrokan, the museum sits on the landfill that now buries much of the ancient waterfront. The site is appropriate in that much of the museum's story focuses on Fukuoka's links with the outside world—what its displays call the story of "Japan's window to the world."

One of the great treasures of Japan, the *Kan no Na no Wa no Kokuo*, is displayed inside. It is a tiny, 3.8-ounce piece of pure sculpted gold just under a square inch in size. The Japanese Government has designated it a National Treasure because it is one of Japan's earliest tangible links with China. This block of gold, capped with a handle in the form of a snake-shaped knob, is a seal sent by the emperor of China's Han Dynasty in or around AD 57 to the Japanese ruler of the area around modern Fukuoka. Engraved with the letters for "Wa no Na," which translates as the "State of Na of Wa" (Japan), the seal is a record of a diplomatic exchange with Han China. The Chinese ruler sent the seal as a gesture of friendship, but it also suggests that the Japanese ruler was a vassal paying tribute to China.

The seal is famous in Japan, not only as a symbol of early exchange, but also because it was found, buried beneath a huge stone, in a farmer's field in 1784. That field, now underwater thanks to the erosion of the seashore, stood at the edge of Hakata Bay on tiny Shikanoshima Island. Across the bay, almost in a straight line east, lie the ruins of the Kōrokan, and sheltered by the island are the waters where Khubilai Khan's fleet anchored during the invasion of 1274. The farmer, a man named Jinbei, brought the seal to his feudal lords, the Kuroda clan, who recognized its importance immediately. The Kurodas kept the seal in their family until 1978, when they donated it to the city of Fukuoka. The story of the seal is important, as we will see. Later, another seal, discovered by a humble fisherman, would give Japanese archaeologists a tangible link to Khubilai Khan's invasion.

To this day, the Japanese believe that the *Kan no Na no Wa no Kokuo* is the same seal mentioned in a Chinese history, *Records of Eastern Barbarians*, written during the late Han Dynasty. "The Na state of the Eastern Tribe, Wa sent a messenger with a tribute to the Emperor in 57 AD," it reads. "The messenger introduced himself as a high official. The state lies in the south of Wa. The Emperor Guanwu conferred a seal with a tassel." The seal is one of the earliest tangible traces of Fukuoka's status as a gateway.

The museum's galleries are filled with other treasures, although to some eyes they may just seem like corroded pieces of metal, broken glass and shattered pots. This debris is the remains of goods brought by sea from Korea, China and Vietnam, evidence of a thriving trade across the Tsushima Strait and beyond. That trade began around AD 300 with planked craft crossing between Hakata Bay and the Korean Peninsula. Three hundred years later, in AD 607, there are records of Japanese diplomats and traders crossing the strait and following the peninsula's shores to reach Mainland China. Where trade flowed, war followed, and in AD 663, a struggle over control of the straits saw the Chinese and their Korean allies fight a pitched naval battle with a Japanese fleet allied with the rival state of Paekche, at the mouth of the Kūm River on the west coast of the Korean Peninsula.

The end of the war—a conflict that historian Bruce Batten calls an "East Asian World War," because of the four kingdoms' involvement—brought a new concept to the waters of Tsushima Strait. That was an international boundary, a line separating Japan and Korea, with Japan's shores a fortified border with "a single designated gateway," the port of Hakata, today's Fukuoka. Previously one of many coastal access points, Fukuoka now became the only one. It was from here that Japanese sailors now sailed to gain access to the Asian mainland, and where Chinese envoys arrived from T'ang China.

The Japanese envoys, the *kentoshi*, probably crossed the South China Sea in Chinese ships, and gradually vessels of their own that drew from Chinese designs. The result, by the eighth century, was regular contact and the beginnings of a more active maritime trade, activities that led to the construction of the Kōrokan. Chinese historian Shen Fuwei writes that between AD 839 and 907, thirty-seven separate voyages sailed in and out of the port of Ningbo and Japan.

What did they carry? The excavations at the Kōrokan and other digs in and around Fukuoka have yielded Korean celadon, Vietnamese ceramics and Chinese coins, as well as evidence of how China's own deep-sea trading outposts were transshipping goods from farther afield. Fragments of Islamic pottery and glassware excavated in Japan first made their way to Guangzhou, Quanzhou and Ningbo and from there to Hakata.

Walking through the galleries of the Fukuoka City Museum, passing huge glass cases filled with fragments of broken pots, corroded bronze coins and models of ships, a visitor gains a sense from these fragments of a long and varied history that seems at odds with the more modern impression of Japan as a closed nation. Instead, the labels talk of how the *kentoshi* voyages not only brought goods but also were intended as opportunities for students and monks to learn and introduce "advanced continental culture in Japan." The exchanges of the seventh and ninth centuries led to a colony for Chinese merchants, and by the twelfth century "Hakata prospered as an international city."

But the same oceanic highway that brought trade also brought invaders. The museum, situated near an excavated and preserved section of the stone wall built to repel Khubilai Khan's navy, also tells the story of the Khan's two failed attempts to take Japan by landing off Fukuoka's shores. As well, it points out that, the stresses of war and the fear of conquest notwithstanding, Japan continued to trade with Khubilai Khan's China, with huge amounts of ceramics continuing to pour into Fukuoka, brought there by Chinese merchants who remained part of the community.

The museum also notes that visiting Chinese monks introduced Zen Buddhism and its culture to Japan at the same time. Standing in the Fukuoka City Museum, especially in front of the case explaining the relationship with Mongol-ruled China, one cannot help but wonder at the irony of intertwining currents of trade and conflict, exchange and demands f submission that have played out on these shores for over two thousand years, with the Mongol invasions of 1274 and 1281 as dramatic, climactic events in the flow of time.

SIX CENTURIES OF TRADE, DIPLOMACY AND CONTACT

The seventh century development of Fukuoka as the gateway into Japan brought more than the construction of the Kōrokan. Fearful of invasion, Japanese officials ordered the construction of fortifications. "The Tsukushi Dazai [the Kōrokan] abuts the Western Sea. Various foreign countries come to pay tribute, their ships and rudders face to face [with Japan's]. For this reason we drill men and horses and sharpen our weapons in order to display our might and prepare for emergencies." Fortresses and garrisons were built and established on the strategic islands of Tsushima, in the middle of the strait, and Iki, closer to Japan.

The officials also built a series of forts and guardhouses on the Fukuoka Plain and manned them with some three thousand *sakimori*, or coastal guards. Camped in the forts or atop the hills overlooking Hakata Bay, these guards kept "their eyes trained to sea 24 hours a day, 365 days a year." A small fleet of warships joined them, ready to intercept naval intruders.

Across the plains—dotted by rice fields and scattered dwellings—Hakata Bay is framed by surrounding hills and mountains. In the eighth century, the main roads followed the Mikasa and Naka rivers to a narrow gap in the Mikasa River Valley between Shiōjisan Mountain and nearby hills. There the Japanese built a fortress whose several-mile-long stone walls encircled the peak of Shiōjisan. Below it, an earthen embankment known as the Mizuki closed the gap between mountain and hill. Built in AD 664, the Mizuki is still standing in the twenty-first century. It is a monumental structure that encompasses 13.5 million cubic feet of earth, which archaeologists estimate took 3,500 men a year to move. The front was protected by a two-hundred-foot-wide moat, crossed by a narrow bridge, which led to a narrow passageway that ran through the embankment. Beyond the Mizuki and several other forts lay the fortified city of Dazaifu, the administrative headquarters of the region. Protected in turn by high walls and a moat and surrounded by forts and troops, Dazaifu became, as a ninth century Japanese account explained, Japan's "barrier-gate between inside and out."

Gradually the fear of invasion from T'ang China or Korea's Silla Kingdom waned, and within a hundred years of the construction of the forts and walls, the Japanese dismantled the *saki-mori* system. Beginning in AD 757, the number of guards declined, until 826, when the last brigades were disbanded and their duties handed over to locally recruited troops.

Overseas wars are expensive and difficult to mount, and success is never assured. Bruce Batten believes that despite the fears of invasion and conquest, Japan's seventh-century leaders never had much to worry about. He argues that the wars of the 660s that witnessed the defeat of Japanese forces in Korea and off the coast were part of a larger international picture, a long cycle of geopolitical competition. The fallout was a realignment of trade and a shift in tributary arrangements, not Chinese or Korean expansion through invasion and conquest. The extensive and costly defenses were meaningless, not even worth much as a strategic deterrent, although their construction and manning brought Kyushu and its citizens into a more centralized, bureaucratic Japan that presaged the empire that would soon arise.

Rather than being overwhelmed by enemy soldiers, the gateway of Fukuoka, fiercely guarded as it was, was instead host to diplomats from Korea and T'ang China, who brought tribute in the form of luxuries and manufactured items. These riches, distributed and sold by the Japanese Court to nobles, gave a new role to the Kōrokan: it was soon full of merchandise.

These purchases were but the beginning of a rich flow of goods. Although diplomatic exchanges declined and faltered in the ninth century, trade blossomed thanks to Japanese desire for Korean and Chinese merchandise. Regular trade voyages between Korea and Japan began in 831, and 842 saw the first recorded arrival of a Chinese trade ship. By 1052, maritime trade, dominated by Chinese traders, had made Fukuoka a busy port.

A Japanese work of fiction of the period, *Shinsarugakuki*, provides a detailed list of "Chinese goods" available in Japan: musk, cloves, frankincense, camphor, sandalwood oil, alum, betel nuts, indigo, cinnabar, leopard and tiger skins, rattan, rhinoceros horns, bamboo, porcelain, brocades, damask, twills, gauze and crape. This demonstrates how seafarers had now linked Japan to an even larger international market thanks to China's more global trade ties. The jungles and forests of Africa and Indonesia yielded wood, animal products and spices. Vietnam, China and Korea produced woven goods. Minerals wrested from the ground in Central Asia joined ceramics and glass from the kilns and shops of China, the Islamic world and the Indianized states of the Near East. All of these goods made their way in the holds of ships to Quanzhou and on from here to Fukuoka.

The flow of goods was soon too great for Fukuoka to remain the only port open to trade. By the early eleventh century, Chinese vessels were seeking other, albeit unauthorized ports to trade in, and by the middle of the century, following a fire that destroyed the Kōrokan in 1047, the center of trade shifted. The first move was several miles to the east. There, on the shores of Hakata Bay, alluvial silt from the Naka and Ishidō rivers provided the foundation for a medieval settlement, named Hakata for the bay. Founded as "a diaspora community of Chinese merchants in the late eleventh century," according to Batten, this Hakata "Chinatown," as Batten calls it, was built by merchants from Ningbo who decided to stay in Japan. They gradually constructed a town ringed by docks and warehouses, inhabited and used by ethnic Chinese who only gradually, through the centuries, became assimilated Japanese.

Medieval Hakata was a city "of, for and by" merchants, says Batten. Bustling, full of merchants selling their wares, sailors busy unloading ships, and laborers hauling goods through the streets, it had grown to 1,600 households by the mid-twelfth century. But at the same time, it had lost its monopoly. Other ports had arisen. The Taira Clan, Lords of Ōwada, built a port for Chinese ships on the shores of Osaka Bay on island of Honshu. This is now the modern port of Kobe. Another rival port, sixty-two miles south of Hakata Bay but also on Kyushu, rose along the shores of Nagasaki's bay. In the centuries that followed, Nagasaki would take on Hakata's ancient role as Japan's official gateway for international trade.

By the twelfth century, Japan was importing massive quantities of silk and other cloth goods, porcelain and ceramics, laquerware, books and scrolls and medicines. Another import was tea, known to the Japanese since the ninth century. After 1200, traders brought in huge amounts of the leaves for brewing, transforming Japan's drinking habits. Japanese exports included large timbers, copper, sulfur and other minerals, inkstands, fans and screens and Japan's famous swords. By far the largest trade commodity was Song copper coins of the eleventh to thirteenth centuries. Shipped by the ton, often as ballast in outbound ships, these Chinese coins became Japan's domestic currency, another symbol of the impact of overseas trade.

From their initial ports of call in Kyushu, where Japanese officials welcomed them, Chinese traders sailed on to other island ports along the Inland Sea and Japan's Pacific coast. Opened to the Chinese-dominated maritime world, Japan had become a strong link in that world, and a regular trading partner and a richer nation as a result. It was that trade, and the links it forged with China, particularly during the heyday of the Song's maritime endeavors in the late twelfth and early thirteenth centuries, that would bring the Mongols to the shores of Hakata Bay.

The oceanic trade route between Korea and Japan had remained largely peaceful for six centuries. The only conflicts of note were pirate attacks in 869, 894 and 940 (when Japanese pirate "rebels" burned Dazaifu), a series of raids between 996 and 999 and a pirate "invasion" from Korea in 1019 that took 374 lives and saw 1,280 Japanese kidnapped and sold into slavery. During those years, Japan traded and developed in relative tranquility, while conflicts roiled the Korean Peninsula and dynasties rose and fell on the Chinese mainland.

Khubilai Khan's attack on the Middle Kingdom changed all that. The Song's trading partners brought in tremendous riches that were a lifeline for the beleaguered rulers of the mainland's southern coast. To strangle that trade, Khubilai turned his eyes to Japan and made plans to subjugate it even while locked in his final struggles with the Song. That is how the Tsushima Strait and the Genkai Sea became an oceanic highway of war.

SEVEN

The Bun'ei War

*Of so great celebrity was the wealth
of this island, that a desire was excited in the breast
of the grand khan Kubilaï now reigning,
to make the conquest of it, and to annex it to his dominions.*
MARCO POLO, *Description of the World*

STANDING ATOP the mountain known as Ibeshi-yama at the northern end of Tsushima Island, you can gaze to the west and there, on a clear day, see the coast of Korea thirty-one miles in the distance, rising out of the haze. Straddling the Korean Strait, Tsushima lies roughly halfway between the southwest coast of Korea and the northern coast of Japan's southernmost island, Kyushu. First settled in Jōmon times thousands of years ago by peoples from both the Korean Peninsula and the Japanese islands, Tsushima has in its long history been a refuge, a bastion and an outpost. Claimed by both Japan and Korea, it was Japanese from the ninth through the fifteenth centuries, then Korean until the nineteenth century. Japanese once again, the island remains an object of desire for Korean nationalists.

The winds that blow across Tsushima carry monsoons from the sea and dust from the deserts of China. The waters that wash its shores teem with fish brought by the warm Kuroshio Current that flows through this narrow, sixty-mile-wide channel linking the East China Sea with the Sea of Japan. The Tsushima Strait, like the island of the same name, has seen numerous craft cross these waters, from the log rafts of the late Neolithic to the junks of T'ang and Song China, from the steel warships of Japan and Russia that fought each other here in 1905 in one of history's most famous naval battles to the fishing boats and nuclear submarines of the twenty-first century. This 269-square mile island, with its 41,000 inhabitants, mostly fishermen and their families, has been a crossroads between the cultures and peoples of the Asian mainland and Japan for millennia. In 1274, the people of Tsushima Island became the first casualty of Khubilai Khan's push across the seas. To them, and to the Japanese, that push is still remembered as the *Bun'ei* war.

During his fourteen-year war (1265–1279) against the Song, Khubilai extended Mongol authority by firming up relations with Korea. In 1258, one of his eldest brother Möngke's generals had led an invasion of Korea, succeeding where two previous expeditions, in 1218 and again in 1231–1233, had failed. The Crown Prince of Korea's Kōryo dynasty presented himself to Khubilai's camp as a vassal. Returning to Korea, he took the throne and became Khubilai's ally, with the new Khan assisting the Korean king to put down a rebellion that with Mongol assistance ended with victory in a battle on Cheju Island in 1273. With this, says Khubilai's biographer Morris Rossabi, Khubilai had "brought Korea within the orbit of his newly formed dynasty."

Khubilai had done more than secure an ally—he had also cut off Song access to Korean trade. With much of the Song's revenues flowing from their taxes on ship-borne imported goods, this helped stifle their ability to raise and equip troops to resist the Mongol invaders. It was also the Song's trade ties to Japan that probably first excited Khubilai's interest in the Japanese. That trade, the culmination of centuries of Chinese and Japanese contact, the growth of Hakata, and the interconnection of that port's expatriate Chinese community to their trading partners in Guangzhou, Ningbo and Quanzhou, had grown to incredible amounts by the late thirteenth century.

The Song taxed exports from Japan into China heavily. The decision to invade Japan, made in 1274, was likely just as attuned to Khubilai's desire to strangle the Song's access to those trade revenues as it was to bring the Japanese into the Mongol orbit, although Marco Polo would later offer a simpler explanation: "Of so great celebrity was the wealth of this island, that a desire was excited in the breast of the grand khan Kublaï now reigning, to make the conquest of it, and to annex it to his dominions."

KHUBILAI'S EARLY APPROACHES TO THE JAPANESE

Khubilai first sent envoys to the Japanese court in 1268 to demand subservience to the Mongols. Khubilai addressed his petition to "The King of Japan" and signed it as "Emperor of Greater Mongolia":

From time immemorial, rulers of small states have sought to maintain friendly relations with one another. We, the Great Mongolian Empire, have received the Mandate of Heaven and have become the master of the universe. Therefore, innumerable states in far-off lands have longed to form ties with us. When we ascended the throne, many innocent people in Kōryo were suffering continuous war. Thereupon we put an end to the fighting, restored their territories, and liberated the captives both old and young. Both the prince of Kōryo and his people, feeling grateful towards us, have visited our country, and while the relations between us and them is that of Lord and vassal its nature is as felicitous as that of parent and child, and of this, no doubt, you, O King, are well aware. Kōryo is situated on the eastern border of our dominion, Japan is near to it, and ever since its founding has carried on relations with Koryo as well as with China. Since the commencement of our reign not a single messenger of peace and friendship has appeared, and as we fear that your country is not fully acquainted with these facts, We have specially sent a messenger bearing a letter to inform you, O King, of Our sentiments. We beg that

*hereafter you, O King, will establish friendly relations with us so that
the sages may make the four seas their home. Is it reasonable to refuse
intercourse with each other? It will lead to war, and who is there who
likes such a state of things! Think of this, O King!*

The Japanese were well aware of the Mongols and the threat
implicit in the letter. The Japanese merchants of Hakata had also
heard about the Mongols from their Song trading partners, who
doubtless imparted a negative impression. Since 1254, the nation-
alist priest Nichiren had been preaching in the streets, whipping
people into a religious fervor, entreating them to repent their sins
and warning that the wrath of heaven would be visited upon them
in the form of a foreign invasion.

While the letter was addressed to the ruler of Japan, it first
landed in the hands of the Japanese military dictatorship, the
bakufu, whose samurai were ruling the nation, but not yet in the
tight grip that would characterize military rule of Japan in the
centuries to come. Political authority was divided, the Emperor's
court wielding diplomatic and religious power while the samurai
ran the secular sphere. The *bakufu* did not want to deal with Khubilai's letter, and so they sent it to the Emperor's court. Imperial
officials also ignored the letter, and sent the envoy back without
an answer. They did issue orders to prepare Japan's defenses; a
letter to a lord in Shugo Province, sent even as the envoy waited
for an answer, told him "recently, we learned that the Mongols
have become inclined toward evil and are now trying to subjugate
Japan. Quickly inform the *gokenin* [conscripts] in your province,
and secure the nation's defense."

Khubilai sent a second delegation in 1268 to try to get an
answer from the Japanese. At the same time he ordered his Kōryo
vassals to build a thousand battleships and raise an army of ten
thousand men, just to be ready. The second envoy's mission was
also unsuccessful, but he returned with two Japanese fishermen
his men had captured in their boat. Taken to Khubilai, the men
were told that the Great Khan wanted only peace, and were then

set free and escorted back to Japan by yet another envoy. This third envoy also returned home with no answer from the *bakufu* other than an order for his expulsion, an act that historian George Sansom called the "equivalent of a declaration of war by Japan." The Japanese were convinced that Khubilai's intentions were far from peaceful.

Another priest, Tōgen Eian, wrote to the government in 1270 arguing that because of the superiority of Japan's soldiers and arms, "the Mongols desire to conquer Japan. Once Japan's warriors are under their control, they will be able to conquer China and India. The country of the Mongols would direct strategy while Japan would fight in the field for their victory. With the strength [of Japan and the Mongols] combined, no country could resist. That is why the Mongols now desire to subjugate Japan." Whatever his motives, Khubilai's overtures were a threat the *bakufu* could not ignore. Amazingly, they did just that. Embroiled in an internal power struggle marked by murders, the *bakufu* were preoccupied. Apart from ordering local lords to keep their *gokenin* nearby, and orders in 1271 and 1272 to send *gokenin* to Kyushu to "defend against the foreigners and protect your holdings against bandits," they made no plans for defense.

THE FALL OF TSUSHIMA AND IKI

In China, Khubilai's war against the Song shifted dramatically in March 1273, when the Song defense line collapsed with the fall of Hsiang-yang after a five-year siege. With his troops now in the Song heartland, Khubilai could open a second front against the Japanese. He detached five thousand Mongol troops to Korea as the advance guard of the Japanese invasion force, and ordered the King of Kōryo to prepare for war. That included building a fleet of nine hundred warships, calling up an army and preparing supplies. There was not enough rice to feed the projected army, so the Koreans ploughed new fields to increase their crops for the coming year.

Khubilai also gathered additional troops. In late October, the official record of his rule noted that captured Chinese troops from

Hsiang-yang arrived in the Mongol capital. "They were released from shackles and spared capital punishment." Instead, "they were allowed to establish squads for themselves in order to subjugate Japan." Khubilai placed these troops under Mongol and northern Chinese commanders, but it is not known whether they were sent to Korea to join the forces massing there. They may have remained behind to fill the gap left when he sent another ten thousand Mongol troops to Korea, building his forces there to a *tümen*, or an army of ten thousand, to supplement the five *mingan*, or battalions, of a thousand already in Kōryo.

Khubilai's orders were for the invasion force to sail in the summer of 1274, but it was not until October 3 that the armada finally left Happ'o (close to modern Pusan) and headed across the strait. The fleet that embarked included 23,000 Mongol, Chinese and Korean soldiers and 6,700 sailors under the command of Hol-Tun, Hung-Tsa-Kiu and Yu-Puk Hyong, whose divisions were called the "triple-winged force." Two days later, they approached the Japanese island of Tsushima. The invaders quickly overwhelmed the island's small garrison of eighty samurai, under a military governor, Sō Sukekuni. Meeting the Koreans and Mongols on the beach, the samurai fell back before a "furious discharge of arrows as heavy as rain." Japanese sources claim that the samurai also fell victim to poisoned arrows. "Through the use of superior weapons the enemy stepped ashore without great loss," and pushed the defenders of Tsushima back from the beach.

As they fought up to the pine barrens, the Mongol-led phalanx cut down individual samurai and attacking horsemen. One samurai, Sukesada, was able to challenge individual soldiers to combat, and according to the legends, cut down twenty-four men before he found himself face to face with a gigantic Mongol soldier. Their fight lasted for "several strokes in hot strife" before Sukesada felled his attacker. In reply, Mongol archers fired from a distance, and three arrows punched through the samurai's armor and laid him low. The Mongol advance continued, and around nightfall, a last-gasp cavalry charge by the Japanese ended in bloody disaster.

Empty horses rode back into the Japanese lines, and the last ramparts fell. The victors massacred the male survivors, burned the town and left with a group of captured women.

The island of Iki, another thirty-two miles distant, was next. The fleet arrived on October 14. The governor of the island, Taira Kagetaka, had received news of the massacre at Tsushima and sent a warning to the mainland. He now prepared to make his own stand. With only a hundred mounted samurai, Kagetaka armed his local populace, mostly fishermen, who assembled with "old hunting spears, rusted blades, poles, sticks and bats, stones and pebbles in sacks, or whatever they could lay their hands on."

The invaders made quick work of these untrained defenders, so Kagetaka and his samurai retreated to his castle, which the Mongols quickly surrounded. Knowing that his island was falling, Kagetaka asked one of his trusted samurai, Sozaburo, to escape with his daughter Katsura through a secret passage to the shore, where they boarded a waiting boat and tried to slip through the Mongol lines. They almost made it, but as their boat passed the Mongol fleet, a rain of arrows killed Katsura. The wounded Sozaburo sailed on and reached Hakata to report that Iki's garrison was all but gone and that the Mongols would soon be upon them.

Back on Iki, Kagetaka faced his final battle. The invaders advanced with a wall of captured Japanese. The last of the samurai, only thirty-six of them, rode out, swords swinging. Only six returned, among them Kagetaka. Riding back on "blood-stained horses" through a burning fortress, the badly wounded Kagetaka and his men reached the inner chamber of Iki Castle to find his wife, family and servants preparing to kill themselves. As the enemy stood at the gates of the burning castle and drummed, the family joined Kagetaka in death, "calmly," as the story goes, turning "themselves to ashes with their palace." According to the Japanese legends, the worst cruelties of the invasion then took place. The Mongols held women down and stabbed through their palms with sharp knives. Stripping the women naked, the Mongols then tied the bloody corpses to the sides of their ships and thus laden, set sail for the shores of Hakata Bay.

THE BATTLE OF HAKATA

Thanks to Kagetaka's warning—and Japanese spies in Kōryo—the samurai stood ready on the beaches of Hakata when Khubilai's fleet arrived on October 19. Groups of samurai and their retainers had rushed to Hakata Bay—in all, modern Japanese historians estimate that some six thousand defenders stood ready to fight the substantial Mongol army. Historian Nakaba Yamada writes of how the *gokenin* and samurai stood with "unnumbered white pennants, with coats of arms painted thereupon, wav[ing] in the north wind." Japanese pride notwithstanding, they were completely outnumbered by the invaders.

The fleet arrived, banners streaming from masts, men pounding huge drums on the decks, and the pale bodies of Iki's women hanging from their prows. At the sound of the drums, "almost all the Japanese horses went mad," and the samurai fought to rein in their mounts. As they did so, the Mongols launched their landing craft, rowed swiftly across the shallows, crunched into the sand and leapt out, ready to fight. The battles that followed were unequal not only in numbers but in tactics and technology. The Mongols wielded superior weapons to their samurai foe. Their bows had greater range, fired poisoned arrows, and the Mongols had the benefit of explosive shells hurled by catapults. The Mongols also advanced en masse and fought as units, while the samurai, true to their code, ventured out to fight individual duels except for occasional cavalry charges.

Among those on the beach was a low-ranking samurai, twenty-nine-year-old Takezaki Suenaga, who with five of his retainers participated in the battles at Hakata Bay. We know more about his experience than any other Japanese defender because of a unique pictorial record: a set of *emaki*, or illustrated handscrolls, now known as the *Moko Shurai Ekotoba* (Mongol Invasions Painting Scrolls). Suenaga had them painted and annotated and presented them to the *bakufu* to obtain acknowledgement for his services. They are an amazing account of the Mongol invasion. The shogun was so pleased by the samurai's devotion that he awarded him a feudal fief. The head of the *bakufu* awards office also gave Suenaga a horse as a special mark of favor.

Suenaga's scrolls begin by showing him and his men riding into the Japanese camp where they meet up with other samurai. They are told to wait for the Mongols to advance, but Suenaga decides there is greater opportunity for glory by attacking at once, shouting, "We won't limit ourselves to merely shooting down the enemy!" He then takes off for the beach, passing two men who hold the severed heads of invading soldiers on the tips of their swords. Spurred on, Suenaga charges. The enemy is waiting, and although Suenaga claims they are in retreat, they clearly are not. Suenaga's retainer Togenda Sukemitsu shouts back, "More of our men are coming. Wait for reinforcements!"

Suenaga responds by yelling, "The way of the bow and arrow is to do what is worthy of reward!" then calls out the command, "Charge!" Arrows rain down, hitting Suenaga's banner man and killing him. Another man takes an arrow through the neck and falls, badly wounded. Suenaga's horse gets bogged down in the wet sand, and as arrows hit him, a catapult-fired shell bursts over his head, sending shrapnel flying into Suenaga and his horse. Streaming blood, they both fall to the sand. Suenaga and his three surviving retainers, all wounded, are then saved by the charge of another soldier, Shiroishi Rokurō Michiyasu, whose "formidable squad of horsemen" drive the Mongols back long enough for Suenaga to escape. He would live to fight another day, but this battle was over.

Elsewhere, men on both sides are felled by arrows, blasts or sword thrusts and slashes. As night falls, the ringing of steel and sparks flying from clashing swords fills the air and the Japanese are forced to retreat from the beach, leaving a third of their force behind, dead on the sand. They are holding their own nonetheless, and large numbers of invaders also lay slain. In the pines, a few dedicated samurai wait for a clear shot and carefully pick off Mongols and Koreans. This does not stop the invaders from reaching Hakata and burning it to the ground, but that is all they are able to accomplish on the first day of the invasion.

Historian Thomas Conlan, reconstructing the battle, believes that the figures for the invading army were exaggerated in the thirteenth century, and that the defending and invading forces were equally matched at several thousand each. Not all samurai fought as bravely or foolishly as Suenaga. Nevertheless, some distinguished themselves, including one by the name of Kagesuye. Pursued by a mounted force, he galloped back toward the Japanese lines. As the Mongols closed, he wheeled his horse around and loosed a single shot from his bow. It struck the lead horseman in the face, knocking him off his mount. The horseman was Yu-Puk Hyong, one of the three generals in command of the invading force. Badly wounded, he was taken back to the fleet as Kagesuye rode off.

As night fell, the two opposing forces hunkered down. A number of Japanese defenders retreated inland to Mizuki and prepared to hold the line there to keep the invaders out of Dazaifu. Back on his ship, the wounded Yu-Puk Hyong caucused with Hol-Tun and Hung-Tsa-Kiu. Hol-Tun pushed hard for a night attack to take Dazaifu before more Japanese reinforcements could arrive, but Hung-Tsa-Kiu argued that the troops were exhausted from a day of fighting and "it is of first importance that we give them a good rest tonight and to supply them with new weapons." He also feared ambushes and traps in the dark. In great pain and feeling no urgency to return to the fight, Yu-Puk Hyong agreed. Rather than risk night attacks by the Japanese, the generals recalled their troops to the ships to wait for daylight. Ashore, as one samurai commented, "we lamented all through the night, thinking that we were doomed and would be destroyed to the last man..."

But when morning dawned, most of the Mongol ships had vanished. According to some sources, a storm rose up and smashed into the fleet, sinking many of the ships and dooming the invasion.

Battered and depleted, the surviving Mongols retreated to Kōryo, arriving home more than a month later on November 27, leaving the Japanese to cheer their salvation. What really happened? Some of the fleet may have weighed anchor and simply headed for home, realizing that the Japanese, alerted to the invasion, were too formidable to beat with the forces at hand. The truth is not clear after seven centuries, but there is a dramatic discrepancy between the official Chinese account, the *Yüan-shi*, and a contemporary Japanese report. According to the *Yüan-shi*, "a great storm arose and many warships were dashed on the rocks and destroyed."

The Japanese source, a diary entry for November 6, 1274, written by courtier Kadenokoji Kanenaka, records that "several tens of thousands of invaders' boats came sailing in on the high seas. Nevertheless, suddenly, a reverse (easterly) wind blew them back to their native lands. A few of the boats were beached." Some fifty hapless Mongol or Korean soldiers and sailors were captured and escorted to the Japanese capital for interrogation and execution. The courtier then excitedly wrote, "The reverse wind must have arisen from the protection of the gods. Most wonderful! We should praise without ceasing. This great protection can only have happened because of the many offerings and prayers at the various shrines... around the nation."

Why the discrepancy? The three generals, back on Kōryo, made their reports to Khubilai with some trepidation, no doubt in fear of their lives. A strong wind would easily become a typhoon, especially on a coast notorious for storms. Official records suggest that three hundred ships and 13,500 men never returned home, which would support the claims of extraordinary bad luck such as an untimely storm. Or do they simply record the number of combat deaths and desertions? There are hints that Khubilai knew that his forces had not been sufficient to carry the day. Nonetheless, he had achieved a major goal. Hakata lay in ruins and the Song would not be receiving trade goods from that port any time soon. The war against the Song would resume, but Khubilai would not forget the Japanese.

As for the Japanese, they prepared for the next round, which the *bakufu* knew would come. For the time being they had been saved by divine intervention, in the eyes of some, sowing the seeds for a myth that would only gain in stature when the Khan's navy came calling again seven years later.

The Mongols Return

The advancing waves
shatter, disintegrating
in the divine wind
sent as a response to prayer
offered by royal command
TAMEUJI, *imperial envoy to Ise Shrine (1281)*

———————

WITH THE retreat of Khubilai Khan's navy from Hakata Bay in 1274, two storms, one literal, the other figurative, had just passed Japan's shores. Whether the weather of 1274 was a typhoon or a strong easterly wind continues to be debated between those who adhere to the legend and those who cannot find verification in the scant historical record. One thing is certain: the southern coast of Japan is frequently lashed by typhoons. The seas between Japan and the south China coast are, according to weather historians, the "most prolific generator of large cyclonic storms in the world," which occur three times more often than the devastating hurricanes of the Caribbean and Gulf of Mexico, such as the notorious Katrina that devastated New Orleans in August of 2005. Weather records of the Northwest Pacific from 1949 to 1976 show that on average there were twenty-nine typhoons *per year*.

Back in December 1274, weather statistics were no doubt the farthest thing from Khubilai Khan's mind. The abortive invasion of Japan was clearly a setback, but also a partial victory against the principal target, the Song. What had transpired in 1274 was, after all, simply bad luck. In the new year of 1275, Khubilai's attention turned back to China as his troops pushed down to take the Song capital. The capitulation of the queen regnant and young emperor soon followed, but the flight of some of the royal family and their supporters locked Khubilai into an ongoing campaign down the southern coast, as his troops pursued and harried the last of the Song loyalists. That campaign, waged on the water, employed the former Song navy, now in Khubilai's hands, and ended in a climatic naval battle near the site of modern Hong Kong. The final victory in 1279 not only cleared the way for a return to Japan, but also underscored the effectiveness of a navy to the Khan, now emperor of a united China.

In 1275, Khubilai sent another envoy to Japan to demand that the "King of Japan" come to China and subjugate himself to Mongol authority. Arriving in April at Nagato, the envoy waited for the next four months to present his message. The *bakufu* finally summoned him and his entourage to their headquarters at Kamakura, and there beheaded them all. They then publicly displayed the severed heads to make the point clear to everyone. There would be no subjugation. There was no turning back. The Japanese had again sent Khubilai an open declaration of war. They now prepared to meet the next, inevitable onslaught. Ordering increased surveillance of the coast and more troops to Kyushu, they also took time to investigate the previous year's conflict and reward those who had contributed to victory and punish those who had not. "It has come to our attention," said an official dispatch, that "a great number of men faced the battlefield but did not attack... This most certainly invites punishment for poor service."

Throughout 1275, the *bakufu* heard from various samurai who had fought the invaders and now sought rewards. Among them was Takezaki Suenaga, who presented his case forcefully. Although remonstrated for not having killed any of the enemy, his perseverance paid off when Suenaga received lands and a horse in recognition of his valor as "first to charge." In all, the *bakufu* rewarded some 120 samurai for meritorious service against the Mongols. However, they deferred punishment for those who had held back, because they needed all the support they could muster. Realizing that a line of men could not hold back invaders, and that after a day of fierce fighting the samurai had retreated to the defensive lines at Mizuki, far from the beach, the *bakufu* decided to draw the line closer—in fact, right off the beach at Hakata Bay.

Peasants, ordered to work by their feudal lords and overseen by samurai, labored for the next five years, breaking their backs to haul stones to build a twelve-and-a-half-mile-long wall, five to nine feet high, 165 feet back from the beach. Remnants of this defensive structure, painstakingly excavated and restored by Japanese archaeologists, emerge in various places around modern Fukuoka, celebrated as the *Ghenkō Borui* or "Mongol Defense Wall."

The samurai also organized their vassals into a compulsory defense force, the *ikoku keigo banyaku*. Small fishing and trading vessels were requisitioned to build a coastal naval force. Not forgetting that some of the samurai who faced the Mongols had not engaged them in battle with any great zeal, the *bakufu* replaced many of the feudal lords of the region around Hakata Bay with samurai allied with the ruling shogun's family. The *bakufu* also prepared to retaliate with an attack on Kōryo, and ordered a naval force built, but those plans came to nought. Japan did not have enough resources to both wage an aggressive war in Korea and defend its own shores.

KHUBILAI'S PREPARATIONS

Khubilai Khan renewed his appeal to the Japanese for surrender in June 1279, just as the last remnants of the Song dynasty crumbled. Mongol power, though, still did not impress the *bakufu*, who executed these envoys on the beach at Hakata just after they had landed, ready to negotiate. Khubilai was prepared for that answer. In 1279, he ordered the King of Kōryo, Ch'ongyol, to start building another invasion fleet, this time a thousand vessels, and to raise an army of twenty thousand men. Khubilai would supply a Mongol army of fifty thousand, effectively doubling the force sent to Japan in 1274. He also established an "Office for the Chastisement of Japan" to oversee the incredible logistical problems around mounting a massive seaborne invasion.

Eager to not only comply but also to curry greater favor with Khubilai, Ch'ongyol traveled to the Mongol Court to ask if Korea could take the lead in the invasion. Although the economic demands of the 1274 invasion had hit the country hard, Kōryo had recovered. So it was that in August 1280, Yüan officials recorded that the King of Kōryo met with the Great Khan. "In consultation with the king and the generals a plan of attack was agreed upon. Ships carrying forty thousand Mongol, Korean and North China troops were to rendezvous off the island of Iki with a fleet carrying 100,000 South China troops, and thence proceed to crush Japan."

The south Chinese forces—both the ships and the men—were made up in large part by the former Song navy, just returned to port after four long years of war hunting down the last of the Song loyalists. But Khubilai needed more ships than he had at hand, so orders went out for additional vessels. In 1279, Khubilai ordered six hundred warships from the Lower Yangtze. P'u Shou-keng, maritime superintendent in Fukien, wrote to complain that his allotment of two hundred ships was simply too much; in the end, he provided only fifty. That put extra pressure on others. Up and down the coast, hillsides were denuded of tress to provide raw materials for warships, and vessels of all description were suddenly pressed into military service, along with their crews. For nearly a decade Khubilai would have to increase his troops in southern China to deal with insurrections aggravated, according to historian Ch'i-ch'ing Hsiao, by this aggressive enlistment of both shipbuilders and seamen for the Japanese invasion force.

The eager Koreans, meanwhile, had assembled a huge fleet of nine hundred ships, massed an army and were hosting a large Mongol garrison at Pusan, where thirty thousand troops under General Hong Da-gu trained at the massive fortress that served as headquarters for the invading force. On the island of Cheju-do, lying off the southern tip of the Korean Peninsula, Mongol horses gathered for the invasion, the descendants of an initial group of 160 animals brought to the island in 1276, raced freely, fattening themselves on the grass. (Seven centuries later, wild horses still run on Cheju-do, and their DNA yields evidence that some of their ancestors were the hardy Mongolian horses of the steppes.) By early 1281, even as harried workers continued to build and repair ships and troops trained in Southern China, the armies on the Korean Peninsula were ready to engage.

THE INVASION BEGINS

Khubilai's battle plan recognized the need for overwhelming force, and it also saw the need for the two fleets to meet offshore from Japan before striking the coast. Khubilai Khan ordered the two fleets—the Kōryo "Eastern Route Division" and the Chinese Chiang-nan Division—to coordinate their attack after rendezvousing at Iki. With a smaller force, and perhaps cognizant that undefeated Japan held a sword at its throat, the Kōryo court was eager to get into combat, as were, perhaps, the Mongol troops with the Korean soldiers and sailors. Ignoring the Khan's orders, the Eastern Route Division's commanders, Hong Da-gu and his Korean counterpart, General Kim Bang-gyong, sailed first, on May 3, 1281.

Again, the Japanese islands of Tsushima and Iki fell easily, with Iki capitulating on June 10. But within a week, without waiting for the arrival of the Chiang-nan Division, the impatient commanders of the eastern route division sailed from Iki and landed at Hakata Bay. Waiting for them were the samurai, among them Takezaki Suenaga, eager to again prove his worth and reap reward.

Suenaga's famous scrolls, the *Moko Shurai Ekotoba*, depict him riding into battle in full regalia, passing samurai and their retainers who had learned the lessons of 1274 and taken position behind and atop the stone defensive walls. The Mongol advance, when it came, came hard up against those walls. There, overpowered by the arrows, spears and sword thrusts of the Japanese, the Mongols retreated, never again to reach the high-tide mark of the beach. Retreating to their ships, the invaders bombarded the beach with catapult fire. To pasture their horses and gain some respite from the sea, the Mongols seized the tiny island of Shika in Hakata Bay and turned it into a base of operations. Occasional skirmishes on the shore notwithstanding, the hoped-for decisive blow at Hakata hunkered down to a stalemated siege. The siege proved to be two-way; when the Mongols would not take to the beach to fight, the Japanese brought the fight to them with their requisitioned small boat "navy," the *ikoku keigo banyaku*.

Small boats filled with samurai eager to cut in close and jump on board an enemy ship. When Suenaga arrived at Hakata in early July, he tried to join a boat crew. As he later recounted, "the enemy is separated from us by the sea. I cannot fight them during this crisis without a ship." Another samurai turned and agreed: "If you don't have a ship, then there is nothing to be done." Suenaga had come all this way to kill the enemy. Desperate to get into the fight, he roamed the beach looking in vain for a ship. Spotting one heading for shore, he and another samurai rowed out to it in a small skiff and jumped aboard. Ordered out, he refused at first, but was finally shamed into leaving and returned to his skiff.

Chastised but not chastened, Suenaga rowed hard to catch up with another boat already loaded with other eager warriors. As he approached them, Suenaga took his helmet off and, standing up, began to badger the boat's crew. Lying that he was there on secret orders, and then that he was a deputy commander, Suenaga lost his cool when told that there was no more room for him. Abandoning his faithful retainers, he yelled, "Since I am a warrior of considerable stature, let me alone get on the boat!" "Why must you make such a fuss?" the boat crew cried in reply, before relenting and letting him on board.

Pulling hard, they headed for the enemy ships as the samurai crouched in their armor and made preparations. Suenaga threw away some of his arrows to lighten his load, and only then realized that in his haste to join the fight he had left his helmet behind.

He implored a younger samurai to give him his, but when the man retorted that if he was killed because he had given Suenaga his helmet, his wife and children would lament—or become Suenaga's responsibility—Suenaga gave up and tied two armored shin guards to his head for protection.

As the boat pulled closer to the Mongol fleet, arrows whizzing by, Suenaga yelled at the oarsmen to "Get close! I want to board!" With this, some of them began to back paddle, and Suenaga jumped into a nearby boat that pressed on, finally grappling with and boarding a large ship filled with enemy soldiers and sailors. Centuries of handling and the ravages of time have erased images and text on the *Moko Shurai Ekotoba*, so here the rascally samurai's words fail him, but the scenes on the scroll show the boat crashing into the side of the ship. Suenaga is first off, throwing away his bow and grabbing a *naginata*, a long, curved blade. At the bow, as his makeshift helmet falls off his head, he cuts a sailor's throat with his short sword, while a second Mongol, blood spurting over the side of the ship, falls to the deck, apparently another of Suenaga's victims. At the stern, while a samurai fends off spear thrusts with his pike and a warrior clambers aboard, three others rush forward into a crowd of defenders, one with his spear before him, the other two samurai with their long swords raised high over their heads as they wade into the bloody melee.

Suenaga and his fellow warriors were not alone. Boat captain Kusano-Jiro raised sail and tacked up to a Mongol ship, sailing through a "shower of darts, one of which took off his left arm." Undaunted, he ran alongside, dropped his masts onto their decks, and he and his men swarmed aboard. Before other vessels could come to the aid of the Mongols, "the daring assailants set the ship on fire and were off, carrying away twenty-one heads." Another group swam out to a ship, clambered aboard and killed its crew of thirty. Another group of samurai, seeing this, tried to capture a junk but all died, cut down to a man once they reached its deck. Unable to "keep themselves within the walls," other "intrepid men of this sort" advanced in boats that "being swifter and lighter were more easily managed," but "many of them were sunk by the darts and the huge stones hurled by the catapults."

Despite their losses, the Japanese did not let up. After the battle, one of Suenaga's superiors praised him for his initiative, exclaiming, "Without your own boat, you repeatedly lied in order to join the fray. You really are the *baddest* man around!" With "bad," almost fanatical warriors like Suenaga, the Japanese forced the invading fleet to close quarters, mooring their vessels together to form a massive floating island so the small Japanese boats could not surround, cut off and take any of the ships. Faced with the Mongol wooden walls, the Japanese shifted tactics. Loading boats with hay, they sent them, on fire, crashing into the chained mass of the fleet. The Mongols and Koreans were forced to cut free the burning ships and re-form their perimeter.

On Shika Island, the samurai harried the Mongol camp, cutting into the horses and driving the soldiers into the sea. Suenaga joined one of these expeditions after landing on the beach fresh from his naval assault. This time the plucky samurai was wounded, as were two of his fighting mates, and lost two horses. But Mongol losses were greater, with a Japanese source claiming that the samurai collected two thousand heads. Harried and badly mauled, the Eastern Route Division pulled anchor and retreated across the straits to Iki Island, with the Japanese pursuing them as they sailed out of Hakata Bay.

THE ARRIVAL AND DESTRUCTION
OF THE CHIANG-NAN DIVISION

Meanwhile the delayed Chiang-nan Division, with 3,500 ships and 100,000 men under the command of former Song General Fan Wen-hu, finally sailed from China in June to rendezvous with the Eastern Route Division. Unlike the Eastern Division, which had had to cross 116 miles of the strait, the ships from China had to traverse 480 miles of open ocean. They did so without incident, but rather than join the stalemate at Hakata, the Chiang-nan Division diverted thirty miles south of Hakata into Imari Bay and poured ashore there. Advancing over the countryside, they could now come in from behind the walls of Hakata and take Dazaifu. The Japanese, however, were ready for the Mongols and met them on the beach. A two-week battle ensued through the less defended, but hilly and rugged countryside. The Mongols took the island of Takashima, with a small population of farmers and fishermen, as a base of operations. The crews of the Chiang-nan ships chained their vessels together just off the island and constructed a planked walkway along its outer edge in preparation for the inevitable waterborne assault by the small defense craft of the Japanese.

As at Hakata, the Japanese boats, including fire ships, struck and probed at the ships in Imari Bay but had little impact on the massive Mongol fleet. The principal fight took place ashore, where losses on both sides mounted as the invasion dragged on. The stalemate lasted for nearly two months. It was finally broken when a sudden storm mauled the Chiang-nan fleet on August 15 and 16. In his diary, courtier Kadenokoji Kanenaka explained that, "a report arrived from Dazaifu… a typhoon sank most of the foreign pirates' ships. Several thousands were killed or captured. Not one [enemy] boat remains at Iki or Tsushima. Most of the foreign invaders who came lost their lives or were captured."

That is all that contemporary Japanese records have to say about what happened to Khubilai Khan's navy. Popular legend, however, adds a great deal more. When the Japanese beseeched the gods to destroy the enemy, "a green dragon had raised its head from the waves… sulfurous flames filled the firmament." With this portent of doom, what followed was inevitable. Clouds quickly gathered over the sea, obscuring the sun, and the wind began to howl. Heavy rain and storm-driven waves followed, smashing into the anchored fleet. While some ships fled, others, still moored together, crashed into each other. "They were butted together like mad bulls. They were impaled on the rocks, dashed against the cliffs, or tossed on land like corks from the spray. They were blown over until they careened and filled. Heavily freighted with human beings and weighty weapons, they sank by hundreds."

A Korean account offers more detail, explaining how the storm came up suddenly from the west and the ships that could clear their moorings headed for the sea. Before they could reach open water, however, "A terrible catastrophe occurred. The vessels were jammed together in the offing, and the bodies of men and broken timbers of the vessels were heaped together in a solid mass so that a person could walk across from one point of land to another on the mass of wreckage."

The final tally, according to the legend, was that nearly four thousand ships sank as the trapped vessels tried to disengage from one another and flee the bay through the narrow harbor entrance. Most did not make it, and nearly 100,000 men were drowned. There were some survivors, among them General Fan Wen-hu, who saved his life by clinging to a plank and riding the waves in to shore. There, he regrouped the survivors; Japanese accounts say 37,000 but the official Mongol history, the *Yüan-shi*, lists much smaller numbers. According to the *Yüan-shi*, Fan Wen-hu left the island in one of few remaining ships, "leaving more than a hundred men at Taka Isle; most of them were before long killed by the Japanese, and those who escaped death and came back were only three."

The exultant Japanese dragged exhausted survivors out of the water and killed them. Troops not aboard the ships and stranded on the beach, demoralized and cut off from escape, were rounded up and executed by the victorious samurai. According to Japanese records, all the captured Mongols and Koreans, viewed as aggressive invaders, were beheaded. The *Yüan-shi* talks of how the Japanese killed twenty to thirty thousand prisoners. Captured Chinese, however, were supposedly spared death because they were enslaved former Song. Three of the men stranded on Takashima ultimately returned home to Southern China, perhaps spared by the Japanese so they could bear witness to Khubilai of what had really happened to his expeditionary force. They were fortunate; Japanese legend tells of twelve thousand of their countrymen left behind in Japan as slaves.

A LEGEND IS BORN

The news of Khubilai's planned invasion of Japan generated more than a military response. Both the Imperial Court in Kyoto and the *bakufu* in Kamakura had urged temples to pray for the destruction of the enemy. In 1271, an Imperial edict told of how friendly envoys from Kōryo had warned Japan and asked for "prayers offered for peace. A *ninnō-e* curse against the Mongols shall be created and recorded." A *ninnō-e* was a high ritual that benevolent kings invoked to protect their countries. In 1281, Emperor Kameyama personally sent a prayer to Ise Shrine asking for the protection of Japan from the Mongols: "I beseech you to take my life if Japan suffers damage from this disturbance in my time."

At the time of the Mongol invasions, Japan was not only undergoing a political crisis; it was also in the throes of a religious revival in which priests like Nichiren preached a potent mixture of religion and incipient nationalism. For those of faith, the prayers offered in the temples by the devout were directly responsible for the defeat of the Mongols and the saving of the country. In writing about the failed 1274 invasion and the "reverse wind" that had swept the invaders from Hakata's shores, courtier Kadenokoji Kanenaka stated his belief that the wind had come because of the "protection of the gods! Most wonderful! We should praise the gods without ceasing. This great protection can only have happened because of the many prayers and offerings to the various shrines... around the realm." The 1281 invasion only strengthened Kanenaka's views. "This event reveals unprecedented divine support. A source of great rejoicing in the realm—what could exceed this? This is no random event... the gods' support has not ceased. One must more fervently worship the gods and buddhas."

In the Imperial Court in Kyoto, the belief of the courtiers was that Japan had been saved as a result of the emperor's prayer and his command that the priests at Ise read the "Great Wisdom Sutra." As the recitations of the priests "reached their climax, a single black cloud suddenly appeared in the clear sky. From its depths, a humming-bulb arrow, fledged with white feathers, sped westward with so fearsome a noise that the enemy host mistook it for a great wind. Huge waves sprang up, and the entire invasion force drowned in the wild waters. It was wondrous proof that ours is indeed the land of the gods."

The storm of 1281, now credited as a kamikaze, or divine wind, thus became firmly settled in the minds of Japan's leaders as not only the means of Japan's salvation, but also as divine. While Khubilai Khan would debate that status, Chinese records and other accounts also show that he viewed the debacle of 1281 as more than just an accident of nature. Defeat by storm might partially save face, not only for him but also for his commanders, including Fan Wen-hu, who returned to the Khan's court to plead his case. According to the *Yüan-shi*, Fan "made false representations... that he had reached Japan and was about to attack... when a storm struck and destroyed the ships."

According to Marco Polo, Khubilai found fault with his commanders. He had:

> sent two of his barons with a great fleet of ships carrying cavalry and infantry. One of these barons was named Abakan, the other Vonsamcin... They set sail from Zaiton and Kinsai and put out to sea and sailed to the island. They landed and occupied some open country and a number of villages, but they had not yet captured a single city or fortified town when the following disaster overtook them... there as great jealousy between the two commanders and neither would do anything to help the other. Now it happened one day that such a gale was blowing from the north that the troops declared that, if they did not get away, all their ships would be wrecked. So they all embarked and... put out to sea... when they had sailed about four miles, the gale began to freshen and there was such a crowd of ships that many of them were smashed by colliding with one another. Those that were not jammed together with others but had enough sea-room escaped shipwreck. Those that succeeded in clearing this island made good their escape. The others who failed to get clear were driven aground by the gale.

FOR YEARS SOME scholars have doubted the veracity of Polo's accounts, but based on what we know from the records, his retelling is surprisingly accurate. Historian Stephen Haw identifies Fan Wen-hu as Vonsancin, based on his rank and military title of Canzheng, and Abbacatan was Abakan, a Mongol general the *Yüan-shi* records as having co-command of the Japan expedition with Fan Wen-hu. Khubilai spared the life of his Chinese general, but demoted him.

The terrible reality of 1281 was more than just a second failed expedition against Japan. Khubilai had squandered much of the massive navy he had inherited from the Song and then built up at great expense, and with it tens of thousands of soldiers, weapons and provisions. For Khubilai, there was only one course to pursue, and that was to build up his navy once again and mount yet another assault against Japan. As he ordered more ships and more men—even pardoning prisoners and criminals to build up his third invasion force—Khubilai probably did not realize that his time to strike Japan had come and gone forever. Other campaigns and defeats awaited Khubilai Khan's navy, but Japan was safe.

Meanwhile the Japanese spent twenty years waiting for the Khan to return. The *bakufu* ran up huge expenses, struggling to reward the samurai who had defended Kyushu, repair and maintain their defenses, and plan for their own counter strike against Korea. The costs of 1274 and 1281 had weakened the Kamakura *bakufu*, and ultimately they would fall to new warriors who sought the power of the shogunate. The Mongol invasions had set in motion powerful forces in Japan, not the least of which was an inspiring legend that would last for seven hundred years and have tragic consequences for the island nation in the twentieth century.

NINE

Kamikaze

*The Japanese have the idea that their land is the
country of the Gods because they have been led to believe
that Japan is under the special protection of the heavenly
Being... No theoretical certainty attaches to this belief. But will
the knowledge of science bring the Gods' power to an end?*

NAKABA YAMADA (1916)

THE JAPANESE belief that their homeland was saved by divine intervention calls to mind another island nation, England, and one of its pivotal historical moments. When the Spanish Armada was defeated in 1588 by a combination of plucky seamanship, rapid gunfire and violent storms, Queen Elizabeth ordered medals struck with the motto "God Breathed and They Were Scattered." Human belief in the gods intervening in battle is ancient and profound, and like many of our deepest and oldest beliefs, is never easy to question. In Britain after the First World War it was unpatriotic, as well as godless, to argue that divine protection—in the form of the "Angel of Mons"—had not saved British troops at the Battle of Mons in Belgium on August 23, 1914.

No stories spread across Japan in the immediate aftermath of 1281, however. Historian Thomas Conlan, after exhaustively studying Japanese contemporary sources, found that at the time, there was very little belief in the concept of a divinely protected

Japan, outside of a "small coterie of courtiers and priests." That is not to say that the disbelievers were not religious; on the contrary, samurai of the time saw the battlefield "as a realm where gods and buddhas mingled with men." Thus warriors like Takezaki Suenaga believed that the gods had protected them. Men caught up in combat often feel a divine presence at their sides, especially when they survive horrific battles or a long war. This feeling finds expression in more modern times. A famous example from the Second World War was American ace Robert L. Scott who, after flying against the Japanese over Burma and China, called his autobiography *God is My Co-Pilot*; it was a bestseller and became a hit Hollywood movie. In the same vein, samurai veterans of the Mongol wars kept their faith, with Suenaga actively supporting the restoration and upkeep of shrines. But there was nothing exceptional in this, and it certainly did not translate into a fervent belief that the Gods alone had saved Japan.

Some did believe it, however, and that belief lasted for decades. In 1309, the chief priest of the Takeo Shrine in Kyushu wrote to the *bakufu* to ask for a reward for the shrine's services in the 1281 invasion, stating that at that time the god of his shrine had fired arrows from his sanctuary at the invaders, and that three purple banners flying from his shrine had pointed toward the Mongol fleet just before the storm hit. However, Conlan points out that even among priests, there was doubt over just what had happened. When a priest named Eison claimed that his prayers had created the kamikaze, Nichiren, who had warned the *bakufu* that Japan's religious uncertainty would lead to divine punishment in the form of an invasion, nonetheless remarked that "little more than an autumn wind and a tiny amount of water" had sunk the Khan's ships. Even the most devout could read the weather, Nichiren seemed to be saying—or perhaps he just knew that the storm had not been heaven sent because he had not prayed for it. Ironically, seven centuries after his death, Nichiren would become a rallying figure for Japanese ultranationalists who made him one of the poster boys for the cult of the Emperor's (and hence Japan's) divine status.

It was those very same ultranationalists who revived the dormant, if not forgotten, tales of the Mongol invasion and the destruction of Khubilai Khan's navy, and who spread the belief of a kamikaze as part of a deliberate campaign linked to the late nineteenth and early twentieth century rise of Japanese nationalism and militarism. The story of the kamikaze would not only help fuel Japan's rise to colonial power and entry into global war, it would inspire some of Japan's most desperate and heartrending acts at that war's end. So it is not surprising that the story of the kamikaze would eventually inspire a search to determine just what happened to Khubilai Khan's navy, and if the old legends have any basis in fact.

JAPAN'S "HISTORICAL MEMORY" OF THE MONGOL INVASION

In the aftermath of the two invasions, the Japanese did not forget Khubilai Khan's aggression or Kōryo's role in the attacks on Kyushu. Japanese pirates, known as *Wakō* (from a pejorative Korean term, *Waegyu*, or "dwarf raiders"), had begun attacking and robbing coastal Korea in 1223, and their ongoing raids, launched from as far away as Kyushu and as close as Tsushima through the following decades, had doubtless played a role in Kōryo's eagerness to support Khubilai's invasion. After the debacle of 1281, it soon became clear that the Khan was not going to be able to muster another large invasion fleet, so the raids began again in earnest, gradually expanding with real vengeance to the southern coast of China—a nation that now was an enemy, not a trading partner.

Nearly a century after the invasions, not long after the fall of the Mongol Yüan Dynasty, China's newly inaugurated Ming Dynasty sent an envoy to the Japanese court to ask that the emperor stop the *Wakō*, who raided with government approval. The envoy arrived in March 1370. The emperor met him, and angrily reminded the Ming envoy about Khubilai's invasions:

> The Mongols, who are barbarians... wanted to turn us into their subjects and our predecessors refused to submit. They,

therefore, dispatched their envoy by the surname Chao to beguile us with sweet words. Hardly before he finished the words, a maritime force of one hundred thousand strong was arrayed against our coast. Thanks to Heaven who brought about the thunder and waves, in no time the whole force was totally annihilated. Now a new Son of Heaven is lording over the Middle Kingdom and the imperial envoy also has Chao as his family name. Is he the Mongol envoy's descendant? Is he going to beguile us with sweet words and attack us by surprise?

Despite the harsh words, the envoy and the emperor ended their audience amicably, which didn't stop the *Wakō* from continuing their raids on the Chinese coast for the next three centuries. They would not desist until the Tokugawa shogunate closed Japan to foreigners in the early seventeenth century and forbade Japanese mariners—even pirates—from sailing out of sight of land.

It seemed that as long as the *Wakō* raids continued, the historical memory of the Mongol invasions remained part of the Japanese consciousness, particularly in Kyushu, Takashima and Hakata, then beginning to transition into Fukuoka. This changed when Japan withdrew into its island borders after 1636 and "foreign" concepts, notably the Christianity introduced by Portuguese and Dutch traders, were ruthlessly stamped out. In its splendid isolation, Japan came to focus on an insular vision of its own uniqueness, and Japanese culture evolved in its own direction, free of foreign taint and influence. Mention of the Mongol invasion was officially prohibited, and in time most people forgot all about it. As late as 1808, when a Japanese novelist wrote a historical drama with a plot involving the Mongol invasion, the Japanese government forced him to remove any mention of the event. The historical memory was not revived until the United States forced Japan to open its doors to outside trade in 1854, when it began to be cited to remind the people that once before Japan had been able to resist the forced introduction of something foreign and alien.

There is a fascinating Japanese woodblock print, dated to the mid-1860s, that depicts Mongol troops fighting on the beach, the invaders of course being overpowered and driven back toward the water. Out on the sea, the enemy ships are taking a pounding, and three of them, hit by cannon fire, are sinking. To look at it, it soon becomes clear that this is a less than accurate depiction of the events of 1281 with some obvious anachronisms. Indeed, a small cartouche on the print says, "despite some inaccuracies in the picture, the public can surely imagine the true scene." Make no mistake—this is an allegory.

The ships in the background in the print are not Khubilai Khan's medieval navy. Instead, they strongly resemble the "black ships" of the American and European navies that had forcibly "opened" Japan, complete with steamship side-wheels and the large black-painted hulls that gave them their Japanese name. The print came at a critical time in Japanese history, not long after British warships bombarded Kagoshima to retaliate for the murder of a British merchant by a feudal lord opposed to the foreigners' presence, and the sinking of two Japanese vessels at Choshū to punish them for firing on European ships. It is part of a revival of the history of the Mongol invasions, a revival that helped reinforce in the public's minds the notion that Japan, a nation of warriors with God—or the gods—on their side, could push off any invader.

THE RISE OF MODERN JAPAN

Opening up to the West had several consequences for Japan, not the least of which was the fall of the *bakufu* and the transfer of power from the shogun to the emperor. Responding to pressure from the Western powers, Japanese patriots—who feared that Japan would go the way of China, recently attacked, defeated and forced to cede both territory and sovereignty in the Opium Wars—maneuvered to end the control of the Tokugawa Shogun and the samurai. In its stead they built a new state centered on the emperor. The goal was to take some of what the West had to offer, notably modern weapons and industrialization, and transform a feudal society in which warriors were beholden to provincial *daimyos*, or lords, to a strong, centralized government with a national army. The *bakufu* fell in 1868, and in its place a new government, headed by Emperor Meiji, arose.

In 1871, the government ordered the end of feudalism, abolished the positions of the *daimyo* and samurai, and abolished the system of clan armies and clan government. The system that had sent Takezaki Suenaga to war against the Mongols in 1274 and 1281 was no more. In its place came national conscription and a new force, the Imperial Japanese Army. The process was not easy—there were almost two hundred rebellions against the new order in the decade between 1868 and 1878—but the emperor's forces were ultimately successful. The determination of Meiji officials to radically change Japan was phenomenal.

As part of this policy the officials encouraged the development of manufacturing facilities and an expansion of trade. When Japan's few wealthy families demurred and refused to invest, the Meiji government put up the money themselves, building arms factories and shipyards as well as glass, sugar, cement and silk works in the 1870s. The success of the new industrial facilities caught on, and in the next decade the government began selling its facilities to new private investors, such as the Mitsubishi family, who bought a government shipyard at a reduced price to encourage their investment. Other families and investors also profited, forming the *zaibatsu* or financial combines that quickly came to dominate Japanese business, as they still do today. Working closely with the government, the *zaibatsu* were partners in creating a modern industrial state, be it a state with a heavy emphasis on producing modern ships, guns and ammunition. The government retained a controlling interest in strategic industries such as the railroads and poured money into military preparation. Even during the economic cutbacks of the 1880s, as they adjusted the economy to deal with the incredible expenditures of the last decade, the Meiji government increased military spending by 60 percent.

To counter an invasion of Japan and to build a strong national force loyal to the government, Meiji officials pursued a policy they called *fukoku kyōhei*: "rich country, strong military." They had built up the army to a force of 200,000 by 1890. Operating under strict discipline on the German model, the army regularly professed its undying loyalty to the emperor. In 1882, the emperor issued an order to the armed forces reminding them of Japan's proud military past and of the need to be loyal and cultivate a "traditional military spirit." The same order was also addressed to the sailors of the new Imperial Japanese Navy, formed in 1872. By 1894, thanks to the purchase of warships from foreign shipyards and the addition of vessels built in Japan's new facilities, the Imperial Japanese Navy was a formidable fighting force with twenty-eight capital ships. The island nation was determined it would never again be invaded by sea.

Japanese society was revolutionized by these developments. Instead of loyalty to a lord or a clan, samurai and the citizenry at large were encouraged to shift their support to the idea of the nation, as symbolized by the emperor, who was portrayed as the living embodiment of the gods. The emperor's advisors, who in truth were the actual rulers of a young and easily manipulated sovereign, chose to reintroduce and reinforce key elements of the "past" to support their main themes, the critical concepts of: resistance to foreigners, the divine nature of Japan and its emperor, the divine protection Japan enjoyed, the idea of a unique Japanese identity, the importance of nationalism and devotion to the state (as represented by the emperor), the concept of ultimate sacrifice to protect the emperor and state and the expansion of the Japanese Empire and the imposition of Japanese values on its neighbors, particularly those who had threatened Japan in the past, notably Korea, China and Mongolia.

In this vein, the story of the Mongol invasions and the powerful myth of the kamikaze were dusted off and polished up for a new generation, who were taught to believe in the legend and the ideals behind it. The story of the invasions was not common knowledge in 1868, or even as late as 1890. It was at this time that Takezaki Suenaga's scrolls "reappeared." The old samurai had placed the precious documents in a shrine controlled by his descendants, but the family lost them in the late fourteenth century as part of a struggle with other samurai. The scrolls went to a rival family, who in turn passed them on to another family, the Ōyano, in the late sixteenth century. The Ōyano, says historian Thomas Conlan, prohibited anyone from reading the passages or even looking at the images on the scrolls. Locked away and badly damaged, the scrolls were not rediscovered until the late eighteenth century, when they were repaired and copied by *bakufu* officials who borrowed them in 1793. Returned to the Ōyano, the scrolls remained under lock and key until 1890, when the family gave them as a present to Emperor Meiji.

The gift was timely, and the Imperial Palace may have even demanded it. Suddenly the scrolls were reproduced and published everywhere, part of a campaign that included the writing of books, poetry and songs and the painting of pictures. The story they held, of the heroism and bravery of Takezaki Suenaga, was retold as an exaggerated legend underscored by the divine intervention that saved Japan from an overwhelming foe. Art historian Mayu Tsuruya, who has investigated the role of art in Japan's militarization, especially in the Second World War, notes that "because of the legendary and supernatural implications that accumulated along with the stories that they told," Suenaga's scrolls became "a favorite of the military and intellectuals during the time of the first Sino-Japanese War" of 1894–1895. "As the first foreign conflict that Japan had encountered in modern times," Tsuruya writes, that conflict "invoked the legend of the kamikaze intervention. The Mongol invasion scrolls were cited as documentary evidence of Japan's superior spiritual power." It would not be the last time; "this invocation of their message of divine invincibility was made again when Japan again fought foreign enemies."

At the same time, artist Ishho Yada created a series of Western-style paintings of the Mongol Invasion that are in the collections of the Mongol Invasion Museum in Fukuoka. Still not widely known to Westerners, they, like the images in Suenaga's scrolls, tell a story. However, Yada's paintings add new elements. They include battle scenes at Tsushima and Hakata, and the Japanese taking the fight to the seas. One painting, *The Mongol Cruelties at Iki Island*, shows women kicked and trussed, their hands pierced as children scream and babies are snatched away from mothers to be killed. Another, *The Heroic Death of Sukesada*, shows individual samurai overwhelmed by groups of leering Mongols. The paintings also include three scenes in which the emperor dispatches envoys with his prayer to Ise shrine; the envoys pray at the shrine; and finally, a frothy sea sinks a fleet of ships. The last work is entitled *The Prayer is Heard and the Divine Tempest Blows*. The paintings, printed on thin, cheap paper, and widely distributed, were a popular means of rewriting the history of the invasion, unsubtly underscoring, through images of brave but overwhelmed samurai, of stalemate and of atrocity—how the emperor's intercession with the gods had saved Japan.

The imagery of the Mongol invasions and the story of divine intervention assisted the Meiji government as their focus shifted from the defense of their shores to Japan's own colonial expansion. The nationalists and militarists had dreamed of just such an expansion since the early decades of Meiji's reign. One of them, Yukichi Fukuzawa, founder of the *Jiji Shimpo* newspaper, had stated as early as 1882 that "we shall someday raise the national power of Japan so that not only shall we control the natives of China and India as the English do today, but we shall also possess in our hands the power to rebuke the English and to rule Asia ourselves." In 1879, Japan forcibly annexed the neighboring Ryukyu Islands, notably Okinawa, into its nascent empire. The next major step, in 1894, was war with China. Japanese interest in Korea, especially to tap into Korean coal and iron to feed the furnaces of Japan's rapidly expanding industrial and military complex, led to a forced treaty between Korea and Japan in 1875 and near war in 1884 when a pro-Japanese coup failed thanks to the intervention of Chinese troops.

An 1885 treaty between China and Japan over Korea only forestalled the inevitable. Both empires sent troops to Korea, and when the Japanese overthrew the Korean ruler in 1894 and established a pro-Japanese state, war followed. Japan struck first, occupying Korea in a bloody land and sea campaign and advancing deep into China, defeating the Chinese army in several battles. Japanese troops also invaded Taiwan. When the war ended in April 1895, China had lost Taiwan and the nearby Pescadores Islands and a large part of Manchuria, and as a condition of the peace treaty was forced to pay a huge indemnity to Japan. Militarists could now boast that the insult of the Mongol invasions had been repaid, and Khubilai's former ally, Korea, had been reduced to a Japanese vassal state.

Japan's next offensive was a response to Russia's colonial interests in Korea and Manchuria, part of the tsar's desires for a Pacific port to tap into Asian trade. The war went badly for Russia, with its fleet smashed more than once by the Imperial Japanese Navy, especially in the decisive naval battle in the Straits of Tsushima on May 27–28, 1905. The Japanese fleet sank all of Russia's eight battleships, crippling Russian sea power and effectively ending the yearlong conflict. The Russo-Japanese War, and especially the Battle of Tsushima, shocked the Western world. Japan was the first Asian power to defeat a Western force in war, and its victories gave homegrown militarism and nationalism a major boost.

During the Meiji era, the government also developed State Shintō, a new religion previously practiced by a small sect that believed the emperor to be a god. This push, beginning in 1871, coincided with the Meiji government's encouragement of Nichiren Buddhism, an obscure denomination that reinforced nationalism, pride in a unique Japanese identity and xenophobia. The merger of Shintō and Buddhism was necessary, because Buddhism and Confucianism, both deeply rooted in Japanese culture, were too strongly supported by the public to be replaced by Shintō. By the turn of the century, clever Meiji officials came to terms with reality, tolerating Buddhism but merging Confucian values into Shintō. Confucius had argued that children must honor and obey their parents, and they adapted this into the concept of the emperor as the "father" of the Japanese—a united nation guided and protected by a living god, a god whose ancestors had saved Japan, not once but twice, when the Mongols came calling.

Nichiren's Buddhist sect, hijacked symbolically by the militarists, was also taken over physically. At the shrine in Fukuoka is a massive eighty-two-ton statue of the monk. It rests on a pedestal surrounded by cast bronze plaques that include scenes similar to those in Yada's paintings, including a disturbing image of Mongol troops killing helpless samurai, babies and the elderly, and a smiling Mongol holding a struggling woman as a Korean vassal cuts through her palms. Admiral Heihachiro Togo, commander of the victorious Japanese fleet at Tsushima, prayed and left poems at Hakozaki shrine. Following the battle, he also worshipped at a newly erected shrine to Nichiren in Fukuoka, built between 1894 and 1904 to let Nichiren's "life-staking activities for establishing righteousness and secure the peace of the nation be remembered forever."

Inside the pedestal, encased like a holy relic, is a section of the mast of Admiral Togo's ship, *Mikasa*, damaged in the battle and taken out, not for scrap, but to form a symbolic link that spanned the centuries and made the point, subtly but dramatically, that Japan's rise in the early twentieth century was an inevitable consequence not only of the invasions but also because of the emperor's powerful military, which, guided and protected by his divinity, was redressing the past and forging a bright new future for Japan.

CONSEQUENCES

Japan's march down the path of nationalism, militarism and expansion continued unabated as the twentieth century progressed. Eager for spoils and glory, Japan joined the Allies in the First World War, sending its navy out to harass the German East Asiatic Squadron and to occupy Germany's Pacific possessions. Fear of the Imperial Japanese Navy sent the German squadron, under the command of the Graf von Spee, out of Asia; the only exception was the auxiliary cruiser SMS *Cormoran*, which ended up interned in Guam by the then neutral United States. Japan's reward, in the Treaty of Versailles, was Germany's former colonies in the Marianas and Marshall Islands. Now a major Pacific power, Japan fortified its newly acquired island territories and made preparations for additional conquest. In the 1930s, Japan's expansion continued. An undeclared war against China led to the Japanese occupation of much of that country and the creation of a "puppet state" in Manchuria. A political alliance with Germany and Italy to form the "Axis" led in time to the Japanese occupation of French Indochina.

Japan's expansion and the brutality of the war it waged in China brought foreign condemnation and an American embargo. The ongoing American presence in the Philippines, Guam and China, as well as European presence in the area—Britain's colonies in Hong Kong and Singapore and the Dutch colonies of Indonesia—would lead to Japan's next military undertaking. Launching simultaneous strikes on December 7 and 8, 1941, Japan delivered a devastating blow, especially to the United States Pacific Fleet at Pearl Harbor. In the aftermath of the attacks, Japan's empire expanded halfway across the Pacific, south to the doorway of Australia and north to the Aleutian Islands of Alaska. With its offensive capabilities crippled by the Pearl Harbor attack, the United States' response was limited at first. By June 1942, however, American industrial capacity and a rapidly expanding military had responded, and the tide of the war began to turn against Japan. By the fall of 1944, the war was effectively lost. For the first time since 1281, an enemy fleet was approaching Japan's sacred shores.

It was then that the venerable story of the Mongols' defeat was invoked in a desperate last measure to stem the tide. There were no prayers, no divine answers, only the sacrifice of over two thousand young men in the *Shinpū*, or kamikaze corps. They went, willingly, to die "for the great cause of our country," as two Japanese naval officers would later write. Their sacrifice "signified a constant and deeply grounded belief in their country and their emperor, and a willingness to die for that belief." The pilots who chose *tokkō*, or suicide tactics, were not alone. On the high seas, other young men squeezed into the tiny cockpits of modified torpedoes—renamed *kaiten*, or "heaven-shakers"—and piloted them into the hulls of enemy ships. Others were trained to attack in bomb-laden high-speed boats. On the battlefields, soldiers rallied in the face of defeat and gave one last charge to the death. Naval ships, their air cover gone and surrounded by few escorts on the sea, sailed into gauntlets of fire. Even Japan's greatest battleships, *Musashi* and *Yamato*, perished under a hail of American bombs, leaving few survivors.

One of the ships that sank near the end of this brutal war was the cruiser *Maya*. In the predawn darkness of October 22, 1944, *Maya* steamed through the Palawan Passage in the Philippines to strike at the battle fleet of the US Navy in a series of actions that history would later call the Battle of Leyte Gulf. As it entered the strait, American submarines ambushed *Maya* and her sister ships *Atago*, *Takao* and *Chōkai*. Hit by torpedoes, *Atago* disappeared within minutes. As *Maya* continued on, the submarine USS *Dace* fired four torpedoes, ripping the cruiser open from bow to stern, blasting into her chain locker near the number one gun turret, a boiler room and the aft engine room. Wracked by explosions, *Maya* listed to port and sank less than ten minutes after the first hit, taking 336 of the crew, including the captain, into the depths.

Rescued from the sea by other ships, *Maya*'s survivors crowded onto the battleship *Musashi*. Their respite was brief. The following day, *Musashi* sank under fierce attack, taking 143 of *Maya*'s crew with her. Out of 1,105 men, 626 survived the Battle of Leyte Gulf. They were luckier than others who went down nearly to the last man with their ships. When the battleship *Yamato* exploded and sank under aerial attack on April 7, 1945, she took all but 280 of her 2,778-man crew with her. The last months of the war did not offer good odds for the survival of Japan's sailors. Among the lucky was a former *Maya* gunnery officer, thirty-one-year-old Torao Mozai. Stricken with tuberculosis at the beginning of the war and sent into the naval hospital, where he was not expected to live,

Mozai did not die. In August 1945 he joined a number of other survivors, numbed by the experiences of war and wondering how they had managed to survive when so many of their friends and family members had died.

Millions of Japanese, Chinese, Indonesians, Pacific Islanders, and hundreds of thousands of Americans, British, Dutch, Canadian, Australian and New Zealand soldiers, sailors, marines and civilians had also perished in the Pacific theater. Their friends and families blamed Japan and its militarists. So too did some Japanese. However, most Japanese went on with their lives, picking up the pieces in a bombed-out, fire-ravaged and nuclear-scarred nation. In time, some of them, including Torao Mozai, would seek answers. For Mozai, the quest for answers took him back to the shores of Hakata Bay, seeking to determine what had really happened in 1274 and 1281. His quest would pit science against belief.

TEN

Takashima

*North-westerly gales frequently occur in the early and latter parts
of the year, lasting from one to three days, and not giving much warning
of their approach, but a heavy swell is usually the first prognostic.*

LORDS COMMISSIONERS OF THE ADMIRALTY,
Sailing Directions for Japan, Korea and Adjacent Seas (1904)

TORAO MOZAI is a short, solidly built, energetic man. When
he, at age 89, last visited the site of Khubilai Khan's naval
defeat, he dominated the room, hiked to the top of a hill
and was known to wink a time or two at pretty girls. "Call me
Tiger," he said with a grin. Proud of his health, stamina and his
many achievements in a long lifetime, Mozai is, to Westerners and
perhaps to more than a few of his fellow citizens, not the stereo-
typical, self-effacing Japanese. He has no reason to be. Mozai is a
survivor of a war that consumed many of his generation. He is also
very much a self-made man. Born on February 9, 1914, in Hōjō at
the foot of Mount Tsukuba in the prefecture of Ibaraki, about an
hour out of Tokyo by fast train, Mozai came into the world on the
day, month and year of the tiger (in Japanese, "*tora*," a word made
famous by the wartime code phrase, "*tora, tora, tora*")—a lucky
star to be born under. And so the boy was named Torao, the word
for a male tiger.

As a boy, Mozai wanted to be a scientist. He also had a power-ful interest in the sea. At age five, the young tiger went to Tokyo and there saw one of Japan's most famous "memorial ships," the 1873-built iron ship *Meiji Maru*, progenitor of the modern Japa-nese Navy. "I was deeply impressed," Mozai later reminisced, "and decided to map a plan for my life" that would take him to sea. That plan led him to Tokyo Nautical College, where he applied for admission, only to fail the entrance examination. Unde-terred, Mozai took the exam again, failing again and again, and finally passed on his fifth try. As a cadet in the college, Mozai at last went to sea, sailing to Hawaii, Fiji and other Pacific islands in the four-masted barque *Taisei Maru*. He also steamed through-out the southern Pacific in the veteran Nippon Yusen Kaisha (NYK) liner *Yokohama Maru*, and then rounded the world twice in the NYK liner *Awata Maru*. Graduating in 1938 with the high-est marks in his class, he might have become the oceanographer he had once dreamed of becoming. Instead, like many other young men of promise, Mozai joined the Imperial Japanese Navy. He did not really have a choice. Japan was at war in China, the Navy was expanding, and Mozai, now a reserve midshipman, headed off to gunnery school at Yokosuka, where he trained as a junior officer before joining his first ship, the cruiser *Maya*.

Mozai's service first took him out into Japan's home waters, but as war broke out with the Allies, Mozai's turn for overseas duty came. But he never made it into combat. An attack of pneumonia in the winter of 1939 led to a diagnosis of tuberculosis. Mozai's doctor told him the disease was fatal, and gave him a month to live. Mozai, however, did not give up. Instead of steaming through the gaunt-let of American submarines that tracked and sank many of Japan's warships and merchant marine, or joining in the surface battles that took the lives of so many of his fellow graduates by aerial bomb or naval gunfire, Mozai instead "fought against illness in bed, not against enemies on the sea," as he relates his wartime years. In the peace that followed, Japan's Imperial Navy was gone for the foresee-able future and there were few jobs for naval officers. But Mozai's skill, knowledge and perseverance paid off with a professorship at the Tokyo University of the Mercantile Marine. While teaching there, he also became a student once again, and in 1962 received his Doctorate in Engineering from the University of Tokyo.

In 1978, at the end of his university career, electrical and mechanical engineer Mozai served as a technical advisor for Inmarsat, the international maritime satellite system. He retired the following year. But rather than go quietly into old age, Mozai turned back to the stories of his youth, particularly to the saga of the Mongol invasions. As a "student of naval history as well as a professor of engineering," Mozai explained, he had long been fascinated by the story of the Mongol invasions. What had really happened in the thirteenth century? How much of the story was true, and more important to Mozai, what was left? "The interpretation of this story," Mozai would later write, "is very controversial." It was, he said, "simply not possible to interpret the story in any logical way."

Mozai knew, like most Japanese of his generation, that the invaders had landed twice at Hakata. Other than the stone wall erected after the 1274 invasion, which Japanese archaeologists had excavated and partially restored before the war, he knew of no discoveries from Hakata Bay that could be traced to Khubilai Khan's navy. Stone anchors had been found, and one was proudly displayed at Hakozaki shrine as a Mongol anchor, but Mozai felt that they could have come from any ships of the period; there was nothing to link them directly to the Khan. But there was another place where for centuries more provocative finds had been emerging from the sea. In 1980, he made his first trip to Takashima, where Japanese histories claimed that the war had been fought. What particularly drew Mozai's attention were tales of how fishermen on the island kept snagging "Chinese pots" from the waters along the southern shores of the seven-square-mile island. A bronze Buddha, also caught in a net in the eighteenth century, was still on the island, placed in a roadside shrine. Mozai's instincts told him what any maritime archaeologist worth his salt knows.

Fishermen are almost always the first to discover shipwrecks, even ones archaeologists spend years or decades searching for.

In the summer of 1980, Mozai took to the waters off Takashima with a small team of engineers and a sonoprobe borrowed from Kokusai Kogyo, a Japanese company that specialized in undersea geology. With the probe, Mozai and the team "crisscrossed" an area where fishermen had said they kept snagging pots. The instrument sent sound waves pinging down through a hundred feet of water, then on through thick mud before hitting buried layers of undersea rock. Mozai's attention, however, was drawn to a series of smaller features that kept showing up on the black-and-white recording paper of the instrument. They might have been "artifacts, scattered debris, individual rocks, or merely buried clumps of seashells," Mozai recalls, but the team had no way of knowing. Frustrated, he realized that the sonoprobe as it was would not do the job.

Returning to Tokyo, Mozai went to see his friend Iso Tanaka, vice president of Koden Electronics, to see if the company's color sonar used to find schools of fish could be adapted to the sonoprobe. Tanaka assigned his engineers to the job and by late 1980 they had successfully merged the two technologies. Now, when Mozai resumed his survey, the device should be able to not only detect buried items but also give the team some idea of what they were. "Objects made of the hardest materials, such as stone, metal or porcelain," said Mozai, would register as red on the screen. Wood, a softer material, would be orange, and silt and sand would show up on the screen as yellow or green. Water, the softest of all, would appropriately be blue. Armed with his improved sonoprobe, and with funding from the Japanese Ministry of Education, Mozai returned to Takashima in the summer of 1981.

TRACES OF THE KHAN'S LOST FLEET EMERGE

The summer of 1981 was a good one for Torao Mozai and his team. Purely by fluke, he claimed, the return to Takashima coincided with the seven hundredth anniversary of the Mongol invasion.

Again guided by local fishermen, the sonoprobe registered a multi-hued array of items buried in the mud. As the instrument kept pinging into the depths, Mozai sent divers down with airlifts and hand tools to extract their finds from the muddy seabed. "In less than two weeks our diving team recovered iron spearheads, iron and copper nails, stone anchors, heavy stone bowls, curiously shaped bricks, iron ingots, and quantities of porcelain and earthenware pots, vases, bowls, and dishes." Mozai's divers also brought up an intact saber that they found sticking upright in the mud, "probably worn by a thirteenth century Mongol cavalry officer," Mozai postulated. Eager to participate in the recovery work, the retired engineer—"no thought nor concern given to my age"—had learned to dive at age sixty-six and joined the team for the twenty days they scoured the bottom.

Mozai returned to Takashima again in the summer of 1982, joined this time by two foreign archaeologists, Jeremy Green of the Western Australian Maritime Museum and Ivan Simeonov Ivanov of the Varna Archaeological Museum. In thirty days of diving, the team recovered even more artifacts, including stone balls—of the type thrown by catapults—and more pots. Catapult balls, another saber, spearheads, stone bowls that could have been used to grind and mix gunpowder, plus thin bricks used, he imagined, to line blacksmith's forges as they repaired and made weapons: Mozai was sure he had found the lost fleet of Khubilai Khan. But he did not have any scientific proof. The discoveries included many thirteenth-century artifacts, and some could be tied to Song and *Yüan* China. The waters off Takashima, however, have seen many centuries of maritime traffic, before and after the Mongol invasion. Mozai's finds could have come from any shipwreck, or even from items tossed overboard by passing vessels.

Mozai was sure they were not. The Buddha pulled from the sea by Takashima fishermen in the eighteenth century was identified by scholars as a Kanzeon Bosatsu Buddha, a symbol of mercy "revered by the Mongols as a protector for their armies." However, the centuries-old Buddha had not been found by archaeologists and the story of its recovery is, as they say in a court of law, not proof enough. Even its rescue from the sea was just hearsay. What Mozai needed was a smoking gun, and he was handed it by a local farmer, Kuniichi Mukae. Several years before Mozai arrived on the scene, in 1974, Mukae went to the beach to dig for clams. As his spade dug through the muddy sand, he hit a heavy object. Brushing it off, he saw it was bronze, and worth keeping, so he tossed it into his toolbox.

As news of Mozai's work spread around Takashima—and that did not take long on an island of only four thousand people— locals started bringing in the finds of years past to show the professor. So it was that Mukae arrived with his piece of bronze. It was a small seal, a stamp used to mark documents. It measured less than a square inch in area, but it was a huge find. "I immediately realized the seal was a national treasure," Mozai recalled. The markings on the front of the seal were in a script Mozai could not identify, but on the back, Chinese writing dated it to "September, fourteenth year of Shigen," or in modern terms, September 1277. That date excited more than Mozai; expert study of the seal by Dr. Takashi Okazaki of Kyushu University revealed the script on the front to be Phagspa, a Tibetan-based writing used by the Mongols. What it said was *"gon geun dzung bayin,"* or "seal of an army commander." The seal, dated to four years before the 1281 invasion, had belonged to a Mongol military commander and it came out of the muddy foreshore of Takashima. At last, Mozai had proof that at least some of the Khan's men had been on the island. And they had left behind something as important as a seal, which could only mean that disaster had struck them during their stay.

Mozai's work, he noted, "caused a great sensation in Japan." It also made international headlines. On August 30, 1981, the *New York Times* broke the story under the headline, "Japanese Says He Has Found Kublai Khan's Fleet." Concluding that a series of color images on the improved sonoprobe represented sunken ships, Mozai reported that "without doubt" seventy-two hulls lay buried under twenty-one feet of mud in about eighty feet of water. The newspaper story went around the world, and soon *National Geographic* magazine invited Mozai to write an article.

The publicity led Mozai to a cross-country speaking tour of the US in the fall of 1982, plus a lecture at the National Maritime Museum in Greenwich, just outside London. Mozai was a celebrity abroad and a hero on Takashima, now firmly on the world map as the site of a great underwater discovery. Japan's Board of Education, eager to capitalize on the media attention, funded the construction of a museum on the island, and there many of Mozai's discoveries were placed alongside others brought in by locals. The pride of the new exhibition was the bronze seal, now formally designated by the government of Japan as a national treasure. A massive granite replica of the seal stands on end in front of the museum—a reminder of the importance of this single piece of bronze. The Takashima museum remains a popular destination on the island to this day, its halls filled with broken pots, stone bowls, the catapult balls and copies of Ishho Yada's paintings.

For all the excitement, though, one question remained. Where were the ships? The team found ten stone anchors from ships, and one provocative sonar image showed a sixty-foot-long, five-foot-deep target, which Mozai described as "extremely interesting." But it was out of reach to his team, and after three seasons in the field, his funding had run out. The initial excitement was gone. As early as 1982, even Mozai had to admit that he was not sure of just what he had found. "We still have not made the discovery of a Mongol ship itself," he confided to audiences on his speaking tour. That task would fall to a new generation of searchers.

SEEKING THE SHIPS

The new generation of Japanese archaeologists was represented by Kenzo Hayashida, recently returned to Japan after completing his master's degree in classical archaeology at the University of Pennsylvania. As a student at Penn, Hayashida heard about another, more famous Penn graduate, George Bass. While at Penn as a

The aircraft carrier USS *Saratoga* (CV-3) burns after an attack by several *kamikaze* aircraft off Iwo Jima, February 21, 1945. *(U.S. Naval Institute)*

ABOVE A fifth-century BC Chinese bronze depicting large, decked
canoes engaged in battle. Men paddle below decks while fighters armed
with halberds and swords face off on deck. *(Author's collection)*

FACING TOP Among a Mongol's greatest military assets were his horse,
saddle with stirrups, and bow, which allowed him to ride and fight quickly
and with accuracy. This image of a Mongol warrior is from an illustrated
Turkish manuscript. *(Author's collection)*

FACING BOTTOM A seagoing Chinese craft of the eighteenth century.
In form and design, these inaccurately named "junks" represented a form
perfected in the eleventh century that enabled China's mariners to rule
the seas. *(Author's collection)*

ABOVE Inspired by a mythic history and a sense of divinely controlled destiny, Japan emerged as a major military power in the late nineteenth century. Memories of the Mongol/Chinese invasions played a role. This contemporary woodblock print depicts the Imperial Japanese Navy smashing a Chinese fleet in the Sino-Japanese War of 1894. *(Author's collection)*

FACING A detail of the *Moko Shurai Ekotoba* or Mongol Invasions Painting Scrolls, commissioned by samurai Takezaki Suenaga in 1293. Suenaga is among the brave samurai in a small boat attacking a large vessel crowded with Mongol invaders. *(Courtesy Museum of the Imperial Collections, Sannomaru Shozokan)*

FACING The early twentieth-century shrine to Nichiren in Fukuoka is decorated with large bronze panels depicting the brutality of the Mongol invasions of 1274 and 1281. Here, a Mongol soldier carries off a baby to kill it; on another panel an invader pierces a woman's hands with a knife to hang her off the side of a ship. These modern monuments helped define Japan's "memory" of the Mongol attacks. *(James P. Delgado, 2002)*

ABOVE One of thousands of prints reproduced from Ishho Yada's *The Prayer is Heard and the Divine Tempest Blows* (ca. 1895) depicting the destruction of Khubilai Khan's fleet by the divine wind, or *kamikaze*. The originals hang in Fukuoka at the Mongol Invasion Museum. *(Torao Mozai collection)*

ABOVE Torao Mozai at the Mongol Invasion monument on Takashima, 2002. Mozai's pioneering discoveries paved the way for the archaeological excavation of Khubilai Khan's lost fleet. (*James P. Delgado, 2002*)

FACING TOP "Mongol" stone anchor weight at Hakozaki Shrine. Unlike the anchor stones recovered by archaeologists at Takashima, this single piece of stone cannot be archaeologically linked to the Mongol invasions, but it has powerful symbolic and religious meaning at the shrine. (*James P. Delgado, 2002*)

FACING BOTTOM Takashima's rugged shores and hillsides were the final battlefield for Khubilai Khan's navy in 1281. (*James P. Delgado, 2002*)

ABOVE Discovered by farmer Kuniichi Mukae while digging for clams off a Takashima beach in 1974, this bronze seal says *"gon geun dzung bayin,"* or "commander of 1,000," in Phagspa, a Tibetan-based writing used by the Mongols. It is dated 1277 and was the initial "smoking gun" that proved that the Khan's fleet had been lost off Takashima. *(James P. Delgado, 2002, courtesy of the Matsura Board of Education)*

FACING TOP Under the direction of archaeologist Kenzo Hayashida (far left), the archaeological excavation and study of Khubilai Khan's lost fleet has progressed for nearly two decades. Here, divers are briefed by archaeologist Mitsuhiko Ogawa before the day's work begins. *(James P. Delgado, 2002)*

FACING BOTTOM A diver carefully removes centuries of mud from the wrecked fleet with an underwater dredge. *(Courtesy of KOSUWA and the Matsura Board of Education)*

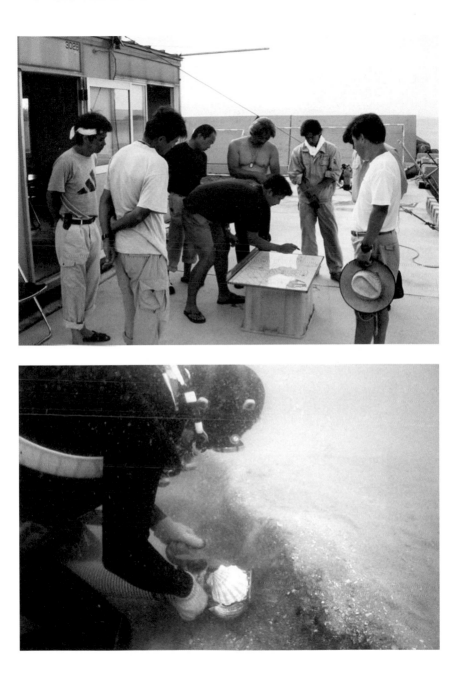

ABOVE LEFT Fragments of lamellar leather armor from a drowned soldier lie exposed on the seabed during excavation. *(Courtesy of KOSUWA and the Matsura Board of Education)*

ABOVE RIGHT This wooden tag, excavated at the wreck site, says "in the first year of ...[name of an official] has repaired and inspected this." It may be from a ship and therefore suggest hasty and not always careful preparations for war by Khubilai Khan's navy. *(Courtesy of KOSUWA and the Matsura Board of Education)*

FACING TOP Randall James "Randy" Sasaki, whose analysis of the broken timbers from Takashima has led to the scholarly reconstruction of some of the Khan's lost ships. *(Courtesy of Randy Sasaki)*

FACING BOTTOM These ceramic shells, some intact, are the world's oldest known seagoing bombs. Known as *tetsuhau*, they were Chinese inventions that gave the Khan's navy a technological advantage. *(Courtesy of KOSUWA and the Matsura Board of Education)*

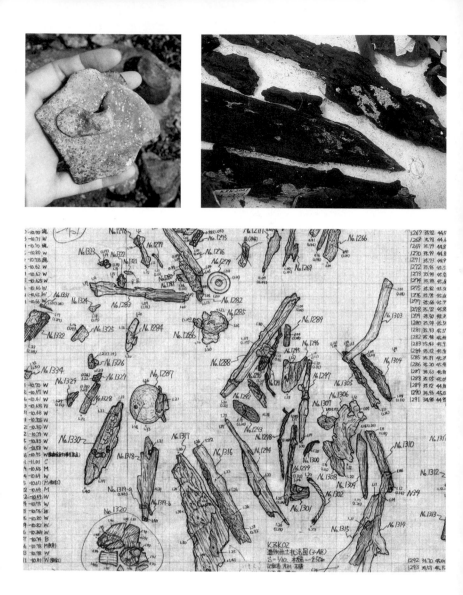

FACING Fragments of history, reconstructed by archaeologists, clockwise right to left: A piece of a ceramic storage jar, discovered in the intertidal zone of a Takashima beach; fragments of shattered ships in a fresh water storage tank; and a drawing by Mitsuhiku Ogawa of scattered timbers as discovered on the seabed during excavation. *(Randy Sasaki, 2004; James P. Delgado, 2002; Mitsuhiko Ogawa, courtesy of* KOSUWA *and the Matsura Board of Education)*

ABOVE These half-flooded paddies lie over the silt-covered remains of the Battle of the Bạch Đằng River, where Khubilai Khan lost another fleet to Vietnamese defenders in 1288. *(James P. Delgado, 2008)*

■戦艦

■抜都児 (バートル)

■水汲船

Preliminary reconstruction of one of Khubilai Khan's lost ships.
The result of generations of Chinese engineering and development,
these were the world's most advanced warships during the Medieval
period. Khubilai Khan squandered his naval advantage with poorly
executed attacks on Japan, Vietnam and Java. *(Courtesy of Yamagata Kinya
and the Matsura Board of Education)*

grad student in 1959, Bass had taken the plunge, literally, going to Turkey to oversee what would become the first scientific archaeological excavation of a shipwreck. That wreck, a Bronze Age ship from around 1200 BC, was a milestone in the developing field of underwater archaeology. The Cape Gelidonya wreck, as it was called, was more than just the first to be scientifically excavated at a time when most archaeologists said that good archaeology could not be done underwater. It also challenged traditional archaeological views of Bronze Age trade in the Mediterranean.

Based on the ship's rich and diverse cargo, remarkably well preserved after three millennia beneath the sea, Bass proposed that instead of ancient Greeks dominating sea trade back then, Semitic peoples from the East—who in time would become the Phoenicians—had played a significant role, if not the dominant one. It was a startling and controversial conjecture, as George Bass would later admit. Cape Gelidonya launched George Bass into more than hot water with a few archaeologists. He became known as the "father of underwater archaeology," and was the founder of the Institute of Nautical Archaeology, the world's leading scientific and educational organization dedicated to the study of shipwrecks. To do so, Bass resigned from the staff of the University Museum at the University of Pennsylvania in 1973, stunning his colleagues by walking away from a tenured professorship. A decade later, when Kenzo Hayashida entered Penn to study the Bronze Age, people were still talking about George Bass, whose institute was now world famous and busy excavating more ancient wrecks in Turkey.

The more Hayashida heard, the more he became interested in underwater archaeology. His opportunity to get more involved came when he returned home to Japan in 1981, just as Torao Mozai was ending his work off Takashima. Hayashida watched the project with interest, but did not join the team because Mozai, an oceanographer and engineer, was not an archaeologist. Hayashida felt that work at Takashima, and underwater excavation work in Japan in general, needed to be conducted by archaeologists. By

1984, with Mozai no longer working on the island, Hayashida's time had come. Construction of harbor improvements resulted in a small rescue dive excavation in Tokonami harbor. The dig recovered animal bones, more pottery, and two fragments of wood that might have come from ships. But all the researchers could learn from the small fragments was that they were a piece of oak and a piece of pine, both had been worked with tools and one had had a nail driven through it. Another of Mozai's contributions was his success in having the government designate the waters around Takashima as an archaeological site. In a little-known Catch-22 in Japanese law, archaeological sites cannot be protected, even from accidental encounters by construction, unless they are known to exist.

Backed by a group of supporters, with whom he formed the Kyushu Okinawa Society for Underwater Archaeology (KOSUWA) in 1986, Hayashida dutifully worked at Takashima through the 1980s and into the early 1990s, taking time off from his day job as an archaeologist for the City of Fukuoka to conduct archaeological rescue campaigns with government money whenever it seemed that underwater construction would destroy remains from the Mongol invasion. Excavations at Tokonami in 1988 and 1989 found more thirteenth-century pottery, but still no ships. The results of eleven separate digs were at hand now, and they were meager, but Hayashida remained optimistic, convinced that more would come. Then, in 1994, at a new site, a small fishing port known as Kozaki Harbor, came the breakthrough.

KOZAKI

Fishermen may find the most wrecks, but the next best way is in a harbor reclamation or development project. In the United States, more wrecks are discovered during projects involving the US Army Corps of Engineers than in any other fashion—except the accidental snags when fishing vessels find a wreck. The greatest irony of Takashima is that construction of a fishing port at Kozaki Harbor finally yielded the remains of at least one if not several of

Khubilai's lost fleet. In 1994, as work began to armor the shoreline and prepare to construct a huge concrete breakwater at Kozaki to shelter fishing boats from the fierce storms that blow in from the sea—yet another irony—KOSUWA returned to the water to examine four targets that the sonar said were buried in the mud 165 feet offshore in about seventy feet of water.

In a two-month season of digging between October 14 and December 12, KOSUWA's divers recovered less than a hundred artifacts from five feet of mud. These included fragments of wood—more than any other dig had yielded—and then the most incredible discovery at Takashima since the bronze seal: three massive wood and stone anchors, still set into the bottom where they had been dropped to moor a ship (or ships), with rope made of plaited bamboo fiber still attached to their shanks stretching toward the shore. All made of red oak, the anchors had stone stocks. The largest one proved to be as much of a smoking gun as the bronze seal. Geologists traced its granite to China's coastal Fujian province.

Archaeologists are able to date organic materials like wood based on the rate of radioactive decay from the solar energy they once consumed when alive. There is always a margin of error, expressed as a plus or minus. The red oak from the big anchor, when recovered in 1994, dated to 770 years before the present, plus or minus ninety years. That meant the tree it came from had lived until sometime between A D 1134 and 1314—a span that neatly covers the invasion of 1281. With its Chinese origin—even the oak was probably from China—and the date, the anchor was, according to KOSUWA, "one of the best archaeological documents for... the Mongolian armada."

The anchors spurred more work at Kozaki. In 1995, KOSUWA returned to excavate deeper into the mud. The new season brought less finds than in the previous year—sixty-one pieces of wood, a fragment of pottery, a piece of bamboo and three animal horns—but when he laid them out alongside the results from 1994, Hayashida was sure that he at last had a site with potential to yield a ship, the elusive goal sought since 1980. It would take a few more years, and in fact it was October 2000, as the harbor work continued, before Hayashida and KOSUWA returned to dig. In the next month, Hayashida and his team, assisted by seven commercial divers hired with money from the developers of the harbor, cleared out the mud from a 4,413-square-foot area of seabed. Using an underwater airlift—essentially a submarine vacuum cleaner that sucked up mud and deposited it through a screen mounted on a barge floating on the surface—the excavators raised 168 artifacts. These included the usual Chinese ceramics, including white porcelain bowls and brown-glazed pots; a piece of Korean celadon ware; fragments of wood; a rusted bundle of iron arrows; several bronze pieces from a belt, and a bronze mirror.

The brown pots were particularly interesting. Hayashida's crew was able to trace them to Yixing in China's Jiangsu province, which they noted was close to the port the Chiang-nan Division had sailed from. The white porcelain also appeared to come from southern China. The evidence was mounting from the seabed; Hayashida had now found a large number of items from exactly the same region as the southern fleet of Khubilai Khan's navy. That was enough to spur a further dig in 2001 which hit a concentrated area of finds: a jumble of planks, a large piece of wood that appeared to be a mast step—a large timber into which a ship's mast was set—and a number of swords, more arrows and round pottery shells that upon examination proved to be *tetsuhau*, or "thunder bombs." One had shown up near the beach in 1993, but its full significance had not become clear until 2001.

The bombs in particular ellicited a great deal of interest. They are the world's earliest examples of seagoing ordnance, and they proved to historians that a scene on Suenaga's scroll, in which the samurai is thrown from his horse, both bleeding, while a shell explodes overhead, had not been added after the thirteenth century by another artist, as some had suggested. Hayashida and KOSUWA now had more than just relics that could be traced to the Khan's invasion; they actually had identifiable pieces of a ship in the form of the mast step and the planks. The next field season, which Hayashida thought would be his last, was scheduled for the summer of 2002.

THE BREAKTHROUGH

On July 11, 2002, KOSUWA's members assembled at Takashima after long drives from Fukuoka and Nagasaki and boarded the little ferry together to take the ten-minute ride from the mainland to the island's dock for the last, winding drive over the hills to Kozaki Harbor. The recently finished harbor now provided a sheltered area for the dig; inside the breakwater, in forty-five feet of water, the divers began to vacuum up the seabed, a process that by year's end, would remove nearly sixty thousand cubic feet of thick, gelatinous mud from the grave of at least one of the shattered ships from Khubilai Khan's navy. The divers doing the digging were professional divers from Nagasaki's Marine Base Kunitomi. Wearing masks that covered their entire faces and allowed them to talk, by microphone, to the diving supervisor on shore, they were also connected by long hoses to air compressors on the dock that allowed them to stay down for hours in the harbor's warm silty waters.

As they vacuumed up the mud, the divers would uncover artifacts: a shattered piece of timber, a hunk of rusted metal, a ceramic jar. Talking to the shore base, they were quickly linked to one of KOSUWA's diving archaeologists, who swam over, stuck a numbered pin in the seabed to "tag" the find, and then called in a team to photograph and map the precise location of the artifact. As the digging continued, artifacts were carefully removed from the seabed, placed in plastic or net bags, carried ashore, and placed in freshwater trays to start the lengthy process of preservation. If allowed to dry out, the wood would crumble, iron would disintegrate and even the ceramics would break if the centuries of salt, dissolved inside, were allowed to crystallize, shattering the clay and glaze as it dried and expanded. It was time-consuming work, painstaking but absolutely necessary. The ship that slowly began to emerge from the mud was not intact; it was shattered and scrambled. "These pieces were put in a blender of sea and were mixed together," maritime archaeologist Randall "Randy" Sasaki would later comment. The meticulous mapping helped the archaeologists understand how each fragment related to the next, so they could put the pieces of the puzzle back together.

The evidence that emerged from the jumble raised from the sea bottom in 2002 was irrefutably from the Mongol invasion. The finds included hundreds of pieces of wood from ships, notably a watertight bulkhead from a lower hull. More than three hundred fragments of ceramic jars, bowls and dishes were also discovered, some in large enough chunks that the archaeologists could piece back together complete vessels. The jars, it now seemed, had been used to carry supplies, and came from kilns near Ningbo, while other dishes were traced to kilns in China's Henan, Jiangsu, Zhejiang and Fujian provinces. Laquerware, wooden combs, bronze spoons, mirrors and coins dating to the Song Dynasty also appeared from beneath the mud, delighting the archaeologists with their hints at daily life aboard the ships.

The ships had come prepared for war. Hayashida's team recovered at least eighteen swords, a helmet, fragments of leather armor, and more of the five-and-a-half-inch diameter *tetsuhau*, ceramic bombs. During the season, in an effort to stir up publicity, KOSUWA released the results of scientific analysis into one of the bombs. Its gunpowder was long gone, but the shell, its powder replaced by silt that had drifted in over the centuries, was still packed with a dozen small chips of metal. When it exploded, it would have sprayed shrapnel over a considerable area. Another was simply packed with mud, suggesting to Hayashida that there may have been different types of bombs, perhaps some filled with powder and chemicals for flash effect. "It is possible there were many uses of this weapon— killing the enemy, blinding the enemy," he postulated.

But perhaps the most telling of the finds was a tightly arranged group of artifacts that, while individually interesting, together spoke volumes, especially once they were mapped in a way that archaeologists could discern a pattern. They seemed to be all that was left of one of the hapless soldiers aboard one of the Khan's ships. There was not much left of him, just half of a hip and the top of his skull, intact to the ridges of his eyebrows. Analysis of the bones suggested that the soldier was around twenty years of age. Close by was a scatter of red leather plates which, when stitched together, formed a layered form of armor called lamellar. Amongst the plates lay a helmet, a bundle of arrows of crossbow bolts rusted into a solid mass, a *tetsuhau*, and a single bowl, face down, with the inscription "Wang, commander of 100" painted on its base.

Archaeologists can never say anything with absolute certainty, but this concentration of bones, leather, metal and laquerware may be the broken remains of Wang, who after seven hundred years, provides us with mute evidence of the human cost of Khubilai's failed invasion. An officer in command of a *ja'un*—one hundred soldiers, in Genghis Khan's decimal-based organization of the Mongol armies—Wang would have been known as a *ja'un-u noyan*, or "centurion." His name, however, is not Mongol but Chinese. Wang is one of the three most common surnames in China, and the second most common in the Yangtze River area. Like nearly everyone else lost with the destruction of Khubilai Khan's naval invasion of Japan, the centurion was Chinese, and probably a former Song soldier now serving a new master.

Swimming around the remains of Wang and his gear, one cannot help but wonder if he ever thought he would end up like this, face down in the mud on a far distant shore, his last purpose to yield some of his secrets to archaeologists seven centuries after his death. If we can learn more about the more intimate, human face of Khubilai's navy through finds like those of 2002, what other insights can the site hold? That question sparked two more seasons of digging at Takashima. The results from all three seasons not only added even more evidence to the unfolding story of Khubilai Khan's navy and its destruction. They also made it possible, for the first time in modern times, to radically reinterpret the events of 1281.

ELEVEN

Broken Ships

There are still thousands of ships to find and analyze.
RANDALL SASAKI (2006)

COLLEGE STATION, Texas, lies inland, an hour and a half from Houston and two hours driving distance from the open waters of the Gulf of Mexico at Galveston. This landlocked city is home to Texas A&M University and it is also the home of the world's premiere educational and scientific organization dedicated to the study of the past through shipwrecks, the Institute of Nautical Archaeology (INA). Founded by archaeologist George F. Bass and a group of friends in 1973, INA relocated in 1976 to College Station to work with Texas A&M to create the Nautical Archaeology Program, at the time the only university program offering degrees to students studying shipwreck archaeology. Proximity to water was not a prerequisite for the institute's move; more important was the support of what is now America's third-largest center of higher education. With the university's support, INA has spent the last four decades creating a multimillion-dollar endowment, bringing in a world-class group of scholars to teach, building laboratories for the study of ships and artifacts and to treat and preserve finds from the sea, and educating many of the world's leading nautical archaeologists.

Occupying the ground floor of the anthropology building on the sprawling A&M campus, the offices, laboratories and classrooms of the Nautical Archaeology Program, INA and the affiliated Center for Maritime Archaeology and Conservation stretch out along a long hallway. At the far end is the J. Richard Steffy Ship Reconstruction Laboratory, filled with long tables, models of long-vanished types of ships, pieces of hulls in small scale and file drawers housing meticulous drawings. On any given day, a small group of students can be seen huddled around computer stations or lining the tables for a lecture by Dr. Filipe Castro, the archaeologist who currently runs the lab and teaches the naval architectural and reconstruction courses. One of those students, a modest, engaging scholar of dual Japanese American heritage, is Randall "Randy" Sasaki. This unassuming young man, his laconic demeanor underscored by a wild mop of hair, an unshaven face and a big grin, is Kenzo Hayashida's and KOSUWA's best hope for the future.

Born in Yokohama, the thirty-year old Sasaki is the child of a Japanese father and an American mother; she was a missionary and he an electrical engineer, and they met on a ship at sea in the middle of the Pacific in the early 1970s. Their son grew up in a port city and developed a love of archaeology. Like Kenzo Hayashida before him, Randy Sasaki's first interests were the ancient, land-locked past of the Bronze Age as well as the great early civilizations of Mesopotamia and the Indus Valley. Because there were more opportunities to learn about his favorite subjects in the United States, Sasaki went there to learn both English and archaeology. Graduating from Southwest Missouri State University in Springfield, where he studied under Dr. Juris Zarins, Sasaki took his education into the field, working as a contract archaeologist in the United States as well as Yemen, Oman and Turkey.

You cannot study the Bronze Age and its complex trade relationships without going to sea, especially after the pioneering work of George Bass and his colleagues at INA, who were busy rewriting history thanks to work on the Gelidonya and Ulubu-run shipwrecks and their cargoes of Bronze Age trade goods. Following the attacks of 9/11, Sasaki began to wonder if there was as future in Middle Eastern archaeology for a foreign archaeologist. He decided to return to school to shift from land to sea, studying the maritime trade of the Bronze Age at Texas A&M. Accepted into the master's program, he settled down to classes in nautical archaeology, conservation and ship construction with an eye toward not only working in the Mediterranean, but also returning home to Japan to work underwater. His active interest in what was happening back home first introduced him to Kenzo Hayashida and KOSUWA's work, but few details were available.

Part of the nautical program's routine includes regular "brown bag" lunch talks by visiting scholars. In early 2003, one of those talks was by an archaeologist who had just returned from diving at Takashima with KOSUWA. As images of the finds—the bronze seal, the bombs, the scraps of leather armor, the bones and the burned and broken timbers from ships—flashed on the screen, Sasaki sat up and took particular notice. It was a career-changing moment. He knew that the skills he had gained at Texas A&M would be an asset for KOSUWA, if he could just get in direct contact with Kenzo Hayashida. An email exchange later, and Sasaki had an invitation. His trip to Japan brought Sasaki to Takashima at the end of 2003.

Since then, Randy Sasaki has revolutionized the work at Takashima and brought a new perspective and skills to KOSUWA. Now being groomed as Kenzo Hayashida's successor, Sasaki has spent four years of his life studying the broken timbers carefully brought up from the bottom in a decade of excavation at Kozaki Harbor. It is not an easy task. The fragmented hulls do not go back together easily. "It is," Sasaki comments, "analogous to reconstructing 4,000 different jigsaw puzzles with only one percent of the pieces remaining and no templates." "Those pieces," he adds, "were put into a blender of sea and were mixed together. It is difficult to figure out which piece goes to which ship."

ENTER RANDALL SASAKI

The successes of 2002, which produced artifacts with identifiable ties to the lost fleet of Khubilai Khan, meant that it would not be Kenzo Hayashida's final season. In December 2003, KOSUWA returned to the site, this time joined by Randy Sasaki. The divers dug a small twelve-by-twelve-foot area, but their finds were not small. A cluster of 88 bronze Song Dynasty Chinese coins, all dated to AD 976, came out of that hole, along with coiled rope, a burned section of planking, iron nails, three black-lacquered knife sheaths and a lacquerware bowl.

That was enough to keep the work going another year, and in 2004, with Sasaki again on the team, KOSUWA opened up more units—the archaeological term for a carefully gridded, precisely excavated hole. A ceramic brick, broken ceramics, cloth and a piece of bone emerged along with a number of timbers, and for the first time the archaeologists were rewarded with a series of planks with joints that showed how they had been fastened together to make a small vessel. With this discovery, Randy Sasaki's specialized training came into play. Arriving for the 2003 dives and excavation, Sasaki's attention was drawn not only to the work in the harbor, but back to the laboratory attached to the Takashima Educational and Cultural Center, the repository of everything recovered from the sea over the last two decades. There, Sasaki found hundreds of wooden fragments in climate-controlled pools of water. Kept wet, they are preserved from the ravages of air. If they dried out, the wood would disintegrate, and so they sat, awaiting costly conservation treatment to let them survive.

Sasaki immediately realized that the project faced a major obstacle: in his words, "nautical archaeology has yet to be developed in Japan." Other than the work of Kenzo Hayashida and his hardworking volunteers, there are no other underwater excavations in Japan, and no funding for this type of research outside of what Hayashida received for Takashima—and then because the seabed is a designated cultural zone and the local people strongly support the ongoing search for the Khan's fleet. Nor was there any interest from the Japanese archaeological establishment. KOSUWA's work is at best condescendingly noted by the other professionals, who do not see how meticulous archaeological work can be conducted underwater.

While, starting in the 1960s, that point was proven elsewhere in the world, it has yet to be demonstrated in Japan. The fact that the Takashima sites were first discovered and "excavated" by a marine engineer, Dr. Mozai, only adds to the archaeological establishment's disdain. The attitude covers more than KOSUWA and Takashima—not too long ago, a visiting UNESCO official was informed by her Japanese hosts that there was *no* underwater cultural heritage in Japan.

Facing this reality, Sasaki, who notes diplomatically that, "no funding from any Japanese institution was available," returned to College Station and sought financial support from the Institute of Nautical Archaeology. Thanks to George Robb, an INA trustee with a strong interest in supporting the students in the program in their field work, Sasaki, aided by fellow A&M nautical student George Schwarz and Kazuma Kashiwagi, a student from Honshu's Ibaraki University, returned to Takashima in May 2004 to begin a detailed six-month study of every piece of wood that KOSUWA had found. He returned again in 2005, this time with Kashiwagi and A&M student Andrew Roberts, for additional work on the timbers.

RECONSTRUCTING THE SHIPS

To better understand Randy Sasaki's work, it is important to first grasp what he had to work with. Sitting in those pools of fresh cold water were hundreds of fragments of wood, almost all of them less than six inches long. Most were isolated finds not closely associated with each other. No complete hulls, or even sections of hulls, had been found. The only more-or-less intact pieces were the four anchors, set deep in the mud with their stone stocks, which KOSUWA had discovered in 1994. One of them, the largest, hinted at the size of the warship it had once moored. Originally measuring nearly twenty-four feet, it would have been about a tenth of the ship's length, suggesting a massive vessel of over two hundred feet. Another large timber, a brace used to set a ship's mast into its hold, also suggested a sizable vessel. Two timbers that Sasaki had been able to fit together clearly came from a bulkhead, a transverse brace in a hull that is watertight. The broken bulkhead measures nearly nineteen feet in length, so Sasaki deduced that it fit into a ship that was nearly forty feet wide and 132 feet long.

Analysis of the timbers dated them to within a hundred years of the Mongol invasions. It also showed that seven large samples came from the same type of tree. Scientist Misutani Takumi of the Nara National Asset Laboratory determined that they were all made of camphor wood, a tree common to southern Japan, Korea, Taiwan, the China coast and Vietnam but most commonly used in the construction of traditional Chinese wooden vessels. This evidence seemed to support the view that the Khan's fleet included large, Chinese-built ships, most likely vessels requisitioned from the defeated Song navy as well as others built on Khubilai's orders in either China or Korea.

The Song's naval prowess was directly related to the seaworthiness of their oceangoing ships and their ability to take punishment. Their deep-water junk became the "model" Chinese warship of the next few centuries, surviving without much modification. When Europeans pushed into the Far East and met the Chinese in skirmishes on the seas, they were astounded at how much shot a junk could absorb without breaking up or sinking, far more so than contemporary European warships. It would clearly take one hell of a storm to destroy such a fleet.

That does seem to be the case. KOSUWA's painstaking work on the seabed, carefully mapping every fragment of wood, every piece of broken pottery and every nail with as much care as the big, "important" artifacts such as helmets and bombs, has allowed them to reconstruct the Kozaki Harbor site on paper. Seemingly meaningless scrambles of artifacts, when analyzed along with waves and currents, start to show patterns. So, too, does an analysis of the silt that covers the compacted sand and shell seabed of

1281, below which no artifacts have been found. Hayashida's work shows a stable rate of deposition for silt washed from Takashima's slopes into the sea since 1281, so that now nearly five feet of loose mud buries the site.

The broken timbers, some of them quite large, lay buried in that matrix of mud close to where the anchors were found in 1994. Smaller, more eroded fragments lay closer to shore along with wave-tumbled pottery. What this all suggests is that there was a major break-up of the vessels. The large pieces of wood, along with heavier artifacts such as large pots, iron arrows, helmets and even human bodies (remember the bones) would have drifted greater distances and come to rest in deeper water, where they were gradually buried in the silt. Only a few of them, close to the beach and continually exposed by seven centuries of storms, continue to break apart, battered and washed by the surf.

The question posed by these pieces is, was there a storm—and if so, was it strong enough to shatter the Khan's fleet? Shinji Takano, an archaeologist with the Nagasaki Prefectural Board of Education, has analyzed the Quanzhou ship and believes that it would have broken apart in a storm with winds gusting to approximately 124 miles per hour—a storm powerful enough to be rated as a "catastrophic typhoon" by the Japanese Meteorological Association. That's enough wind, on the Saffir-Simpson Hurricane Scale, to form a Category 3 "major typhoon" capable of generating storm surges of nine to twelve feet. The first major Pacific typhoon of 2005, Haitang, swept over Taiwan and hit Mainland China as a Category 3 storm in mid-July, forcing the evacuation of nearly three quarters of a million people and flattening more than 2,600 homes. Out on the open sea, the force of such a storm would only be worse. In those kinds of seas, wooden ships, especially ones tied together as historical accounts suggest, would be dragged toward the beach, breaking apart as the churning waves battered them against each other.

"The bay was packed with their ships," says Takano. "They must have tied their ships to one another to stay together," but he believes that the wind-driven waves overwhelmed even the strongest of Khubilai's Navy. The anchors set into the mud, when excavated in 1994, had their broken cables stretched in a line toward shore, showing that the ships they tethered, moored close to shore, had been caught in a strong surge that came in from the south and drove them toward the beach. Only those ships anchored in deeper water would have survived, and then only if they had cut their cables and run to the open sea to ride out the storm—just as Marco Polo reported some of them did.

MORE THAN A STORM

However, there is more at play in the demise of Khubilai Khan's navy than just a storm, no matter how powerful it was. Sasaki's detective work with the broken pieces of wood has reassembled a more complex tale of different types of ships, of shoddy workmanship or what appear to be hasty repairs and of evidence of a careful strategy undone by human factors as well as weather. The catastrophic destruction of the ship or ships at Kozaki Harbor in 1281 could be explained by the wave energy of a super typhoon, except that such a storm would not have left intact jars and pots, or a closely associated group of artifacts like those around Wang's bowl—the armor, helmet, arrows and human bones—that suggest a ship breaking apart and quickly settling down onto the seabed. Why did the ship or ships break apart so completely?

As he sorted through hundreds of fragments of wood, Sasaki noticed that nearly two hundred of them had holes; rust marks in some of these suggested that they had once held long-vanished nails. Many of these nail holes were not neatly driven. There were timbers with nail holes in different directions, sometimes with two or three nails driven within less than half an inch of each other. Anyone who has ever tried to nail a section of garden fence or fix a broken drawer knows the technique; it is a less than perfect way to repair or reattach pieces of wood that have come apart. These multinailed fragments suggested to Sasaki that not every ship had sailed to Japan in good repair.

That fit nicely with a wooden tag with writing on it that also emerged from the mud. It reads, "in the first year of... [name of an official] has repaired and inspected this." The tag comes from a large item. It could be from a large weapon such as a catapult, suggests Sasaki, but to his mind it more likely comes from one of the ships. The tag and the banged-together timbers are suggestive evidence that some of Khubilai Khan's navy were less than perfect for the invasion; in the rush to fit out the fleet, some vessels were made ready or passed by officials because they were simply good enough for government work. Sometimes archaeology comes along and reminds us that despite the differences of time, culture and language, some things never change.

Sasaki also found evidence that some of the ships were not as well built as they should have been. One of the "smoking guns" is a four-foot-long mast step. Essentially the base of support for a ship's mast, the step has rectangular holes cut into it where braces helped hold the mast in place. Archaeologists studying the Quanzhou ship, and another period wreck from Korea, the Shinan wreck, found mast steps with carefully carved holes for the support pegs that fit into them and fasten the mast. But the mast step from Takashima is a poor shadow of them. It is a sloppy piece of work, with two off-center holes and a misplaced third hole that looks like a mistake.

To Sasaki, the mast step looks like it was built in a hasty or careless manner, perhaps by inexperienced workers hired to build this and other ships. Ordered by Khubilai to build more ships for the invasion of Japan, the Southern Chinese may have had to compromise quality.

Sasaki has a similar reaction when he looks at the bulkhead. This integral piece of the ship's structure is made up of several pieces joggled together instead of a few larger, stronger timbers, as in the Quanzhou ship. It looks to Sasaki like the shipwright did not have enough quality wood to do the job properly. Instead of being fitted with iron brackets and wooden pegs that locked it into place in the hull, the bulkhead also had closely spaced but shallow nails every five inches. This feels like a rushed job, which took less time than the superior yet labor-intensive method of cutting and drilling to fit braces and pegs.

There is other evidence of haste or carelessness. The largest stone anchor, recovered in 1994, was fitted with a stone stock to help weigh it down. The "standard" for Asian anchors of the period is a stock carved from a large, single piece of rock. Archaeologists have recovered numerous examples of this type of stock from the coast of China, and a number have also been found in Japan, especially in Hakata Bay and along the now landfilled waterfront of Fukuoka, including the one displayed at Hakozaki as a Mongol anchor from the invasion fleet.

Unlike all the others, the Takashima anchor stock is in two pieces, and is crudely carved. It was easier to take two smaller stones and shape them into the weights for both sides of a wooden anchor than to go to all the bother of carving a large single stock. It may have been faster and cheaper to make anchors that way, but therein lay a flaw. Double anchors are weaker, and the large anchor pulled from Takashima's mud in 1994 had separated, making it fail. In the same vein, an off-center mast step would easily twist apart and topple the mast, and a bulkhead loosely nailed into a hull would pull free, leaving planks to break away as the ship disintegrated.

With this comes even more evidence of a fleet rushed into existence, with many corners cut. The fragments of jars and pots from the site, when reassembled by the archaeologists, show signs of not being well formed or well fired. All this evidence points in one direction. They were part of a hasty set of preparations that saw a large amount of provisions, weapons and men packed into ships that were freshly and poorly built, or others that had seen long service and needed lengthy repairs to get them ready—and remember that the records of the 1281 invasion mention that the Khan's large fleet from southern China was plagued by delays and was late for the rendezvous with the Korean fleet. While Sasaki and Hayashida are basing their conclusions on just 502 pieces of timber, that's enough of a sample to support their theory that inadequate preparations may have been "the real cause for the failure of the invasion." There was a storm, but "if the ships were built more carefully," says Sasaki, it "might not have inflicted such havoc."

Some of the timbers also suggest more at play than a storm. Several of them are charred. It is impossible at this stage to determine exactly what this means. Did some of the ships, equipped with galleys ready to cook meals, catch fire as hot coals scattered in the storm? Or are these char marks the handiwork of the Japanese fire ships mentioned in some accounts—small vessels filled with straw and kindling, set ablaze and sailed into the packed Mongol ships to start a fleet-wide conflagration? If so, they are material evidence of the valor of the defenders of Kyushu's shores. Historian Thomas Conlan, analyzing the accounts of the battles of 1274 and 1281, believes that the samurai had "little need of divine intervention," and that the explanation of the defeat of the two invasions is far more complex than the simple legend of the *kamikaze*.

The samurai were effective warriors who, despite what seemed like overwhelming odds, struck back at the massive invading army by shifting tactics from ill-fated and ill-advised charges and individual duels to sniper-style archery and attacks by small boats loosed on the Khan's ships, with the boats either packed full of firewood and in flames, or bristling with warriors. In 1281, the combination of the stone wall and the determination of the defenders kept the Mongols and Koreans from landing at Hakata. That same determination and the fighting abilities of the samurai kept the Khan's fleet, moored well offshore at Takashima, unable to land the troops and supplies they needed to establish a strong beachhead and advance into the interior. In the opinion of historian Stephen Turnbull, all these factors meant that even a massive storm would have been "minimal in its effectiveness."

The archaeology of the lost fleet reinforces the view of these historians, and also points to a tragic irony. The exceptional, life-risking and at times suicidal bravery of the samurai played a key role in the victory over Khubilai Khan's navy. That message was later overshadowed, if not forgotten, in the late nineteenth century as the legend of the *kamikaze* took hold. When the gods failed to answer Japanese prayers in 1944–1945 and defeat in the Pacific war loomed, the descendants of the samurai conjured up the name of that legend when they once again turned to fierce, brave and suicidal tactics to avert the tides of war. That time, they failed.

KHUBILAI KHAN'S NAVY

The excavations at Kozaki Harbor also provide a more intimate look at the composition of the Khan's navy. Archaeologists never accept any written document at face value. That distrust is based on an anthropologist's understanding of human nature—deeply ingrained habits such as dissembling, exaggeration and outright lying, particularly in battle. The key questions to be asked about the archaeology of the Mongol invasion are not only what caused them to fail, but also if the accounts of thousands of ships and as many as 140,000 men—an invasion fleet larger than any in history other than the Normandy landings of June 1944—are exaggerated. And was the invasion truly a "Mongol" invasion? The Mongols were some of history's most formidable and successful warriors; how could they be defeated if not by a storm?

The full answers to these questions are not yet known. Out of the entire area of the ocean floor where the fleet is believed to lie, the work of the last few decades has excavated at most only 1 percent. The exceptional work of Kenzo Hayashida, Randall Sasaki and KOSUWA is, as journalist Hideko Takayama has said, "hardly the last word." However, there are tantalizing suggestions. The KOSUWA team believes, based on their finds, that the wrecked ships off Takashima represent for the most part the Chinese contribution to the invasion—supply ships and a few warships, mainly veterans of the conquered Song navy. The preponderance of large jars would suggest storage of provisions, especially rice and water. There are timbers from small vessels, and these vessels appear to have had flat bottoms and an intricate, almost handcrafted aspect to their fastenings. This is indicative of the Korean-built warships, which while small were capable of close in-fighting on inland waters.

Khubilai Khan's ingenuity, Sasaki believes, can be seen in his adoption of Chinese weapons such as catapults, rapid-firing cross-bows and exploding bombs. It is also evident in his recognition that the Koreans excelled at building warships suited to the straits of Tsushima and the coast. That is why Khubilai demanded they build hundreds of warships, and that is why the bulk of the Mongol and northern Chinese troops sent for the subjugation of Japan based themselves and their horses in Korea. The fighting force would cross en masse from Korea. Their back-up—some troops, but mostly in terms of provisions and arms—would come from southern China, in the larger, slower ships built there. The Koreans did not and could not feed all of the invasion force, but China's vaster rice fields could. The two fleets would meet to combine their respective strengths off Takashima, establish a beachhead, fortify it and then strike inland, gradually subjugating Kyushu and then the rest of Japan.

It would have worked except for the disparate nature of the two fleets. What Marco Polo described as a lack of cooperation, based on jealousy on the part of the two commanders, may have been more complex. The Koreans were eager to fight, given their King's desire to please Khubilai as a vassal; the recently subjugated Song were less motivated, not just to go into battle but also, as the historical records show, to build the hulls to carry the troops and supplies the Khan demanded. With Khubilai's impatience came hasty, rushed work to build and equip the fleet. There may have also been a bit of subtle sabotage on the part of the former Song.

All these factors led to a delayed departure by a fleet with a less than eager contingent of sailors and soldiers, which then did not link up with the Korean fleet as planned. As a result the two groups failed to become a cohesive, effective invasion force. The gung-ho Koreans, with all their ships and a preponderance of Mongols, pushed ahead, only to be repelled from the beaches of Hakata. When the fleets met, the element of surprise was gone, the Japanese were ready and denied an easy landing, and without a beachhead, the heavy Chinese ships, laden down with grain, rice and drinking water, had to anchor off Takashima.

There, instead of offloading and returning to deeper water or back to China, they waited like sitting ducks, exposed to Japanese attacks and to the inevitable typhoon that arose to smash into them. Despite the overwhelming strength of the Khan's forces, the technological achievements of these great ships and deadly weaponry they carried, and the presence of skilled warriors who had spread the Mongol banner from the shores of the Pacific to the gates of Vienna, Khubilai Khan's navy lost its advantage. It was squandered on the shores of Japan by impatience, mismanagement, and the determined defense of an entrenched enemy who fought as if heaven was on its side. It is a timeless and eminently human story.

TWELVE

Distant Seas,
Distant Fields

*When the enemy advances roaring
like fire and wind, it is easy to overcome them.*

TRẦN HƯNG ĐẠO (1300)

T HE DESTRUCTION of Khubilai Khan's ships off Takashima
ended the second Mongol invasion of Japan. That defeat, and
the destruction of hundreds, if not thousands, of ships, did
not mean the end of the Khan's navy. On the contrary, a number
of ships survived and returned to Korea with many of their sailors and soldiers alive. These were the Korean-built warships sent
by Kōryo to support Khubilai's invasion and to carry his troops
who had assembled on the Korean Peninsula. A Song official in
1123 described a typical Kōryo warship as "especially simple, with
a single mast standing in the middle of the ship, there was no fore-
castle, and there was a steering oar."

This basic design had not changed a century and half later, and
the remains of Kōryo-built ships can be discerned from the larger
southern Chinese ships of the Mongol invasion. The excavations
at Takashima have yielded traces of such flat-bottomed, light and
intricately built ships: small planks fitted with tenons of wood, not

nails. But Randall Sasaki has not found many of them. Most of the ship timbers are apparently Chinese, meaning that the Korean ships got away. Korean histories are clear on that issue; they say that most of the nine hundred ships sent to Japan returned. The *Yüan-shi*, Khubilai's court history, confirms this, adding the Khan's opinion that "Korean vessels were strong, but small, while Chinese vessels were weaker but with a larger hold."

The return of hundreds of ships to Korea meant that the fighting core of a navy was still available for Khubilai if he wanted to go after Japan a third time. To do so he would have to build or commandeer more supply ships. He would also need an even larger army, and so the Khan would have to build additional fighting ships in China. The two disastrous invasion attempts had left Khubilai short of funds, however, and so, against the objections of his advisors, Khubilai imposed additional duties and taxes and began to squeeze the money for a third invasion out of the Chinese. Ironically, he also turned to the policies of the defeated Song and encouraged an increase in China's overseas trade. Taxes on imported goods had played a large role in financing the Song government, and Khubilai had tried to cut that trade in order to subjugate it. Now, as ruler of China and with two expensive failed wars to pay for, he turned to that same trade to fill his own coffers.

Once he had built up a sufficient cash reserve, Khubilai gave orders for more ships and troops in 1284. The following year the Khan pardoned a number of criminals, some of them reportedly captured pirates, and conscripted them into the army to again invade Japan. Everything seemed to be proceeding, albeit slowly. Perhaps he had learned his lesson about being too hasty. As early as 1282, however, Khubilai was showing signs of being less than the man he had once been. Old, overweight and drinking heavily after the loss of Chabi, Khubilai's judgment was becoming clouded, and in 1286 he abruptly cancelled the plans for a third invasion of Japan. Historians believe there were a number of factors involved in the decision, among them the hardships the taxes were wreaking on the Chinese, leading to further dissension and revolt; the inability to mount sufficient resources; and the influence of strong advisors. There were also the demands and the humiliation of yet another failed invasion and the destruction of another fleet, this time in what is now Vietnam.

THE CHAM, ĐẠI VIỆT AND THE MONGOLS

The coast of Vietnam curves northeast at the Gulf of Tonkin and into southern China, its shores lined with white sand beaches and the muddy deltas of low-lying rivers. Relatively shallow, the gulf is only 180 feet deep in most places, and large rocks hidden offshore have made navigation dangerous for centuries. And yet these waters served as another highway of war, not once but three times, when Khubilai Khan sent his navy to subjugate the Vietnamese kingdoms of Champa and Đại Việt in 1282, 1285 and 1288. The target, situated on the banks of the Sông Hồng or Red River, which flows into the Gulf at Haiphong on Halong Bay, was Hà Nội, then known as Thăng Long, the capital of an independent Vietnam ruled by the Trần Dynasty.

The people of Đại Việt, as the land was then known, were not the initial target of the Khan; rather, he was striking farther south against the Cham, a seafaring people whose capital, Vijaya, was on the central coast near today's Đà Nẵng. Khubilai's rationale for his invasion was the presence of former Song Dynasty officials who had fled to Đại Việt after the fall of southern China to the Mongols. But a desire to dominate the maritime trade of the coast, extract revenues from the Cham and the Việt, and just perhaps to regain some of the prestige lost in Japan, were at the heart of the southern strikes.

Beginning at around the second century AD, the Champa Kingdom based much of its coastal economy on piracy, going so far as to build a fleet of armed boats for riverine incursions up the Mekong against the neighboring Khmer of Cambodia. The Cham also raided north against the Đại Việt, who did not yet possess a navy. They responded by building a fleet and defeating the Cham ruler in 1044. In 1069, a new Đại Việt king returned south with a fleet to sack the Cham and remind them of their now subjugated status, seizing control of the region's rich maritime trade, which the Cham had dominated for centuries, especially to and from China.

Chinese accounts first mention the Cham in the fifth century AD, and by the time of the T'ang Dynasty, regular trade between the Cham and China introduced a rich flow of goods to the Chinese market, carried by South Asian and Arab traders. That trade grew in the succeeding centuries, and by the time of the Song Dynasty, pearls, aromatic wood, precious metals, elephant tusks and rhinoceros horns brought tremendous revenues to the rich merchants of Guangzhou and Quanzhou, with the taxes and duties on them filling the government's coffers. Eager to not only maintain but also increase trade and revenues, the Khan followed the policies of his Song predecessors, opening more Chinese ports to trade. He also sent envoys to the Cham and Đại Việt and the neighboring kingdoms in Java, to impress them with his preeminence and demand their submission as vassals of his empire, just as he had done with the Japanese.

The Cham and the Đại Việt were well aware of Mongol power, particularly after the Mongol conquest of Yunnan, which bordered the Đại Việt to the north. As well, Song refugees had made their way by sea to Vietnam. The Đại Việt in particular were fiercely independent. The proximity of northern Vietnam had invited Chinese invasion and domination for centuries. Occupied by the Chinese as early as the third century BC, northern Vietnam had become a vassal state ruled by strong local clans allied with China. This situation persisted for nearly a thousand years, until a weakened and fragmented China lost its grasp on Vietnam in the sixth century AD. The T'ang reasserted control in the eighth century, making northern Vietnam a protectorate and founding a provincial capital at Hà Nội.

One of the strong local clans, the Ly, took advantage of the fall of the T'ang and established the kingdom of the Đại Việt, defeating invading forces in 980–981. The Chinese would never again regain control of Vietnam. Following their earlier subjugation of Champa in 1044 and again in 1069, the Đại Việt launched a raid on Song China, hitting the island of Hainan. The Song retaliated with an invasion in 1076, but intense fighting and guerilla warfare by the Đại Việt ended the war leaving their independence intact. In 1225, a new Dynasty, the Trần, had come to power. They felt the wrath of the Mongols in 1257. Following Khubilai's conquest of Yunnan, the Mongols demanded access through Đại Việt territory to encircle the Song by coming up from the south.

The Đại Việt refused, and so the Mongols invaded Đại Việt, sacking and capturing the capital. The Đại Việt responded by retreating into the jungles and mounting a protracted campaign of guerilla warfare and resistance. Ambushed constantly and weakened by tropical disease, the Mongols withdrew in 1258, but neither they nor the Đại Việt would forget. When Khubilai demanded Đại Việt submission as vassals in 1267, the Tran rulers did not refuse outright—but they chose to ignore the Mongol demands for personal subjugation, taxes, princes to be sent to Khubilai's court as hostages, and conscription of their people for the Khan's army, opting instead to send rich tribute to the Khan. It was, as one historian has noted, a dangerous game, but the Đại Việt played it successfully for nearly twenty years. The Cham also played for a time, but not as well.

THE INVASION OF CHAMPA AND ĐẠI VIỆT

Jaya Indravarman, the king of Champa, roused Khubilai's anger by mistreating his envoys, or so the Khan claimed, and in 1281 he ordered an invasion. Because of the Japanese debacle, Khubilai could only muster a fleet of one hundred ships, which sailed with a force of five thousand men under the command of Mongol general Sogetu. Landing near the Cham capital of Vijaya in 1282, Sogetu's army took it without resistance when Jaya Indravarman abandoned the city and fled into the mountains of the interior. The king was too old to fight but his son, the crown prince, turned to guerilla warfare. Unable to advance much beyond the capital,

ambushed at every turn, Sogetu's army nonetheless held Vijaya for
the next few years. There they were gradually worn down, sapped
by the Cham war of attrition and the Vietnamese climate. Khubilai was unable to send much help by sea because he had lost so
much of his navy, especially his large transport and supply ships,
in Japan. So the Khan demanded that the Đại Việt let his troops
cross into Champa by marching overland from Yunnan. Khubilai
either hadn't read his history or chose to ignore it, nor did he seem
to have a clear sense of who he was dealing with—but then he had
proven that with the Japanese.

The fall of the Cham would trap the Đại Việt between two
Mongol-controlled states, Yunnan and Champa, and the Đại Việt
had been quietly aiding the Cham resistance. When Khubilai's
demand for free passage came, the Đại Việt were backed into an
untenable position and had to refuse, despite the fact that this
would invite retaliation. It came as an invasion of fifteen thousand
troops, who poured across the border in 1285. Sogetu's army set
out from Vijaya to link up with them; united, they would take the
peninsula. But the Đại Việt, unlike their rivals, knew their history. From centuries of experience they knew how to beat invaders, and so the royal court, guarded by the army, abandoned the
capital and retreated south, burning crops and villages behind
them. Their scorched-earth policy denied the invading army the
supplies they needed.

The Đại Việt forces were led by a royal prince, Trần Hưng
Đao. Even today, the traveler to Vietnam sees this thirteenth century general, the country's greatest military hero, commemorated
in place names, shrines and statues, including a huge one in his
hometown of Nam Dinh. Many Vietnamese see him as the pro-
totypical Vietnamese hero, a soldier who would have rather been
a poet but who instead, forced by circumstance, turned to war and
became a general who was never defeated, using tactics of strategic
retreat, hit and run raids, and letting Vietnam's wet, humid landscape and climate take their toll. Trần Hưng Đao's military trea-
tises were avidly studied and adopted seven hundred years later in

the decades-long struggle against the Japanese, French and Americans in the twentieth century. The military architect of that struggle, General Võ Nguyên Giáp, a former teacher, was a passionate advocate of history. Knowledge of it, he said, was "indispensable to our task in military, political, economical and diplomatic activities." In particular Giáp studied Trần Hưng Đao, and learned his lessons well, for they were in many ways the key to North Vietnamese victory in 1973.

Vietnamese and Cham strategy played brilliantly in 1285. The Cham killed Sogetu in battle, then defeated his army as they struggled north, denying the invaders from the north the link-up they were fighting to achieve. When Trần Hưng Đao felt that the northern force was sufficiently weak from disease and hunger, he launched a counterattack, selecting battlefields where the Mongols' tactical advantage, their cavalry, could not be used. The muddy plains of the Red River, which bogged down the Mongol horses, proved to be the turning point. The Mongols fell back, retreating to Yunnan through the mountains, harried all the way by the Đại Việt who, aided by fighters from the Hmong and Yao—the peoples of the mountains—made sure very few Mongol or Chinese soldiers made it out of Vietnam alive.

THE BATTLE OF BẠCH ĐẰNG

As you approach the coast of North Vietnam through the Gulf of Tonkin, the myriad islands of Halong Bay rise out of the sea in a maze of eroded stone and white sand. The dramatic scenery is broken by the occasional group of small boats moored in semi-permanent communities of fishermen, pearl divers and merchants. Beyond the islands, the coastline appears in sharp contrast, low, flat and muddy. The mouth of the great Red River spills silt into the sea, its marshy banks home to numerous villages and hamlets that you pass as your ship enters the main channel and begins the long run toward the capitol, Hà Nội. Unless you are a keen student of history, you cannot see what lies hidden in a back channel as you enter the river, often submerged by the tide. There, preserved by fresh water and mud, lie the archaeological traces of Vietnam's war with the Mongols, and another defeat for Khubilai Khan's navy.

If the failed invasions of Japan are not proof enough of Khubilai's stubborn, and ultimately, disastrous determination, then the third Mongol invasion of Vietnam should be all the proof you need. With conscription and another drain on his military resources, the Khan prepared an even larger invasion force in Yunnan in just two years. Vietnamese sources of the period say as many as half a million invaders poured into Đại Việt in 1287, but modern historians believe these numbers may be exaggerated anywhere from five to seven times. Even if the number of troops involved in the third push was only seventy thousand, that still means the Khan sent forth four times more men than he had in 1285.

His application of overwhelming force worked—at first. Mongol cavalry rolled over Đại Việt troops stationed at the border and made short work of the northern stations of Phú Lương and Đại Than. The next move was to enclose the Đại Việt in a pincer. A fleet with troops landed and defeated the Đại Việt at the Battle of Vân Đôn, the Đại Việt's principal port on the coast near the mouth of the Red River. The attack on Vân Đôn, like the Mongol push against the Japanese at Hakata, was a move to seize the country's main trading outpost. It was also part of a strategy that saw the land troops moving south link up with those landed at Vân Đôn, and together push up the river to again take the capital of Thăng Long (modern Hà Nội). The other part of the strategy was a fleet of supply ships, full of rice and other food, to counter the inevitable Đại Việt scorched-earth strategy to starve out the invading troops.

The king and court had already abandoned the capital and prepared to fight the invaders as they had before. The Mongols had adapted, however, and the Đại Việt needed something more. It came in the form of Trần Hưng Đạo's recapture of the fallen garrison at Đại Than, and the disobedience of another, defeated Đại Việt general, Trần Khánh Dư', who had lost at Vân Đôn.

Recalled by the king for court-martial, Trần Khánh Du' ignored the summons, mustered his surviving troops, and from the banks of the river, attacked the Mongol supply ships heading up the river behind the troops. The loss of the ships—and more importantly, the supplies—left the invaders cut off. As the Đại Việt again turned to guerilla tactics and scorched-earth retreats, the Mongol-Chinese army, suffering from attrition, finally decided to retreat. They had won some battles but it was clear that they were again isolated, with no reliable means of supply and reinforcement except by sea.

The main body of the army, under the command of Mongol general Toghan, would retreat back into Yunnan, while the fighting fleet and supply ships left afloat, a force of about four hundred vessels under the command of Mongol general Omar, would return down the river, exiting at the main channel near Vân Đôn. That channel is now known as the Bạch Đằng River. There, Trần Hu'ng Đao was waiting. A student of history, Trần Hu'ng Đao had studied the Chinese invasion of Đại Việt in the tenth century, and how the victorious general of the day, Ngô Quyền, had set wooden stakes in the riverbed to trap the Chinese fleet. Trần Hu'ng Đao marshaled his men to cut hundreds of ironwood stakes out of trees as big as a foot or two in diameter. Sticking out of the mud as much as five feet, the stakes were sharpened and laid out to block the channel at low tide.

The Đại Việt did such a good job in setting their trap that seven centuries later it remains in place, in part thanks to the gradual silting of the river. The Bạch Đằng River is no longer the main route into the interior, and instead is a placid backwater where the people of the Yên Giang commune make their living through rice and fish farming. The stakes first reappeared in 1953 when a dyke cut through centuries of silt exposed them. Archaeological excavations in 1959 documented and recovered a number of the stakes, which today are proudly displayed in the capital's History Museum. In late 2005, more of the stakes, still set at forty-five degree angles, were exposed by new work on the fish ponds.

These were preserved, and the Bạch Đằng Stake-Yard, as it is now known, is being developed by the Vietnamese as a tourist attraction. It is a reminder of Vietnam's incredible victory at this site on April 9, 1288.

As the invaders sailed down the river, Trần Hưng Đạo sent small boats out to harass the Khan's fleet. They then turned and fled, with the Mongols in pursuit. The chase played out on the changing tide until the Mongol fleet suddenly found itself trapped in the midst of the stake-yard, with some ships pinned and impaled as the tide continued to drop. Standing on the banks, Đại Việt archers prepared their fire arrows. Streaming flame, the arrows arched through the sky, striking the mass of trapped ships closest to shore. The ships farther out in the channel were not spared; bamboo rafts, filled with tinder, were set ablaze and launched into the stream. As these crashed into the trapped ships, the firestorm spread throughout the fleet. Some of the sailors and soldiers leapt into the water and mud to escape, while others perished on their blazing ships.

The modern Vietnamese point to a stretch of beach near Ha Long City, close to the river's mouth, as the site of the fleet's funeral pyre. Known as Bai Chay, or "scorched beach," its sand is dark. The color, they say, comes from the ships and the forest that once stood here. As the tide rose, the burning ships drifted ashore, and the wind carried the flames into the trees. The conflagration raged for days, and when it finally died down, the sand was dark with charcoal that the centuries have not been able to wash away. The sands are actually stained with mineral deposits, not ash, but the name and the veneration of the beach is a reminder of how the defeat of the Mongols and the destruction of the Khan's navy still play a powerful role in the Vietnamese national consciousness. The same is true for the river itself. The Vietnamese claim that the color of the mud that tints the water is also a reminder, for "since the past, the Bạch Đằng has been red with blood."

The vaunted power of the Mongols had broken in the face of stiff resistance and clever tactics by the Vietnamese. More pragmatic than the Japanese, perhaps from their long history of foreign intervention and conquest, the Vietnamese drew no religious message from their victory, only justified pride in their martial prowess.

THE JAVA EXPEDITION

Historians tend to see Khubilai's attacks on Japan, Champa, Đại Việt and Java as either attempts to assert his authority as the ruler of a new Mongol dynasty of the Chinese empire—the region's dominant cultural and economic and military power for over a millennium—or to show that he, like his grandfather, was capable of carrying the family banner into distant lands, spurred by his contested ascension as Grand Khan and murmurs of his unworthiness to sit on that throne. While there may be elements of truth in both assertions, there is another, underlying motive, and that is control of trade routes and their revenues. The overseas kingdoms attacked by Khubilai were all wealthy and active trading partners with China, important sources of the Middle Empire's fantastic riches, and the Khan wished to add them not only to his Chinese kingdom but also to the free trade zone sometimes referred to as *Pax Mongolica*, just as his grandfather Genghis had added the countries of the west to his growing empire at the beginning of the century.

One of those kingdoms was that of Singasari in east Java, which dominated the spice trade of Indonesia. Marco Polo described it as a land of "surpassing wealth... frequented by a vast amount of shipping, and by merchants who buy and sell costly goods from which they reap great profit. Indeed, the treasure of this island is so great as to be past telling." The kingdom of Śrīvijaya, which controlled the Straits of Malacca and the Sunda Strait from the seventh to the eleventh century, dominated the lucrative spice trade of Indonesia. The riches of Śrīvijaya reached T'ang ports, exciting Chinese interest and introducing a regular maritime trade that continued even when this kingdom's influence waned in the early eleventh century. Beginning in 1025, a new set of rulers in east Java under the leadership of King Airlangga conquered Bali and central Java, built improved ports, and dipped into their own coffers to encourage trade, including regular contact with Song China. The commerce that followed became so rich that in 1225 the commissioner of foreign trade at Quanzhou, Zhao Rugua, complained that the Javanese were taking too much copper coin out of China in response to the Song demand for spices, especially pepper.

So it comes as no surprise that following his conquest of the Song, Khubilai Khan would turn his attention to Java and send his navy there. Like all of the Khan's maritime adventures, however, the Javanese expedition failed, although not as dramatically as the debacles in Japan, Champa and Đại Việt. Starting in 1268, when it came under the rule of Kĕrtanagara, Singasari had risen to dominate the east Java trade and then expanded overseas. Building a navy, Kĕrtanagara captured the Sumatran port of Jambi-Malāyu, on the Straits of Malacca, in 1275, then extended his reach to Bali in 1284. By 1286, the king controlled the entire straits region, including several former Śrīvijayan areas that had sent tribute to Khubilai's court following the defeat of the Song in an effort to revive the lucrative trade with China.

Kĕrtanagara's success was too much for the Khan. Here was a rival who, although distant, was in a position to directly challenge Khubilai's efforts to dominate maritime trade, a ruler into whose coffers the riches from that trade was now flowing. The Khan reacted in typical fashion, sending envoys to Kĕrtanagara's court to demand immediate submission as a vassal. Kĕrtanagara's response was swift and brutal: he sliced off the noses of the Khan's envoys and sent them home, disfigured and in disgrace. Enraged, Khubilai ordered an immediate invasion of Singasari. According to the *Yüan-shi*, southern China was again tasked with providing troops, provisions and ships, with its governor ordered in February 1292 "to send out a thousand ships and to equip them with provisions" and to amass an army of twenty thousand under the command of generals Shih-pi, I-k'o-mu-ssu and Kao Hsing.

The Khan's demand was not met until the end of the year, when the fleet sailed south from Quanzhou. It was a long and difficult voyage that lasted over a month. The official account complains that "the wind was strong and the sea very rough, so that the ships rolled heavily and the soldiers could not eat for many days." Denied landing by the Cham, who doubtless knew that they could now refuse the Khan's demands with little fear of retaliation, the Yüan-Mongol fleet finally reached Java.

There they found that Kĕrtanagara was dead. But they were greeted by his successor, his son-in-law Raden Vijaya, who was embroiled in a conflict with the kingdom of Kadiri, which had just defeated Singasari forces and occupied the capital, apparently killing Kĕrtanagara. Raden Vijaya had established a new capital, Majapahit, just as Khubilai's navy arrived. Seizing the opportunity, he told the Mongol leaders that the offending state of Singasari was no more, that its ruler had been punished with death, and that he, as the ruler of Majapahit, pledged his fealty as a vassal to Khubilai Khan. The Kadiri, however, needed to be punished, and by force made into vassals so that all of Java would answer to the Khan.

Khubilai's generals plunged into the midst of the Javanese war, pushing back the Kadiri forces—which were poised to take Majahapit and then striking into the interior with their troops and their Majahapit allies to defeat the Kadiri in a final battle that lasted from morning until noon. In the aftermath of victory, Raden Vijaya asked to return to Majahapit "in order to prepare a new letter of submission" and to assemble his tribute to the Khan. Two officers and a force of two-hundred Mongols were sent to escort Raden Vijaya, but as they entered the forest, the canny Javanese ruler turned the tables on the invaders, ambushing and killing them all. The Khan's army now found itself trapped inland in a hostile country and had to fight its way back to the ships, losing about three thousand men in the long march to safety. Outfoxed by Raden Vijaya, the Khan's three commanders sailed back to China to face the Khan's wrath. Another expedition had ended badly. Fortunately for the returning generals, they were able to return with their holds crammed with enough loot that Khubilai ultimately forgave them, though that process took many years.

The failure to subjugate Java marked the end of Khubilai Khan's use of his navy for Mongol conquests across the seas. When he defeated the Song and took control of China, Khubilai had inherited more than a vast inland empire. Thanks to centuries of Chinese development of maritime trade and the intensive efforts of the Song to extend it by creating more ports, a larger merchant fleet and China's first great deep-sea navy, he also gained a fleet and men who knew how to build, navigate and fight in ships.

The key to earlier Mongol successes had been swift action, cavalry charges, ruthlessness and a willingness to adopt and adapt foreign forces and weapons. Some historians see Khubilai's use of the Song navy and ships as another Mongol adaptation. But it would seem that he never quite understood just what he had inherited or how to best use it. Over-extended in his campaigns across the sea, particularly in consistently having to build more ships and equip and provision them, Khubilai Khan squandered the vast maritime forces he had inherited and expanded. His prestige in shambles, his empire beset with internal problems, the Great Khan died in 1291, just after the fleet returned from Java, bedraggled and defeated. In less than a century, the Yüan Dynasty Khubilai had created would also fall, and the new rulers of China, the Ming, would push the Mongols back beyond the limits of the Great Wall.

The Legacy of
Khubilai Khan's Navy

I sent my fleet against men,
not against the wind and the waves.
PHILIP II OF SPAIN, 1588

THE DEFEATS of Khubilai Khan's navy in Japan, Vietnam and Java paved the way for the downfall of the Yüan Dynasty. Whether Khubilai fully grasped the potential of his navy remains a subject of debate, with most scholars feeling that no Mongol leader, accustomed to a nomadic, horse-centered lifestyle, could ever understand the concept of sea power. Khubilai was not your average Mongol, however. His adoption of Chinese customs, and his ability to create an eastern empire that continued China's age-old cycle of dynastic rule, was certainly not typical. So to point to the Khan's lack of adaptability to the concept of a navy is unsatisfactory.

Khubilai's defeats stem more from his not fully grasping how to project sea power. In all his maritime forays he overreached, acted hastily, and sought victory at all cost, without ever fully backing up his initial thrusts with sufficient numbers of ships, properly built and maintained, and sent at the right time. He relied on overwhelming force and refused to plan beyond the first victory. In that, Khubilai was not so different from Philip 11 of Spain, who rushed what was then the world's mightiest fleet against a beleaguered England in 1588 only to lose his armada.

But historians now agree that English sea dogs and their nimble fighting ships had already defeated the much larger but less maneuverable Spanish Armada by the time the great storms claimed many of Philip's fleet as they struggled home. Philip's reaction to news of the disaster—"I sent my fleet against men, not against the wind and the waves"—could have come from the officials of the Yüan court, who preferred to attribute the failures of 1274 and 1281 to the weather. There was far more at play than stormy seas and skies, however.

It is far easier to accept defeat by a force that cannot be controlled, such as a storm, than to accept the blame oneself. Despite Marco Polo's claims that the Khan's commanders had erred, the blame for the defeats in Japan, Vietnam and Java rests firmly with Khubilai himself. His principal biographer, Morris Rossabi, points to Khubilai's widespread mismanagement of his empire and its fiscal problems as evidence of a less than organized mind and the qualities needed to effectively govern what he had conquered. Ultimately, the battles had been lost on the beaches of Japan before the storms hit. The 1274 invaders arrived with advance warning and in insufficient numbers; had they succeeded, the debacle of 1281, against an even better prepared Japan, would never have been necessary. The latter invasion clearly over-taxed the resources of the Chinese, who protested that they could not send enough ships. Khubilai did not listen and simply demanded more than could ever be delivered. When the time came he then proceeded as if all was well, either in self-delusion or because he was lied to.

The oft-repeated numbers of ships and troops are debatable. Scholars such as Thomas Conlan believe that these numbers may be grossly exaggerated, perhaps by a factor of ten. When asked how many ships might have come to Takashima, Kenzo Hayashida agrees with Conlan, answering that there may have been four hundred, not four thousand. That would make sense given the difficulties involved in assembling a fleet for the invasion while maintaining a naval presence on the Chinese coast and keeping ships to attack Champa. In the aftermath of defeat, though, would it not make sense to "increase" the numbers of ships lost, to underscore how a powerful storm could undo even the best and largest fleet of all time?

There is also the matter of the delay in the sailing of the two fleets. This delay not only split Khubilai's forces but also removed the element of surprise, so that the Japanese were waiting, in force, for the second landing. Denied a sufficient beachhead, the Mongols were unable to mass cavalry charges, to forage, or to even dig in beyond the confines of the beaches of Takashima. Their late arrival left the invading fleet sitting ducks for a storm that any prudent mariner would have forecast. That a few of the ships escaped suggests that some of the Khan's captains were indeed cautious men who knew the precarious position they had been placed in.

Imagine the circumstances of June 1944 if the Allies had followed Khubilai's plan when they invaded Nazi-held Europe on the beaches of Normandy. The landings of the Second World War came after years of preparation, the construction of an overwhelming force, extensive training. All the participants understood that the key to success was a rapid, surprise landing, which would allow them to establish a firm beachhead and then create the infrastructure for the ongoing shuttle of supplies, ammunition and men to the front. The numbers were impressive: almost 5,000 ships and 156,000 men. In the next few days, another 156,000 more men landed. The beachheads and port facilities they created kept the lifeline open even when a devastating storm hit on June 19 and lasted for several days.

After D-Day, three million troops poured into Europe through the doors the initial landings had kicked open. Had the landings been rushed, with fewer ships and men and a small beachhead that kept ships huddled off the beaches offloading supplies, the storms of June 1944 might well have gone down in the history books as the heaven-sent wind that saved a Nazi-dominated continent from the Allied invaders.

In the end, the story that Khubilai Khan's navy was destroyed by the kamikaze was a convenient fiction that worked well for both sides. For the Japanese, it was a perfect demonstration that their homeland was a *Shinkoku*, a divine land protected by the gods. The Yüan court was also well served by a tale that told how the best-laid plans could be undone by the vagaries of the weather. That it happened not once but twice, and that Khubilai then somehow managed to repeat his failures in both Vietnam and Java, should arouse our suspicion.

THE LEGEND LIVES ON

Much of the Western world's understanding of Asia is, at best, muddled, often romantic and often completely wrong. This stems from more than the geographical distance across continents and oceans, and the different languages and customs. It also derives from the centuries-old link between Asia and Europe, the desire for what Asia had to offer, especially its riches, and the complexities of that economic and cultural exchange that have marked East-West relations for centuries. Much of the "modern" worldview of Asia was shaped by the events of the Renaissance, when Europe rediscovered its sense of world geography, albeit distorted, and the knowledge of the Islamic world, which had traded with Asia for centuries, reached the trading cities and ports of Italy.

It was at this time that a remarkable book appeared, the result of a prison-cell collaboration between a captured Venetian traveler and an imprisoned writer of Pisa. Both were jailed by their Genoese enemies in 1298 as a result of the wars between the Italian city states. The traveler was Marco Polo, the writer, Rustichello, and the result of Polo's weaving tales of his incredible travels was Rustichello's publication *The Description of the World*, which has remained in print for seven centuries, in numbers that some scholars suggest rival printings of the Bible. Controversial, amazing and an instant (in terms of its time) bestseller, the book of Marco

Polo's travels was read with as much amazement and disbelief in Renaissance Europe as we might read the account of a traveler who claims to have visited other stars and planets, filled with new life and new civilizations.

While the truth of its tales were doubted—the popular nickname for the book was *Il Milione*, for the "million lies" it was said to hold—*The Description of the World* was translated into many languages and read avidly, heavily influencing European opinions about Asia, especially given the all-to-recent history of the Mongol invasions and the near-fall of Vienna. The tales of Khubilai Khan, at whose court Marco, his father and uncle were guests, especially captivated attention, and it is because of the popularity of *The Description of the World* that Khubilai became a celebrity. Described by Polo as the "Great Lord of Lords," this "Great Khan is the mightiest man, whether in respect of subjects or of territory or of treasure, who is in the world today or who ever has been."

The Description of the World related Marco Polo's stories of Khubilai's kingdom, its customs, peoples, trade and its battles. In this fashion, Europe first learned of Japan, which Polo called "Zipangu" and described in a way that only inspired a quest to reach its shores:

> They have gold in the greatest abundance, its sources being inexhaustible. To this circumstance we are to attribute the extraordinary richness of the sovereign's palace according to what we are told by those who have access to the place. The entire roof is covered with a plating of gold, in the same manner as we cover houses, or more properly churches, with lead. The ceilings of the halls are of the same precious metal; many of the apartments have small tables of pure gold, of considerable thickness; and the windows have also golden ornaments. So vast, indeed, are the riches of the palace that it is impossible to convey an idea of them. In this island there are pearls also, in large quantities, of a pink color, round in shape and of great size, equal in value to, or even exceeding, that of the white pearls. There are also found there a number of precious stones.

Marco Polo not only introduced Europe to Japan for the first time, albeit via hearsay, but he also told of the Mongol invasion of Japan and of the storm that defeated it.

At the same time that Japan, reopened to the world by western force in the nineteenth century, rediscovered the Mongol invasions, learned Europeans read Polo and experienced the serendipity of mutual rediscovery of the Khan's failed invasion, with that particular resonance that comes when something once thought too fantastic for belief is suddenly proven true. In many ways, the late nineteenth-century revival of the Mongol invasion story was also the beginning of the modern rehabilitation of Marco Polo as a truthful, if exaggerated, source.

What followed were inevitable comparisons between the Mongol invasions and the Spanish Armada—not surprising given that this was a period of strong British-Japanese bonding, only broken by the Second World War. The rise of a nationalistic, militaristic Japan, with all its tragic consequences, and the revival of the story as a powerful legend all played a role in ensuring the ongoing fame of not only Khubilai Khan's invasions, but also of the "divine wind" that ended them. The story was kept alive by a potent mix of romance, violence, other-worldliness and heart-rending sacrifice.

At the dawn of the twenty-first century, interest in China, the Mongols, Genghis, Khubilai and the latter's invasions of Japan are again at a peak. The "discovery" of Chinese seafaring and nautical expertise, as revealed in a popular book from 1994, *When China Ruled the Seas* by Louise Levathes, was then whipped to a fever pitch by a controversial follow-up by retired naval officer Gavin Menzies. His 2003 book, *1421*, remains a major bestseller and spurs ongoing research by followers and detractors. Recent biographies of Genghis and Khubilai have also become bestsellers; the best of these is Jack Weatherford's portrait of Genghis, an epic work of accessible and readable scholarship. On the fictional side, author Clive Cussler draws on Khubilai's navy and the mystery of his final resting place in his 2006 bestseller *Treasure of Khan*, which opens with the naval battle off Japan and the storm of 1281 and ends with an underwater excavation of a sunken ship.

The impact of the story is there in other media, too. One of the bestselling virtual reality games of the twenty-first century, Electronic Arts' *Shogun Total War: The Mongol Invasion*, gives PC gamers the opportunity to take sides and fight the campaign on the ground in Japan. Despite the view of some gamers that it shows what might have been without the storm of 1281, the game is perhaps best seen as a perfect opportunity to see what could have happened if the Khan had sent his invading force in with maximum resources and sufficient preparations against the Japanese in 1274.

Finally, there is the physical reality of the lost fleet itself. Accounts of the work off Japan have also inspired a tremendous response in the Western world, beginning with Torao Mozai's *National Geographic* article and continuing with more recent accounts, especially of KOSUWA's incredible finds. Major magazine stories, television documentaries, and news releases have made big splashes, if you can pardon the pun, in the world media. An estimated 200 million viewers in 172 countries viewed the 2003 *National Geographic* special "Kublai Khan's Lost Fleet."

In Japan, the story also lives on, as does the legend. Under both lies an almost imperceptible strain between the tale of the divine wind and the modern, "scientific" archaeology; listening to the debate one is reminded of Nakaba Yamada's question, posed way back in 1916: "Will the knowledge of science bring the God's power to an end?" The question hangs in the air over the divers at Takashima, especially given modern scholarship's—and the modern media's—role as myth buster. Inevitably, every visitor to KOSUWA's dig asked, sometimes obliquely, about the nature of the storm whose consequences Kenzo Hayashida and his crew have excavated. In some quarters, at least, there seems to be relief that the digs have shown that there was a great storm, leaving the factors behind it as a matter of personal belief or faith.

THE LEGACY

In the twenty-first century, the legacy of Khubilai Khan's fleet is less about faith or the exact circumstances of the fleet's final destruction, and more about what these lost ships represent as links to the past. They are a tangible reminder of a famous, near-mythical event linked to a ruler whose fame still resounds after seven centuries. They also speak to the promise inherent in underwater archaeology.

That promise is that many aspects of human history, particularly ones that have been lost or forgotten or are little understood, may yet be rewritten based on finds that emerge dripping from the sea. Just as digs in ancient cities and tombs can and do reveal much new information, so the discovery and excavation of lost ships has also added to our understanding of the past. They give us real objects we can see and touch where once all we had was a name or an image: an actual Viking ship, a magnificent galleon, a sunken ocean liner once thought lost forever to the depths, or a famous warship from the last great global conflict.

Before Torao Mozai, Kenzo Hayashida, Randall Sasaki and their colleagues began their work, the Mongol invasions of Japan had been represented by toppled stone walls and anchor stocks. Now we have the immediacy of a shattered ship, a broken skeleton pressed face down on the seabed in a scatter of torn leather armor, a fallen helmet and dropped weapons, a battle forever frozen in the embrace of sea and mud. There are certainly more items to be found, particularly considering that less than 1 percent of that underwater battlefield has yielded its secrets. When asked how he felt about the ongoing work at Takashima, eighty-nine-year-old Torao Mozai replied, "there are still so many wonders... that need to be unearthed. And so, therefore, I wish this generation of scientists the very best of luck in their activities."

That luck was demonstrated by KOSUWA's discoveries, some made even as Mozai stood at the dock and wished them well. What is clear is that the waters of Imari Bay cover not only a site important to Japan and its history, but to the world. The Mongol conquests, and in particular the legacies of Khubilai Khan's invasions, had a figurative and literal impact across the globe, from their role in forging the national identities of Japan and Vietnam to their part in the fall of the Yüan dynasty and the end of Mongol power in east Asia, to the power of the legend of the kamikaze and its effect on the global war fought in the Pacific during the Second World War.

And we mustn't forget that the lost fleet of the Khan remains elusive. Fragments, no matter how carefully reconstructed, do not make an intact ship, nor give us a comprehensive understanding. There should be more, maybe even whole vessels in deeper water and thick mud that sank intact, laden with supplies, weapons and men. Randall Sasaki believes it, as does Kenzo Hayashida. "Hundreds of vessels may still lie" in the bay, says Sasaki. "I believe that further investigation will one day reveal the true nature of this event, the largest maritime disaster until modern times, which shaped the history of the world."

Those ships would give us a better sense, not only of the invasion but also of the technologies of Chinese seafaring and naval warfare that Khubilai inherited, as well as those of Kōryo. Archaeologists know of more than two thousand Roman shipwrecks and have undertaken hundreds of excavations and surveys of underwater sites around the world. The notable exception is Asia. The hints of advanced technology, of ships built larger and better than their contemporaries in Europe, of advances like the *tetsuhau*, the world's oldest known seagoing ordnance, all suggest that what lies off Japan is a world-class nautical archaeological site with value beyond that of just understanding the events of 1281.

KOSUWA's work beneath Takashima's waters is over for now. Renamed the Asian Research Institute of Underwater Archaeology (ARIUA), the society has taken on the larger mission of building up professional underwater archaeology in Japan and collaborating with colleagues elsewhere in Asia. The development of Takashima's shoreline is now complete, so the archeological project has also ended: the pumps have been shut down, the dredges are silent and fishing boats anchor over the dig site in Kozaki Harbor. The work continues in the laboratory, but at a slower pace brought not only by the need for meticulous forensic scholarship but also by a lack of funds. The work at Takashima began, unfortunately, during times of deep economic recession in Japan.

There is only enough money to start the process of conservation: excavating large lumps of corrosion to see what lies within them, and preserving the fragile wood, iron and even stone so that they will not disintegrate when they are taken from the water. Conservation costs ten times more than excavating, and so the present budget only allows for this work to be done for 10 percent of the finds—no one expected that so much would emerge from the digs. This is a great shame, not only for science but also for those who would come to Takashima as visitors to observe and be inspired. Those funds need to come, and from those who care, all over the world.

That is the greatest need for now, and the wrecks hidden by shrouds of mud in Imari Bay will one day be found. Not too far from Kozaki, scattered ceramics and stone bowls hint at another shipwreck closer to shore in another cove, but this is probably another mix of shattered timbers and hundreds if not thousands of artifacts, and for now they have no champion or deep-pocketed sponsor to pay for their recovery and treatment. As one swims over that seabed, though, one cannot help but wonder about what lies beneath, even if it is broken and ravaged by time and sea. The "Holy Grail" is what is needed now, think some, to revive the interest in the quest.

That means more searching, and it may not be long before it brings results. Others have already picked up the baton, and even now, vessels carefully cross the waters of the bay, pinging the seabed with sonar to map its contours and hopefully reveal what lies below. Ironically, the quest is again in the hands of an oceanographer. Dr. Kenji Nemoto, with the Faculty of Marine Science and Technology at Tokai University, has during his long career spent decades mapping the seafloor in many distant seas. Today he is poring over the bottom of Imari Bay, systematically sweeping it, one piece at a time, with a high-resolution sonar that reveals every contour of the ocean floor.

Nakaba Yamada's question, of whether the knowledge of science will ever "bring the God's power to an end" by telling us what really sent the Khan's fleet to the ocean bottom, may never be answered. But what is certain is that as the tools of science improve and the quest goes deeper—as is happening now—it is only a matter of time before the next round of discoveries. When they are made, more of Khubilai Khan's navy will rise from the depths to reveal their watery secrets.

Acknowledgements

THE GENESIS of this book was the unique opportunity to dive at the site of the wreck of Khubilai Khan's navy off Japan's Takashima Island in August 2002. That trip involved more than diving. It also gave me a detailed and intensive look at a number of locations associated with the 1274 and 1281 Mongol invasions of Japan, and allowed me to meet with a number of prominent archaeologists, historians and priests. This trip was part of the filming of an hour-long episode of National Geographic International Television's *The Sea Hunters*, which I hosted for all of its five seasons from 2000 to 2006; the episode "The Lost Ships of Kublai Khan" was released in the fall of 2003. *The Sea Hunters* was created and produced by Eco-Nova Productions Ltd. of Halifax, Nova Scotia. I am particularly indebted to John B. Davis, President of Eco-Nova, for agreeing to do a show on the Khan's lost fleet, and for his generous and gracious inclusion of time and opportunities during filming. John is a friend of archaeology, going the extra mile for solid scholarship, a staunch believer in cultural sensitivity and multiple points of view, and a good friend.

The Sea Hunters team also included Susan McDonald, who made many of the arrangements, researcher Lisa Bower, who conducted background research and facilitated our time in Japan, and Eco-Nova CFO Phil Sceviour, who arranged the financing for a complex and expensive episode. I would also like to thank *The Sea Hunters* field crew of Marc Pike, John Rosborough, Mike and Warren Fletcher and Bill Jardine. In Japan, interpreters Manami Ikeda and Tomoko Nishizaki went far beyond interpreting to making arrangements, opening doors, facilitating and greatly assisting not only our filming but also the research. Ms. Ikeda is forever in my thoughts for scouring the bookstores of Fukuoka to find a rare, large-format edition of Takezaki Suenaga's fabled scroll of the Mongol invasions, the *moku shurai ekotoba*, as well a two-volume set of manga that tell a very traditional tale of the invasions.

I also owe a huge debt of gratitude to Dr. Torao Mozai, the "father of underwater archaeology in Japan." Mozai-*sensai* first introduced me to the detailed story of Khubilai's fleet, graciously shared his research, ideas and imagery of his work at Takashima, and introduced me to the Kyushu and Okinawa Society for Underwater Archaeology (KOSUWA). I would also like to thank Kenzo Hayashida and his team from KOSUWA, especially Mitsuhiko Ogawa, senior researcher, who made us very welcome at Takashima, graciously and generously shared their site and the work being done there, and copies, some now rare, of their entire library of archaeological reports and site maps. Archaeologists can be a tight-lipped, private bunch, especially when it comes to their ongoing research, but Hayashida-*san*'s openness and sharing, far above what is usually offered by colleagues, was greatly appreciated. He offered their research to help bring the story of their work to a non-Japanese, English-speaking audience. I hope I have lived up to his expectations in making the story of KOSUWA's incredible work better known to the Western world.

I would also like to thank Randall Sasaki, who I had the good fortune to meet while visiting the Nautical Archaeology Program at Texas A&M University and lecturing on KOSUWA's work in 2003. I was able to connect Randy with Kenzo Hayashida and KOSUWA simply by providing an email address. Randy's incredible drive, his intensive research and scholarly contributions greatly assisted KOSUWA's work. Kenzo Hayashida is another of Japan's fathers of underwater archaeology, and as part of his belief in what he does, he has provided opportunities for younger scholars of merit like Randy. If Sasaki-*san*'s work at Takashima, and his subsequent work in Japan, is any measure, the second generation of Japanese nautical archaeological scholarship is in excellent hands. I would also like to join Randy in thanking the sponsors of his work in Japan, especially George Robb, the RPM Nautical Foundation, and the Institute of Nautical Archaeology, as well as his professors at Texas A&M, especially Dr. Filipe V. Castro and Dr. C. Wayne Smith.

The *Sea Hunters* visit to Takashima and work at the site was authorized by Hideyuki Tatsuguchi, Superintendent, Takashima Board of Education, and Toyohide Kanaida of the Takashima Town Office. The Takashima Board of Education has supported and funded work off the island's shores for more than two decades now, and all of Japan, indeed the whole world, owes them a debt of gratitude for their support of underwater archaeology and the quest to find the lost fleet of Khubilai Khan. I would also like to thank Akiko Matsuo, Curator at the Takashima Cultural Properties Center, for her gracious sharing of time, a tour of the exhibits and laboratories of the center, and for sharing research on the finds made by Dr. Mozai's team and KOSUWA. I will always remember Matsuo-*san*'s kindness and enthusiasm as she handed me the bronze seal of the commander of one thousand—a national treasure—to hold in my hands, followed soon after by several *tetsuhau* bombs and the skull of a young man who might just be Wang, commander of one hundred.

In Fukuoka, I would like to thank the staff of the Kōrokan for a special tour and explanation of the site and the adjoining center and exhibitions, and the Fukuoka Board of Education for access to the *Ghenkō Borui* (Mongol invasion wall) sections. The priests provided access to the Nichiren shrine, and the adjoining Mongol Invasion Museum, which houses the provincial treasures known as the Ishho Yada paintings of the Mongol invasion. I would also like to thank the Fukuoka City Museum for a tour of their excellent facilities and exhibitions, with particular thanks for Daizou Tasaka, Deputy Chief Executive of the Museum, and Mr. Kato, curator and member of KOSUWA. A highlight of the time in Fukuoka was a tour of Hakozaki Shrine, one of Japan's most sacred places, and a rare viewing of the shrine's copy of Suenaga's scroll. I am particularly indebted to the Chief Priest of the Shrine for his hospitality and for a forthright discussion of the legacy of the Mongol invasions. I also want to thank him for drawing my attention to Admiral Togo's affinity for Hakozaki and the Nichiren Shrine, and for showing me poems done in Admiral Togo's calligraphy for the shrine. It was also at the shrine that I was treated to the schoolgirls' song of the Mongol Invasion, again arranged, thankfully, by our intrepid interpreters in response to a request.

In Tokyo, I would like to thank Toshiharu Konada for graciously sharing his wartime reminiscences as a *kaiten* pilot, and for his open discussion of the role of the story of the Mongol invasions in the decisions to adopt the policies that led to the *kamikaze* and *kaiten* corps. I would also like to thank the priests of Yasukuni Shrine, especially Yasuhiro Noda, who allowed for the interview to take place there, as well as the curators and priests of the nearby *Yashukan*, Yasukuni's museum. My understanding of Meiji Japan, and particularly of Admiral Togo and the Battle of Tsushima, was also assisted by a tour of Togo's flagship *Mikasa* at Yokosuka. I am particularly indebted to Admiral Tameo Oki and his staff.

My research in Vietnam was spurred, facilitated and made possible by my good friend of many years, George Belcher, and his wife, Nyugen Lan Huang, who arranged a magnificent tour of Vietnam's many history and archaeology museums and introduced me to Hoi An, port of the ancient Cham, as well as many of Vietnam's leading journalists and archaeologists with an interest in their country's rich maritime past. Indeed, it was George who first introduced me to Asia's incredible maritime story, founding the Asia Maritime Institute and asking me to join its board, sending me a number of hard-to-get publications and his own images of the Quanzhou ship. I am deeply indebted to him. I would also like to thank the staff of the Bao Tang Lich Su, the Vietnamese History Museum and the Army Museum in Hà Nội for excellent tours and an understanding of the role and significance of Trần Hưng Đạo and the Battle of the Bạch Đằng River in Vietnamese history.

My research in Vietnam was also granted a tremendous boost with a coastal sailing tour from Ho Chi Minh City (Saigon) to Hà Nội, with stops at a number of Cham ports, and especially a tour of Halong Bay, including the cave on the islands where the wooden stakes used to trap the Mongol fleet on the Bạch Đằng River were stored before the Đại Việt defenders emplaced them in the river, and a trip up the Red River, retracing the route of the Khan's naval forces as they penetrated the heart of Đại Việt in 1287–1288. I would like to thank my friends Werner Zehnder, Scott Fitzsimmons and Mike Messick for another tremendous opportunity to learn through cultural travel. My trip was also greatly enhanced by Mason Florence, author of the Lonely Planet guidebook for Vietnam, who proved to be an excellent guide. A return trip to Vietnam in May 2008 brought new insights into the Battle of the Bạch Đằng River and the strategies employed by the Vietnamese. The trip was funded by the RPM Nautical Foundation and was arranged thanks to Dr. Vu The Long.

My research outside Japan was assisted by thoughtful contributions from many. I particularly want to thank Dr. Jack Weatherford of MacAlester College, Vice Admiral Yoji Koda of the Japanese Self Defense Force, and Pai-lu Wu of the Taiwan National Museum for their insights. I would also like to thank the staffs of the exceptional libraries I conducted my research at the Cushing Memorial Library at Texas A&M University, the W.B. and M.H. Chung Library at the Vancouver Maritime Museum and the National Palace Museum Library in Taipei, Taiwan.

I am grateful for the review of the manuscript and suggestions made by Jack Weatherford, John Man, Randall Sasaki and my assistant Kathy Smith. Any errors are mine. I have been more than fortunate in the last decade to be associated with my Canadian publisher, Douglas & McIntyre. I want to thank editor Scott Steedman for his advice and encouragement, and my friend Scott McIntyre for publishing yet another esoteric history and archaeology book. My wife, Ann, is as always my muse, my inspiration and the one who always covers the bases when I am away diving, researching and writing. Thank you, darling.

SOURCES

BOOKS

Aikens, C. Melvin and Takayama Higuchi, *The Prehistory of Japan*. Academic Press, New York, 1982.

Ballard, George Alexander, *The Influence of the Sea on the Political History of Japan*. John Murray Publishers, London, 1921.

Barnes, Gina L., *The Rise of Civilization in East Asia: The Archaeology of China, Korea and Japan*. Thames and Hudson, Ltd., London, 1999.

Bass, George F., *Archaeology Beneath the Sea: A Personal Account*. Harper and Row, New York, San Francisco and London, 1975.

Batten, Bruce L., *To The Ends of Japan: Premodern Frontiers, Boundaries and Interactions*. University of Hawai'i Press, 2003.

Batten, Bruce L., *Gateway to Japan: Hakata in War and Peace, 500–1300*. University of Hawai'i Press, 2006.

Bix, Herbert P., *Hirohito and the Making of Modern Japan*. HarperCollins Publishers, New York, 2000.

Boyle, John Andrew, translator, *The History of the World Conqueror by 'Ala-ad-Din' Ata-Malik Juvaini*. Manchester, 1958.

Chaliand, Gerard, *Nomadic Empires: From Mongolia to the Danube*. Translated by A.M. Berrett. Transaction Publishers, New Brunswick, New Jersey, 2004.

Clark, Hugh R., *Community, Trade and Networks: Southern Fujian Province from the Third to the Thirteenth Century*. Cambridge University Press, Cambridge, New York, Port Chester, Melbourne and Sydney, 1991.

Conlan, Thomas, *In Little Need of Divine Intervention: Scrolls of the Mongol Invasion of Japan*. Cornell East Asia Series, No. 20. Cornell University Press, Ithaca, New York, 2001.

———, *State of War: The Violent Order of Fourteenth Century Japan*. Center for Japanese Studies, University of Michigan, Ann Arbor, Michigan, 2003.

Curtin, Jeremiah, *The Mongols: A History*. Little, Brown and Company, Boston, 1908.

Deng, Gang, *Chinese Maritime Activities and Socioeconomic Development, c. 2100 B.C.–1900 A.D. Contributions in Economics and Economic History*, Number 188. Greenwood Press, Westport, Connecticut and London, 1997.

———, *Maritime Sector, Institutions, and Sea Power of Premodern China*. Greenwood Press, Westport, Connecticut and London, 1999.

Franke, Herbert and Dennis Twitchett, editors, *The Cambridge History of China: Volume 6: Alien Regimes and Border States, 907–1368*. Cambridge University Press, Cambridge, 1994.

Fuwei, Shen, *Cultural Flow Between China and the Outside World*. Foreign Languages Press, Beijing, 1996.

Gabriel, Richard A., *Genghis Khan's Greatest General: Subotai the Valiant*. University of Oklahoma Press, Norman, 2006.

Graff, David A., *Medieval Chinese Warfare, 300–900*. Routledge, London and New York, 2002.

Hall, John W. and Jeffrey P. Mass, *Medieval Japan, Essays in Institutional History*. Yale University Press, New Haven and London, 1974.

Haw, Stephen G., *Marco Polo's China: A Venetian in the Realm of Khubilai Khan*. Routledge, London and New York, 2005.

Henthorn, William E., *Korea, The Mongol Invasions*. J.E. Brill, Leiden, 1963.

Hiên, Lê Nǎng, *Three Victories on the Bach Dang River*, Culture-Information Publishing House, Hà Nôi, 2003.

Hourani, George F., *Arab Seafaring*. Princeton University Press, Princeton, New Jersey, 1951.

Hsiao, Ch'i-Ch'ing, *The Military Establishment of the Yüan Dynasty*. Harvard East Asian Monographs; 77. Harvard University Press, Cambridge, 1978.

Inoguchi, Rikihei, Tadashi Nakajima and Roger Pineau, *The Divine Wind: Japan's Kamikaze Force in World War II*. United States Naval Institute Press, Annapolis, 1958.

Jansen, Marius B., editor, *Warrior Rule in Japan*. Cambridge University Press, Cambridge, New York and Melbourne, 1995.

Johnstone, Paul, *The Archaeology of Ships*. Henry Z. Walck Company, New York, 1974.

Keene, Donald, *Emperor of Japan: Meiji and His World, 1852–1912*. Columbia University Press, New York, 2002.

Kierman, Frank A., Jr., editor. *Chinese Ways in Warfare*. Harvard University Press, Cambridge, 1974.

Langlois, J.D., Jr., editor, *China under Mongol Rule*. Princeton University Press, Princeton, New Jersey, 1981.

Levathes, Louise, *When China Ruled the Seas: The Treasure Fleet of the Dragon Throne, 1405–1433*. Simon and Schuster, New York, 1994.

Lords Commissioners of the Admiralty, *Sailing Directions for Japan, Korea, and Adjacent Seas, from Yalu River, The Boundary Between Korea and China, to the Komandorski Islands, Also the Ogasawara (Bonin) Islands, &c., Southward of Japan, and the Kuril Islands, Formerly Published as China Sea Directory, Vol. IV, First Edition*. Published for the Hydrographic Office, Admiralty, by Eyre and Spottiswoode, London, 1904.

McGrail, Sean, *The Ship: Rafts, Boats and Ships from Prehistoric Times to the Medieval Era*. Her Majesty's Stationery Office, London, 1981.

Man, John, *Kublai Khan: The Mongol King Who Remade China*. Bantam Press, London, Toronto, Sydney, Auckland and Johannesburg, 2006.

Martin, Colin and Geoffrey Parker, *The Spanish Armada, Revised Edition*. Mandolin (Manchester University Press), Manchester, UK, 1999.

Mote, F.W., *Imperial China, 900–1800*. Harvard University Press, Cambridge and London, 1999.

Murdoch, James, *A History of Japan* (reprint of the 1903 edition). Routledge, London and New York, 1996.

Needham, Joseph, Ho Ping-Yü, Lu Gwei-Djen and Wang Ling, *Science and Civilization in China, Volume 4: Physics and Physical Technology Part 3: Civil Engineering and Nautics*. Cambridge University Press, London, New York, New Rochelle, Melbourne and Sydney, 1971.

——, *Science and Civilization in China, Volume 5: Chemistry and Chemical Technology, Part 7: Military Technology; The Gunpowder Epic*. Cambridge University Press, London, New York, New Rochelle, Melbourne and Sydney, 1971.

Nester, William R., *Power across the Pacific: A Diplomatic History of American Relations with Japan*. New York: New York University Press, 1996.

Nicolle, David, *The Mongol Warlords: Genghis Khan, Khubilai Khan, Hülegü, Tamerlane*. Brockhampton Books, London, 1990.

Nishimura, Shinji, *Ancient Rafts of Japan*. The Society of Naval Architects, Tokyo, 1925.

Ota, Kouki, *Moko Shurai—Sono Gunjiteki Kenkyu (Military Aspects of the Mongol Invasion)*. Kinseisha, Tokyo, 1997.

Perkins, Dorothy, *Encyclopedia of China: The Essential Reference to China, Its History and Culture*. Checkmark Books, New York, 1999.

Perkins, George W., editor and translator, *The Clear Mirror: A Chronicle of the Japanese Court During the Kamakura Period (1185–1333)*. Stanford University Press, Stanford, California, 1998.

Polo, Marco, *The Travels of Marco Polo*, translated and edited by Ronald Latham. Penguin Books, London and New York, 1958.

Prawdin, Michael, *The Mongol Empire: Its Rise and Legacy*. Transaction Publications, New Brunswick, New Jersey, 2006.

Rossabi, Morris, *Khubilai Khan: His Life and Times*. University of California Press, Berkeley, Los Angeles and London, 1988.

Sansom, George, *A History of Japan to 1334*. Stanford University Press, Stanford, California, 1958.

Saunders, J.J., *The History of the Mongol Conquests*. University of Pennsylvania Press, Philadelphia, 1971.

Sawyer, Ralph D., *Fire and Water: The Art of Incendiary and Aquatic Warfare in China*. Westview Press, Boulder, Colorado, 2004.

Schaffer, Lynda Norene, *Maritime Southeast Asia to 1500*. M.E. Sharpe, Armonk, New York and London, 1996.

Schottenhammer, Angela, editor, *The Emporium of the World: Maritime Quanzhou, 1000–1400*. Brill Academic Publishers, Leiden, Netherlands, 2001.

Sheftall, M.G., *Blossoms in the Wind: Human Legacies of the Kamikaze*. New American Library, New York, 2005.

Shiba, Yoshinobu, *Commerce and Society in Song China*. Translated by Mark Elvin. Center for Chinese Studies, University of Michigan, Ann Arbor, 1970.

So, Billy K.L., *Prosperity, Region and Institutions in Maritime China: The South Fukien Pattern, 946–1368*. Harvard University Asia Center and Harvard University Press, Cambridge, Massachusetts and London, 2000.

So, Kwan-wai, *Japanese Piracy in Ming China During the 16th Century*. Michigan State University Press, Lansing, 1975.

Stuart-Fox, Martin, *A Short History of China and Southeast Asia: Tribute, Trade and Influence*. Allen & Unwin, Crows Nest, New South Wales, Australia, 2003.

Swanson, Bruce, *Eighth Voyage of the Dragon: A History of China's Quest for Seapower*. Naval Institute Press, Annapolis, Maryland, 1982.

Tarling, Nicholas, editor, *The Cambridge History of Southeast Asia, Volume 1, Part 1: Early Times to c. 1500.* Cambridge University Press, Cambridge, New York, Port Chester, Melbourne and Sydney, 2000.

Ting, Joseph S.P., editor, *The Maritime Silk Route; 2000 years of trade on the South China Sea.* Hong Kong Museum of History, Hong Kong, 1996.

Totman, Conrad, *A History of Japan, Second Edition.* Blackwell Publishing, Malden, Massachusetts, Oxford and Carlton, Victoria, 2005.

Turnbull, Stephen R., *The Samurai: A Military History.* Osprey Publishing, London, 1977.

———, *Genghis Khan & the Mongol Conquests, 1190–1400.* Osprey Publishing, Botley, Oxford, 2003.

———, *Warriors of Medieval Japan.* Osprey Publishing, Botley, Oxford, 2005.

———, *The Samurai and the Sacred.* Osprey Publishing, Botley, Oxford, 2006.

Turnbull, Stephen and Wayne Reynolds, *Fighting Ships of the Far East (1): China and Southeast Asia 202 BC–AD 1419.* Osprey Publishing, Botley, Oxford, 2003.

———, *Fighting Ships of the Far East (2): Japan and Korea AD 612–1639.* Osprey Publishing, Botley, Oxford, 2003.

———, *Mongol Warrior, 1200–1350.* Osprey Publishing, Botley, Oxford, 2003.

United States Strategic Bombing Survey, *United States Strategic Bombing Survey Summary Report (Pacific War).* U.S. Government Printing Office, Washington, D.C., 1946.

Wang, Gungwu, *The Nanhai Trade: The Early History of Chinese Trade in the South China Sea,* reprint edition. Times Academic Press, Singapore, 1998.

———, *The Chinese Overseas: From Earthbound China to the Quest for Autonomy.* Harvard University Press, Cambridge, Massachusetts and London, England, 2000.

Weatherford, Jack, *Genghis Khan and the Making of the Modern World.* Crown Publishers, New York, 2004.

Wilkinson, Endymion, *Chinese History: A Manual.* Harvard University Asia Center and Harvard University Press, Cambridge, Massachusetts and London, 1998.

Williams, E. Leslie, Jr., *Spirit Tree: Origins of Cosmology in Shintō Ritual at Hakozaki.* University Press of America, Lanham, Maryland, 2006.

Yamada, Nakaba, *Ghenkō: The Mongol Invasion of Japan.* E.P. Dutton & Company, New York, 1916.

Yamamura, Kozo, editor, *The Cambridge History of Japan, Volume 3: Medieval Japan*. Cambridge University Press, Cambridge, New York, Port Chester, Melbourne and Sydney, 1990.

ARTICLES

Delgado, James P., "Relics of the Kamikaze," *Archaeology Magazine*, vol. 56, no. 1, January-February 2003, pp. 36–42.

———, "Shooting Down the Kamikaze Myth," *Naval History*, vol. 17, no. 3, June 2003, pp. 36–42.

Ellwood, Robert S., Jr., "Shintō and the Discovery of History of Japan," *Journal of the American Academy of Religion*, vol. 41, no. 4, December 1973, pp. 493–505.

Flecker, Michael, "A 9th-century Arab or Indian Shipwreck in Indonesian waters," *The International Journal of Nautical Archaeology*, vol. 29, no. 2, 2000, pp. 199–217.

———, "A 9th Century AD Arab or Indian Shipwreck in Indonesia: First Evidence for Direct Trade with China," *World Archaeology*, vol. 32, no. 3, 2001, pp. 335–354.

———, "The South-China-Sea Tradition: the Hybrid Hulls of South-East Asia," *The International Journal of Nautical Archaeology*, vol. 36, no. 1, 2007, pp. 75–90.

Gaunt, G.D. and A.M. Gaunt, "Mongol Archers of the Thirteenth Century," *Journal of the Society of Archer Antiquaries*, vol. 15, 1973, pp. 20–21.

Green, Jeremy, "The Song Dynasty Shipwreck at Quanzhou, Fujian Province, People's Republic of China," *The International Journal of Nautical Archaeology*, vol. 12, no. 3, 1983, pp. 253–261.

Green, Jeremy, Nick Burningham, and the Museum of Overseas Communication History, "The Ship from Quanzhou, Fujian Province, People's Republic of China," *The International Journal of Nautical Archaeology*, vol. 27, no. 4, 1998, pp. 277–301.

Green, Jeremy and Kim Z. "The Shinan and Wando Sites, Korea: Further Information," *The International Journal of Nautical Archaeology*, vol. 18, no. 1, 1989, pp. 33–41.

Groeneveldt, W.P., "The Expedition of the Mongols Against Java in 1293 A.D.," *China Review*, vol. IV (1875–1876), pp. 246–254.

Hazard, Benjamin H., "The Formative Years of The Wakō, 1223–63," *Monumenta Nipponica*, vol. 22, no. 3/4, 1967, pp. 260–277.

Hori, Kyotsu, "The Economic and Political Effects of the Mongol Wars," in John
    W. Hall and Jeffrey P. Mass, editors, *Medieval Japan: Essays in Institutional
    History*, pp. 184–198.

Jung, Yong-Hwan, Sang-Hyun Han, Taekyun Shin, and Moon You-Oh, "Genetic
    Composition of Horse Bone Excavated from the Kwakji Archaeological Site,
    Jeju, Korea," *Molecules and Cells*, vol. 14, No. 2, 2002, pp. 224–230.

Kapitan, Gerhard, "Ancient Two-Armed Stone-Stocked Wooden Anchors—
    Chinese and Greek," *The International Journal of Nautical Archaeology*, vol. 19,
    no. 3, 1990, pp. 243–245.

Keith, Donald H. and Christian J. Buys, "New Light on Medieval Chinese
    Seagoing Ship Construction," *The International Journal of Nautical Archaeology*,
    vol. 10, no. 2, 1981, pp. 119–132.

Kenderdine, Sarah, "Bai Jiao 1—The Excavation of a Song Dynasty Shipwreck
    in the Dinghai Area, Fujian Province, China, 1995," *The International Journal
    of Nautical Archaeology*, vol. 24, no. 4, 1995, pp. 247–266.

Kimura, Jun, "Recent Survey and Excavation on the Mongolian Fleet Sunk off
    Japan: The Takashima Underwater Site," *Bulletin of the Australasian Institute
    for Maritime Archaeology*, vol. 30, 2006, pp. 7–13.

Kogawa, Tetsuo, "Japan as a Manipulated Society," *Telos: A Quarterly Journal
    of Critical Thought*, no. 49, Fall 1981, pp. 138–141.

Li, Guoqing, "Ancient Chinese Anchors: The Rigging and Conservation,"
    The International Journal of Nautical Archaeology, vol. 27, no. 4, 1998,
    pp. 307–312.

Lo, Jung-Pang, "Maritime Commerce and Its Relation to the Song Navy," *Journal
    of the Economic and Social History of the Orient*, vol. 12, no. 1, January 1969,
    pp. 57–101.

———, "The Emergence of China as a Sea Power During the Late Song and Early
    Yüan Periods," *Far Eastern Quarterly*, vol. 14, 1955, pp. 489–503.

Martin, H.D., "The Mongol Army," *Journal of the Royal Asiatic Society*, 1943,
    pp. 46–85.

Michiaki, Okuyama, "Religious Nationalism in the Modernization Process:
    State Shintō and Nichirenism in Meiji Japan," *Nanzan Bulletin*, vol. 26, 2002,
    pp. 19–31.

Mozai, Torao, "The Lost Fleet of Khubilai Khan," *National Geographic*,
    vol. 162, no. 5, pp. 634–648.

————, "The Mongol Invasion Fleet of 1281: Recent Underwater Archaeological Finds," *Journal of the Pacific Society*, no. 18, April 1983, pp. 24–53.

Pearson, Richard, Li Min, and Li Guo, "Quanzhou Archaeology: A Brief Review," *International Journal of Historical Archaeology*, vol. 6, no. 1, March 2002, pp. 23–59.

Rambelli, Fabio, "Religion, Ideology of Domination, and Nationalism: Kuroda Toshio on the Discourse of *Shinkoku*," *Japanese Journal of Religious Studies*, vol. 23, nos. 3–4, 1996, pp. 387–426.

Rossabi, Morris, "All the Khan's Horses," *Natural History*, vol. 103, issue 10, October 1994, pp. 48–58.

Sasaki, Randall, "The Legend of Kamikaze: Nautical Archaeology in Japan," *The INA Quarterly*, vol.32, no. 1, Spring 2005, pp. 3–8.

————, "Where the Vessels Were Built: Reconstructing the Mongol Invasions of Japan," *The INA Quarterly*, vol. 33, no. 3, Fall 2006, pp. 16–22.

Shimin, Lin, Du Genqi, and Jeremy Green, "Waterfront Excavations at Dongmenkou, Ningbo, Zhe Jiang Province, PRC," *The International Journal of Nautical Archaeology*, vol. 20, no. 4, 1991, pp. 299–311.

Suzuki, Kazahiro, Hirotaka Oda, Mitsuhiko Ogawa, Etsuko Niu, Akiko Ikeda, Toshio Nakamura, and Akiko Matsuo, "C14 Dating of Wooden Anchors and Planks Excavated from Submerged Wrecks Located at Takashima in Imari Bay, Nagasaki Prefecture," *Proceedings of the Japan Academy, Series B, Physical and Biological Sciences*, vol. 77, no. 7, 2001, pp. 131–134.

Takayama, Hideko, "The Bay Was Packed With Ships," *Newsweek International Edition*, August 16, 2006, p. 52.

Tana, Li, "A View from the Sea: Perspectives on the Northern and Central Vietnamese Coast," *Journal of Southeast Asian Studies*, vol. 37, no. 1, February 2006, pp. 83–102.

Tōno, Haruyuki, "Japanese Embassies to T'ang China and Their Ships," *Acta Asiatica* 69 (1995): 39–62.

Williams, Richard, "The Divine Wind," *Weatherwise*, vol. 44, no. 5, October/November 1991, pp. 11–15.

Yang, Qin Zhang, "South-Song Stone Anchors in China, Korea and Japan," *The International Journal of Nautical Archaeology*, vol. 19, no. 2, 1990, pp. 113–121.

MANUSCRIPTS, DISSERTATIONS AND THESES

Hori, Kyutsu, "The Mongol Invasions and the Kamakura Bakufu," Ph.D. Dissertation, Columbia University, 1967.

Inoue, Takahiko, "A Nautical Archaeological Study of Kublai Khan's Fleets,"
M.A. Thesis, Texas A&M University, 1991.

Mozai, Torao, letter to James Delgado, December 23, 2006, in the possession
of the author.

Tsuruya, Mayu, "*Sensô Sakusen Kirokuga* (War Campaign Documentary
Painting): Japan's National Imagery of the "Holy War," 1937–1945," Ph.D.
Dissertation, University of Pittsburgh, 2005.

INTERNET RESOURCES

Blunt, Peter, "Mongolian Horse Talk—in the Home of Arvaiheer," http://mirror.
undp.org/momgolia/archives/ger-mag/issue3/horse.htm (accessed November
22, 2006).

China News, "Typhoon Haitang Causes Heavy Loss to Wenzhou," http://news.
xinhuanet.com/english/2005-07/20/content_3243247.htm (accessed
November 27, 2006).

Conlan, Thomas D., Kevin Travers, David Hamilton, Jennifer Snow, Christina
Goto, Greydon Foil, and Danny Yingst, "The Scrolls of the Mongol Invasions
of Japan" website, http://www.bowdoin.edu/mongol-scrolls/ (accessed
December 4, 2006).

"The Corner of the World," http://www.thecorner.org/hist/japan/meiji2.htm
(accessed December 3, 2006).

Heidorn, Keith C., *The Saffir-Simpson Hurricane Damage-Potential Scale* © 1999,
http://www.islandnet.com/~see/weather/elements/safsimp.htm (accessed
November 27, 2006).

Ichiyûsai Kuniyuki ga, Ôban triptych nishiki-e of the Mongol Invasion,
mid-1860s, http://www.osakaprints.com/content/artists/info_pp/kuniyuki_
info/kuniyuki_01a.htm (accessed November 15, 2006).

Kapur, Nick, "Divine Wind and Ancient Heroes: Reconstructing the
Kamikaze Idealogy," 1999, http://www.stanford.edu/~nickpk/writings/
Kamikaze.html (accessed March 9, 2002).

KOSUWA (Kyushu and Okinawa Society for Underwater Archaeology),
"Project Takashima: Takashima Underwater Site, The Report of the
Takashima-cho Cultural Asset Survey, 1992," http://www.h3.dion.
ne.jp/~uwarchae/project%20takashima.htm (accessed October 8, 2006).

———, "Project Takashima: Takashima Underwater Site II, The
Report of the Takashima-cho Cultural Asset Survey, 1993,"

http://www.h3.dion.ne.jp/~uwarchae/project%20takashima.htm (accessed October 8, 2006).

———, "Project Takashima: Takashima Underwater Site III, The Report of the Takashima-cho Cultural Asset Survey, 1996," http://www.h3.dion. ne.jp/~uwarchae/project%20takashima.htm (accessed October 8, 2006).

———, "Project Takashima: Takashima Underwater Site IV, The Report of the Takashima-cho Cultural Asset Survey, 2001," http://www.h3.dion. ne.jp/~uwarchae/project%20takashima.htm (accessed October 8, 2006).

———, "Project Takashima: Takashima Underwater Site V, The Report of the Takashima-cho Cultural Asset Survey, 2001," http://www.h3.dion. ne.jp/~uwarchae/project%20takashima.htm (accessed October 8, 2006).

———, "Project Takashima: Takashima Underwater Site VI, The Report of the Takashima-cho Cultural Asset Survey, 2002," http://www.h3.dion. ne.jp/~uwarchae/project%20takashima.htm (accessed October 8, 2006).

———, "Project Takashima: Takashima Underwater Site VIII, The Report of the Takashima-cho Cultural Asset Survey, 2003," http://www.h3.dion. ne.jp/~uwarchae/project%20takashima.htm (accessed October 8, 2006).

———, "Project Takashima: Takashima Underwater Site IX, The Report of the Takashima-cho Cultural Asset Survey, 2003," http://www.h3.dion. ne.jp/~uwarchae/project%20takashima.htm (accessed October 8, 2006).

———, "Project Takashima: Takashima Underwater Site X, The Report of the Takashima-cho Cultural Asset Survey, 2004," http://www.h3.dion. ne.jp/~uwarchae/project%20takashima.htm (accessed October 8, 2006).

Maritime Asia, "Asian Maritime & Trade Chronology to 1700 CE," http:// maritimeasia.ws/topic/chronology.html (accessed December 3, 2006).

———, "Ship Construction," http://maritimeasia.ws/topic/shiptypes.html (accessed December 3, 2006).

Olsen, Sandra L., "Nomadic Pastoralists, their Livestock, and their Landscape," www.carnegiemnh.org/anthro/olsen/mongolia4.html (accessed December 3, 2006).

Royal, Debbie, "The Mongol Invasion of Japan, The 'Divine Wind' Case," ICE Case Studies, number 181, Spring 2006, Inventory of Conflict and Environment (ICE), http://www.american.edu/ted/ice/divine-wind.htm (accessed December 4, 2006).

Sasaki, Randall, "Not So Divine Wind," (analysis of the ship timbers from the 2002–2004 seasons), http://nautarch.tamu.edu/shiplab/randall/ Upgrade2005/Notsodivinewind.htm (accessed November 20, 2006).

Wade, Geoff, "The Pre-Modern East Asian Maritime Realm: An Overview of European-Language Studies," Asia Research Institute Working Paper Series No. 16, National University of Singapore, http://www.ari.nus.edu.sg/docs/ wps/wps03_016.pdf (accessed December 6, 2006).

NOTES

Numbers at left refer to page numbers

PROLOGUE

8 "Soaring into the sky of the southern seas," is from Matsuo's final letter home, which is translated and reproduced in Inoguchi and Nakajima's *The Divine Wind*, p. 190.

9 Teruo Yamaguchi's final letter home is translated and reproduced in Inoguchi and Nakajima's *The Divine Wind*, pp. 187–189.

11 There are many accounts of the kamikaze corps; I have primarily drawn from Inoguchi and Nakajima, *The Divine Wind* and Sheftall, *Blossoms in the Wind*.

12 The comments made to Toshiharu Konada were related in an interview conducted by the author and translator Tomoko Nishizaki at Yasukuni Shrine, Tokyo, on August 30, 2002.

13 Neal Nunnelly's remarks are from his manuscript, *The Yellow Brick Road is Longer Than I Thought: Fifteen Years of Depression and War,* which details his personal experiences onboard USS *Anzio* (CVE-57) between April 1943 and February 1946. It is available online at www.historycentral.com/navy/stories/Anzio.html.

CHAPTER ONE

15 The story of Hakozaki Shrine was graciously provided by the priests and monks of the shrine. Information and images of the shrine are also available online in Japanese at http://www/yado/co/jp/tiiki/fukuoka/hakozaki/hakozaki.htm. E. Leslie Williams' *Spirit Tree: Origins of Cosmology in Shintō Ritual at Hakozaki* offers what the publisher describes as a "unique social psychological interpretation" of the rituals at Hakozaki, which Williams sees as an affirmation of the cognitive link between woman and earth.

17 Yamada describes the song in the introduction to *Ghenkō: The Mongol Invasion of Japan*, p. x.

18 The words to the song are reproduced in Yamada, *Ghenkō*, p. xx.

20 The story of the *Ghenkō Borui* is found on a detailed multipage handout, *Historic Site: Ghenkō-Borui*, by the Board of Education of Fukuoka City. The document offers an excellent summary of the wall's history, construction and archaeology and includes a detailed map of the sites where it and the monuments and memorials can be seen. On a trip in August 2002 I was able to visit sections of the wall. Bruce Batten, in *Gateway to Japan*, describes the wall and its construction and resurrection on pp. 48–49. There is also information online at http://bunkazai.city.fukuoka.jp/.

CHAPTER TWO

23 "Where roll the waves, there arises civilization," comes from the first page of an early twentieth-century Japanese history book by Yosaburo Takenokoshi, *Nisengohyakunen-shi* (2500 years of Japanese History), which Nishimura quotes on p. 6.

25 Gina Barnes's observations on the Yellow Sea Basin are found in *The Rise of Civilization in East Asia*, pp. 10–12.

27 The Suzhou and Xiaoshan boats were discussed in a November 21, 2002 release from the Xinhua News Agency, which quoted Jiang Leping, a "researcher with the Zhejiang Institute of Cultural Relics and Archaeology."

27 On the origins of the word "sampan," Needham, p. 380, note b.

27 On bamboo as the origin of bulkheads, Needham, pp. 389 391.

28 Nishimura on rafts and creation myth, pp. 6–23.

28 On the comparison between the Jōmon and the Native peoples of the Northwest Coast of America, Barnes, *The Rise of Civilization in East Asia*, p. 69.

28 Nishimura on the reed boat on the bronze bell—pp. 114–116. The bell was discovered in 1868 at the village of Oishi, in Echizen Province.

29 Japanese archaeological discoveries of ancient logboats and sea craft including the Yayoi fragments are discussed in Aikens and Higashi, *The Prehistory of Japan*, pp. 124, 238.

29 Chinese accounts from A D 32 on Korean embassies sailing to China, Turnbull, *Fighting Ships of the Far East*, p. 14.

29 Most heavily populated trading area, entry on Grand Canal, Perkins, *Encyclopedia of China*, p. 188.

29 The discussion of Yue's naval forces and trade is from Needham, pages 440–441, and "Asian Maritime & Trade Chronology to 1700 A D."

29   The fifth century BC bronze is discussed in Needham, p. 445.

30   The account of a King of Wu is discussed in Needham, p. 424.

31   Needham discusses and illustrates the Han tomb models on pp. 447–448.

31   Needham discusses the wooden tomb model on p. 447. It is also illustrated in Ting *et al*, *The Maritime Silk Road*, p. 49.

31   The *T'ai Pai Yin Ching* is discussed in Needham, pp. 685–686.

32   The description of the tower ships is cited by Needham, p. 685.

32   The Grand Canal discussion is drawn from Perkins, *Encyclopedia of China*, p. 188.

33   "the crews of the ships lived on board, they were born, married and died there," and "the sea-going junks are foreign ships" is cited by Needham, pp. 452–453, drawing on a T'ang document, *T'ang Yu Lin* (Miscellanea of the T'ang Dynasty).

33   Ibn Faqih's account is cited in Shen Fuwei, *Cultural Flow Between China and the Outside World*, p. 163.

34   The Belitung wreck is described in Flecker, "A 9th-century Arab or Indonesian Shipwreck."

34   The shift to the Yangtze Delta and "the center of Chinese civilization" is from Lo, "Maritime Commerce and Its Relation to the Song Navy," p. 59.

CHAPTER THREE

35   "In a hundred battles I have been at the forefront," is cited by Nicolle in *The Mongol Warlords*, page 9.

36   The discussion of Mongolian horses comes from the website of Carnegie Museum of Natural History curator Dr. Sandra L. Olsen, who discusses them in a larger article on these nomadic pastoralists, their livestock and their landscape at www.carnegiemnh.org/anthro/olsen/mongolia4.html.

36   "… horses and people depend on each other in Mongolia," is from "Mongolian Horse Talk—in the Home of Arvaiheer," a blog posted by Australian scholar and horseman Peter Blunt after a United Nations Development Programme trip to Mongolia, online at http://mirror.undp.org/momgolia/archives/ger-mag/issue3/horse.htm.

37   "… conquered and ruled the largest land empire in world history" is from Rossabi, *All the Khan's Horses*, p. 48.

37   On the speed of Mongol horsemen, Kennedy, *Mongols, Huns and Vikings*, p. 114.

37 On the accoutrement of a Mongol horseman, Rossabi, *All the Khan's Horses*, p. 49.

37 On the Mongolian bow, the best source is Gaunt and Gaunt, *Mongol Archers*.

37 I have based the discussion of Genghis's life on Weatherford, *Genghis Khan*, as well as Mote, *Imperial China*, pp. 414–434.

38 Minhaj al-Siraj's description of Genghis as "a man of tall stature, of vigorous build, robust in body" is cited by Weatherford, *Genghis Khan*, p. 6.

39 Genghis's organization of the Mongol Army is from Hsiao, *The Military Establishment of the Yüan Dynasty*, p. 9. It is also described and commented on in Weatherford, p. 52, Mote, *Imperial China*, p. 421, and Nicolle, *The Mongol Warlords*, p. 28.

39 "... based on mutual commitment and loyalty that transcended kinship, ethnicity and religion," and "a type of modern civic citizenship based upon personal choice and commitment," Weatherford, p. 58.

39 "... diehard collection of Mongol holdouts," Mote, *Imperial China*, p. 421.

40 "Mongol World War," Weatherford, p. 79.

40 "... overrun everything from the Indus River to the Danube, from the Pacific Ocean to the Mediterranean Sea," Weatherford, pp. 85–86.

40 On Mongol tactics under Genghis, Weatherford, p. 91. "There is no good in anything unless it is finished" is cited in Weatherford, p. 92.

41 "... the Mongols ordered that, apart from four hundred artisans whom they specified and selected," is from Juvaini's *History of the World Conqueror*, p. 162.

42 Ibn al-Athir's quote, "... have done things utterly unparalleled in ancient or modern times" is cited in Nicolle, *The Mongol Warlords*, p. 46.

44 "... swept through the city like hungry falcons attacking a flight of doves," is from Arab historian Wassaf, as quoted in Nicolle, *The Mongol Warlords*, p. 132.

CHAPTER FOUR

47 "... everyone should know that this Great Khan is the mightiest man," Marco Polo, *The Travels*, p. 113.

48 "... huge palace of marble and other ornamental stones... halls and chambers... all gilded," Marco Polo, *The Travels*, p. 125.

48 "... with gold and silver and decorated with pictures of dragons and birds and horsemen and various breeds of beasts and scenes of battle," "... extensive apartments, both chambers and halls, in which are kept the private

possessions of the Khan," and "The roof of the palace, ablaze with scarlet and green and blue and yellow and all the colours that are, so brilliantly varnished…" Marco Polo, *The Travels*, pp. 125–126.

49 "… for I can assure you that the Great Khan has such a store of vessels of gold and silver that no one who did not see it with his own eyes could well believe it…" Marco Polo, *The Travels*, p. 136.

49 "… remarkable feats… and the guests show their amusement by peals of laughter," Marco Polo, *The Travels*, p. 137.

50 "… splendidly adorned with pearls and gems and other ornaments," and "The cost of these robes, to the number of 156,000 in all, amounts to a quantity of treasure that is almost past computation…" Marco Polo, *The Travels*, p. 140.

50 The discussion of Khubilai in this chapter is derived from Rossabi's masterful biography of the Khan, Marco Polo, *The Travels*, Man, *Khubilai Khan*, and Mote, *Imperial China*. The comment on Khubilai's successful transition from a nomadic conqueror to the effective ruler of a sedentary society is from Rossabi, p. xi.

51 Rossabi's comments on the portrait are from Rossabi, *Khubilai Khan*, p. 66.

51 "… a man of good stature, neither short nor tall but of moderate height," Marco Polo, *The Travels*, pp. 121–122.

52 On Khubilai's second portrait, see Rossabi, p. 66.

52 Rashīd al-Dīn's comments on Sorghaghtani being "extremely intelligent and able," and a woman "who towered above all the women in the world" are cited in Rossabi, p. 12.

53 On Sorghaghtani's religion and character, see Rossabi, p. 13.

53 "… by his own valour and prowess and good sense; his kinsfolk and brothers tried to debar him from it, but by his great prowess he won it," and "… he showed himself a valiant soldier and a good commander," Marco Polo, *The Travels*, p. 113.

54 "… characteristically minute, even exhaustive preparations… leaving nothing to chance," and "his troops must be ready for any obstacle they encountered," Rossabi, *Khubilai Khan*, p. 24.

54 "… an aura of illegitimacy" that "would continue to haunt Khubilai through his reign," and this "may indeed have motivated some of his later military campaigns," Rossabi, p. 53.

55 "… there will be no punishment. But if the proposals are useful, the Court

will liberally promote and reward the persons who make the proposals" is cited by Rossabi, p. 118.

56 "... you might well say that he has mastered the art of alchemy," and "The... issue is as formal and as authoritative as if they were made of pure gold and silver," Marco Polo, *The Travels*, pp. 147–148.

56 "... rather miniscule for the size of the population, the nature of the opposition, and the level of violence at the time," Rossabi, *Khubilai Khan*, p. 130.

57 "Prisoners are not a mere flock of sheep," is cited by Rossabi, p. 130.

57 "... the most beautiful girls according to the standard of beauty" and the subsequent quotes and discussion of the selection of women for the harem is from Marco Polo, *The Travels*, pp. 122–123.

58 "... and I do honor and reverence to all four, so that I may be sure of doing it to him who is greatest in heaven and truest," Marco Polo, *The Travels*, p. 119.

58 "... he presented himself in different guises to the different audiences he faced," Rossabi, p. 175.

59 Sydenham's description of a gout attack, originally written in Latin, was translated and published as "A Treatise on Gout and Dropsy" in *Medical Classics* 4:354 (1939).

CHAPTER FIVE

61 "Our strength lies in cavalry which is unbeatable," is from the *Yüan shih*, the official Chinese dynastic history of the Yüan, which is cited by Lo in "China as a Sea Power," p. 492.

61 The discussion on Quanzhou is drawn from Clark, *Community, Trade and Networks*, pp. 3–4, 17, 33, 135, and So, *Prosperity, Region and Institutions in Maritime China*.

62 The Nanhai trade discussion is from Wang, *The Nanhai Trade*.

62 "... unmatched economic expansion," is from Clark, *Community, Trade and Networks*, p. 120. The discussion of the population increase is from Clark, pp. 3–4, and p. 74.

62 "... there are three prefectures that carry on trade relationships with the lands of the South Seas" is from the *Juazhai Wenji* (c. 1160), as cited by Clark, *Community, Trade and Networks*, p. 127.

63 Ibn Battuta's quote, "among the inhabitants of China" is cited by Needham, p. 470.

63   The discussion of the Quanzhou ship is taken from Keith and Buys, "New Light on Medieval Chinese Seagoing Ship Construction," Green, "The Song Dynasty Shipwreck at Quanzhou," Green, Burningham and the Museum of Overseas Communication History, "The Ship from Quanzhou," and from observations made by my good friend George Belcher of the Asia Maritime Foundation during his visit to the museum and ship in February 2006.

63   "… as large as any merchant vessel known from the same period in the West" is from Keith and Buys, p. 124.

65   "… the product of an evolutionary development of considerable antiquity" is from Keith and Buys, p. 124.

65   The discussion of the Quanzhou ship as a possible Southeast Asian and Chinese hybrid is from Green, Burningham and the Museum of Overseas Communication History, "The Ship from Quanzhou," pp. 296–297. It is also summarized and discussed on the Maritime Asia website's section on ship construction at http://www.maritimeasia.wa/topic/shiptypes.html Another good source is Flecker's "The South-China-Sea Tradition" article.

66   The discussion of the Song navy is from Lo, "The Emergence of China as a Sea Power," Lo, "Maritime Commerce and Its Relation to the Sung Navy," and Needham's excellent summary in Science and Civilization.

66   "China must now regard the Sea and River as her Great Wall" is from a naval memorial drafted by Chang I, Minister of Finance, in 1131, as cited in a 1635 document, Li-tai ming-ch-en tsoui (Memorials of Famous Ministers in History), in turn cited by Lo, "China as a Sea Power," p. 502.

67   The numbers of squadrons and naval troops is from Lo, "The Emergence of China as a Sea Power," p. 491.

67   The discussion of the Song's technological adaptations for the navy is from Lo, "China as a Sea Power," pp. 500–501.

67   "All of a sudden they appeared, and finding us quite unready they hurled incendiary gunpowder projectiles on to our ships" is cited by Needham in Science and Civilization in China, Volume 5, Chemistry and Chemical Technology, Part 7: Military Technology; The Gunpowder Epic, p. 157.

68   "… rushed forth from behind [the island] on both sides" is from Needham, p. 166.

69   Marco Polo's description of Zaiton is from The Travels, p. 237.

69   Al-Idrisi's account is from his Geography, cited in Fuwei, Cultural Flow Between China and the Outside World, pp. 159–161.

70 The description of the Nanhai-1 wreck is from an article, "Song Dynasty Shipwreck to Emerge from Water" in the *People's Daily* of March 7, 2003, which was available online at http://www.china.org.cn.

70 The shifting nature of China's port city urban dwellers is from So, *Prosperity, Region and Institutions in Maritime China*, pp. 281–282 and Shiba, *Commerce and Society in Sung China*, pp. 126–128. The minister who described city dwellers as either merchants or artisans was Wang Chieh, as quoted in Shiba, p. 127.

70 "... profits from maritime commerce are very great. If properly managed, they can amount to millions" is cited by Levathes in *When China Ruled the Seas*, p. 41.

70 The discussion of the *Shih-po ssu*, duties and government revenues is from Lo, "Maritime Commerce," pp. 66–69, and is also discussed at length by Clark, So and Shiba.

70 "... unending vistas of tea-shrubs and mulberry trees" that looked like "a sea on land" is from an account by Yeh Shao-weng, *Ssu-ch'ao wen-chien lu (Experiences of Four Reigns)* as cited in Shiba, *Commerce and Society in Sung China*, p. 46.

71 "... the rest of the men were weary, dispirited, deaf, moronic, emaciated, short and frail," is cited by Lo in "Maritime Commerce and its Relation to the Sung Navy," p. 92.

71 "... the defense of this gateway to the country is now left in a state of impotence," Lo, "Maritime Commerce," p. 93.

72 The role of the Persian artillery is discussed in Franke and Twichett, *The Cambridge History of China*, vol. 6, p. 453.

72 The discussion of the fall of the Song and the various battles is drawn from *The Cambridge History of China*, vol. 6, pp. 431–435.

CHAPTER SIX

75 Ōtomo's poem, from the *Man'yōshū* poetry anthology, is reproduced in Batten, *Gateway to Japan*, p. 42. His source was Paula Doe's *A Warbler's Song in the Dusk: The Life and Works of Ōtomo Yakamochi (718–785)*, (University of California Press, Berkeley and Los Angeles, 1982), pp. 219–220.

76 The destruction of Fukuoka is detailed in the reports of the United States Strategic Bombing Survey and in the history of the 9th Bomb Group.

79 The story of the Fukuoka City Museum is from the museum's website as well as the City of Fukuoka's English-language online tourism guide. Details of

the exhibitions and a sense of this amazing museum also come from a visit to the Fukuoka City Museum in August 2002.

79　The story of the gold seal is from the museum website, and Barnes, *The Rise of Civilization*, p. 218.

81　"… advanced continental culture in Japan" and "Hakata prospered as an international city," are from the Fukuoka City Museum website's description of the permanent exhibition.

82　The rise of and role of the *sakimori* is related by Batten in *Gateway to Japan*, pp. 41–45.

82　"24 hours a day, 365 days a year" is from Batten, *Gateway to Japan*, p. 33.

83　The Mizuki construction estimate is from Batten, *Gateway to Japan*, p. 31, who cites an exhaustive Japanese report that summarizes thirty years of excavation at and around Dazaifu. Batten's own scholarship is just as impressive, and this chapter is indebted to his masterful summary of Japanese and English language sources.

83　The description of Mizuki is from Batten, *Gateway to Japan*, p. 35.

83　Dazaifu as a "barrier," is from the *Nihon Montoku tenno jitsuroku*, Ninju 2, correspondence dated 2/8/852, and cited in Batten, *Gateway to Japan*, p. 41.

83　The disbanding of the *sakimori* is described by Batten, p. 46.

83　The concept and the wording of the "geopolitical competition" is from Batten, *Gateway to Japan*, p. 48.

83　Batten summarizes why Japan was not in danger of a real invasion on pp. 48–49.

84　The purchases of the nobles in AD 752 are summarized by Batten on p. 63.

84　The dates of the first Korean and Chinese trade ships at Hakata are from Batten, p. 112.

84　The *Shinsarugakuki* account of Chinese trade goods is summarized by Batten on pp. 114–115.

85　Hakata as a "diaspora community" and "Chinatown," is from Batten, *Gateway to Japan*, p. 122. Also see Batten, *To the Ends of Japan*, p. 189.

85　Hakata, "of, for and by" merchants, Batten, *Gateway to Japan*, p. 124.

85　The commodities of twelfth-century maritime trade are cited by Totman, *A History of Japan*, pp. 109 and 155 and Sansom, *A History of Japan to 1334*, p. 423. The discussion of Song coins is also from Totman, page 109 and Sansom, p. 423.

86 Batten summarizes the pirate raids and the Toi invasion in *Gateway to Japan*, pp. 86–101.

CHAPTER SEVEN

87 "Of so great celebrity was the wealth of this island, that a desire was excited in the breast of the grand khan Kublaï now reigning," Marco Polo, *The Travels*, p. 244.

88 The discussion of the reasons for the invasion is drawn from Rossabi, *Khubilai Khan*, Sansom, *A History of Japan*, Mote, *Imperial China*, Yamada, *Ghenkō*, and Conlan, *In Little Need of Divine Intervention*. The first to suggest the invasion as a means to strangle the Song trade link to Hakata was Hori in "Mongol Invasions," pp. 107–111. Rossabi agrees, commenting, "by defeating the Japanese, he [Khubilai] could sever the trade links between his two enemies, thus weakening the Sung," p. 102.

88 "… brought Korea within the orbit of his newly formed dynasty" Rossabi, p. 97.

88 The discussion of the shift in the Hakata trade is from Batten, *Gateway to Japan*, and So, *Prosperity, Region and Institutions in Maritime China*.

89 "From time immemorial, rulers of small states have sought to maintain friendly relations with one another." Khubilai's letter has been translated more than once, and there are differences in the wording. I have drawn from Murdoch's more flowery and extensive translation in *A History of Japan*, pp. 499–500, but have made note of significant interpretations by Yamamura in the *Cambridge History of Japan* (p. 132), which smooth out some of the more awkward phrasing.

90 "… recently, we learned that the Mongols have become inclined toward evil and are now trying to subjugate Japan", is cited by Yamamura in the *Cambridge History of Japan*, p. 136.

91 "… equivalent of a declaration of war by Japan," Sansom, *A History of Japan*, p. 441.

91 "… the Mongols desire to conquer Japan. Once Japan's warriors are under their control, they will be able to conquer China and India" is cited by Conlan, *In Little Need of Divine Intervention*, p. 201.

91 "… defend against the foreigners and protect your holdings against bandits," is cited by Conlan, *In Little Need of Divine Intervention*, p. 202.

92 "They were released from shackles and spared capital punishment" and "they were allowed to establish squads for themselves in order to subjugate Japan," Hsiao, *The Military Establishment of the Yüan Dynasty*, p. 82, which quotes the *Yüan-shih*, the official dynastic history or record of Khubilai's rule.

92 "... furious discharge of arrows as heavy as rain," Yamada, *Ghenkō*, p. 110.

92 "Through the use of superior weapons the enemy stepped ashore without great loss," Yamada, p. 111.

92 "... several strokes in hot strife" Yamada, p. 113.

93 "... old hunting spears, rusted blades, poles, sticks and bats, stones and pebbles in sacks, or whatever they could lay their hands on," Yamada, p. 118.

93 On "blood-stained horses," Yamada, p. 128.

93 "... calmly," says the legend, turning "themselves to ashes with their palace," Yamada, p. 129.

93 Yamada recounts the stripping, palm-piercing and hanging of the women from the ships on pp. 129–130. The scene is also depicted in Japanese prints and starkly in bronze at the Nichiren monument in Fukuoka.

94 "... unnumbered white pennants, with coats or arms painted thereupon, wave in the north wind," Yamada, p. 134.

94 "... almost all the Japanese horses went mad," Yamada, p. 135.

95 "We won't limit ourselves to merely shooting down the enemy!" Suenaga's account is cited by Conlan, *In Little Need of Divine Intervention*, p. 40.

95 "... more of our men are coming. Wait for reinforcements!" and "The way of the bow and arrow is to do what is worthy of reward!" Conlan, citing Suenaga, p. 64.

95 "... formidable squad of horsemen," Conlan, citing Suenaga, p. 64.

95 The image of ringing steel and sparks in the darkening sky is from Yamada, p. 140.

96 Conlan's discussion of the battle and the numbers of troops is recounted by him in *In Little Need of Divine Intervention*, pp. 261–263. Conlan does a masterful job in reconstructing the invasions and sorting through Suenaga's scroll. I have also relied on Yamada and Turnbull, *The Samurai* in my discussion of the battle.

96 "... it is of first importance that we give them a good rest tonight and to supply them with new weapons." Yamada, p. 142.

96 "… we lamented all through the night, thinking that we were doomed and would be destroyed to the last man." As cited in Turnbull, *The Samurai*, p. 91.

97 "… a great storm arose and many warships were dashed on the rocks and destroyed," from Conlan's citation of the *Yüan-shi*, p. 266.

97 Kadenokoji Kanenaka's diary entry about "several tens of thousands of invaders' boats came sailing in on the high seas" is cited by Conlan, p. 266.

CHAPTER EIGHT

99 Tameuji's poem is cited in Perkins, *The Clear Mirror*, p. 125.

99 "… most prolific generator of large cyclonic storms," Williams, "The Divine Wind," p. 15.

100 "It has come to our attention… a great number of men faced the battlefield but did not attack," from the records of the Kamakura *bakufu*, the *Kamakura ibun*, as cited by Conlan, *In Little Need of Divine Intervention*, p. 207.

102 "In consultation with the king and the generals a plan of attack was agreed upon," is cited by Sansom, *A History of Japan to 1334*, pp. 448–449.

102 I have based my discussion of Khubilai's preparations on Sansom, Rossabi, *Khubilai Khan*, and Hsiao, *The Military Establishment of the Yüan Dynasty*. The discussion of unrest in Southern China because of the demands for ships and seamen is from Hsiao, p. 203.

103 The discussion of the Mongol horses on Cheju-do Island is from Jung, Han, Shin and Oh, "Genetic Composition of Horse Bone…"

104 "I said 'the enemy is separated from us by the sea. I cannot fight them during this crisis without a ship,'" and "If you don't have a ship, then there is nothing to be done" is from the *Moko Shurai Ektoba*, as cited by Conlan, p. 133.

104 "Since I am a warrior of considerable stature, let me alone get on the boat!" and "why must you make such a fuss?" Conlan, citing Suenaga, p. 154.

105 "… get close! I want to board!" Conlan, citing Suenaga, p. 179. In describing Suenaga's actions on the enemy ship, I have relied on a full-color, bound reproduction of the scrolls and line drawings of the scenes in Conlan, pp. 157–160.

105 "… the daring assailants set the ship on fire and were off, carrying away twenty-one heads," "keep themselves within the walls," "intrepid men of this

sort," "being swifter and lighter were more easily managed" and "many of them were sunk by the darts and the huge stones hurled by the catapults," from Yamada, *Ghenkō*, p. 185.

106 "... without your own boat, you repeatedly lied in order to join the fray. You really are the *baddest* man around!" Conlan, citing Suenaga, who cites *shugo* Gōta Gorō, p. 155.

107 "... a report arrived from Dazaifu... a typhoon sank most of the foreign pirates' ships" is from the diary of Kadenokoji Kanenaka's as cited by Conlan, p. 272.

107 "They were butted together like mad bulls," Yamada, pp. 193–194.

108 "A terrible catastrophe occurred. The vessels were jammed together in the offing," is cited by Murdoch in *A History of Japan*, p. 522.

108 "... leaving more than a hundred men at Taka Isle," is from the *Yüan-shi*, as cited by Yamada, p. 195.

108 The number of executed prisoners is from the *Yüan-shi*, as cited by Conlon, pp. 269–270.

109 "A *ninnō-e* curse against the Mongols shall be created and recorded" is from the private diary of courtier Yoshida Tsunenaga, who recorded the edict. It is cited by Conlan, pp. 246–247.

109 "I beseech you to take my life if Japan suffers damage from this disturbance in my time," was reportedly sent to the shrine in a prayer written in Emperor Kameyama's own hand as cited in Perkins, *The Clear Mirror*, p. 125.

109 "... protection of the gods! Most wonderful! We should praise the gods without ceasing," is from the diary of Kadenokoji Kanenaka, as cited and translated by Conlan, pp. 266–267.

109 "This event reveals unprecedented divine support," is from the diary of Kadenokoji Kanenaka, as cited and translated by Conlan, p. 272.

109 "... reached their climax, a single black cloud suddenly appeared in the clear sky," is in Perkins, *The Clear Mirror*, p. 125.

110 "... made false representations... that he had reached Japan" is from the *Yüan-shi*, as cited by Conlon, p. 266. Fan's role is also discussed in Hsiao, *The Military Establishment of the Yüan Dynasty*, p. 201.

110 "... he sent two of his barons with a great fleet of ships carrying cavalry and infantry," is from Marco Polo's *Description of the World*. I have drawn from the Penguin Classic edition edited by Ronald Latham,

pp. 244–246. The discussion of its accuracy is from Haw, *Marco Polo's China*, pp. 160–162.

111 The consequences of the Mongol invasions for the *bakufu* are discussed in Yamamura, *Cambridge History of Japan*, reproduced in Jensen, *Warrior Rule in Japan*, pp. 44–76, and Hori, "The Economic and Political Effects of the Mongol Wars."

CHAPTER NINE

112 "The Japanese have the idea that their land is the country of the Gods," is from Yamada's introduction to *Ghenkō*, p. ix.

113 "... as a realm where gods and buddhas mingled with men" is from Conlan, *State of War*, p. 166. I also consulted Turnbull's *The Samurai and the Sacred*.

113 *God is My Co-Pilot.* Ballantine Books released Col. Robert L. Scott's bestseller as a mass paperback in 1943; its success led to a 1945 Warner Brothers film by the same name.

113 "... little more than an autumn wind and a tiny amount of water" is cited by Conlan, *In Little Need of Divine Intervention*, p. 275.

113 The account of the priest of the Takeo Shrine is from Hori, "Economic and Political Effects of the Mongol Wars," p. 187.

114 My discussion of the *Wakō* is based on Hazard, "The Formative Years of The Wakō, 1223–63" and So, *Japanese Piracy in Ming China During the 16th Century.*

114 "The Mongols, who are barbarians... wanted to turn us into their subjects," is from the *Ming-shi*, the official Chinese history of the Ming Dynasty, as quoted in So, *Japanese Piracy in Ming China*, p. 162.

116 "... despite some inaccuracies in the picture, the public can surely imagine the true scene," is from the website of Osaka Prints, which was offering the triptych wood block print for sale in November 2006. Attributed to the artist Kuniyuki, it was online at http://www.osakaprints.com/content/artists/info_pp/kuniyuki_info/kuniyuki_01a.htm (accessed November 15, 2006).

117 The discussion on the rise of Meiji Japan is drawn from Keene, *Emperor of Japan*, and was greatly assisted by "The Corner of the World," a history educational website from Hong Kong, which has an excellent summary outline of the rise of Meiji Japan at http://www.thecorner.org/hist/japan/meiji2.htm.

119 The discussion of the fate of Suenaga's scrolls is from Conlan, *In Little Need of Divine Intervention*, pp. 7–11.

119 "Because of the legendary and supernatural implications that accumulated along with the stories that they told," is from Tsuraya, *Sensô Sakusen Kirokuga*, p. 109.

119 Yada's paintings are reproduced in the 1979 reprint of Yamada, *Ghenkô*. I have seen prints of the paintings on Takashima. The originals are at the Mongol Invasion Museum next to the Nichiren shrine in Fukuoka. Designated a Prefectural cultural treasure, they were recently restored by the Fukuoka Art Museum. Yada's painting of atrocities against the women of Iki inspired a very different response in the 1930s, when a series of lithographed drawings appeared as a form of *hentai*, or pornography. One particular aspect of Japanese pornography, prevalent for decades, is *Ero Guro*, the depiction of rape, savagery and brutality against women, and the Mongol actions on Iki fit the bill perfectly.

120 "… we shall someday raise the national power of Japan so that not only shall we control the natives of China and India," is cited by Nester, *Power across the Pacific*, p. 63.

121 The discussion of Meiji religious policies is from Michiaki, "Religious Nationalism in the Modernization Process: State Shintō and Nichirenism in Meiji Japan,"and Kogawa, "Japan as a Manipulated Society." "The Corner of the World" website was also helpful with its synthesis of ideas.

122 "… life-staking activities for establishing righteousness and secure the peace of the nation be remembered forever," is from the English language handout at the Nichiren shrine and statue in Fukuoka.

123 Bix, in *Hirohito and the Making of Modern Japan*, comments that the Emperor's naval aide, Lt. Commander Eiichirō Jō, was a descendant of Kyushu warrior Takefusa Kikuchi, a veteran of the Mongol wars. "This background surely figured in Jō's later determination to save Japan from the American fleet by drawing up the first detailed plan for a "kamikaze" Special Attack Corps in June 1943," p. 451.

123 "… for the great cause of our country" and "signified a constant and deeply grounded belief" is from Inoguchi and Nakajima, *The Divine Wind*, page xvi.

CHAPTER TEN

126 The discussion of Torao Mozai's life is based on interviews and conversations with Dr. Mozai at Takashima on August 23, 2002, from materials provided by him, and in a detailed letter he wrote in answer to several questions on December 23, 2006.

128 "The interpretation of this story is very controversial," "simply not possible to interpret the story in any logical way" and "student of naval history as well as a professor of engineering," is from Mozai, "The Mongol Invasion Fleet of 1281," p. 51, and "The Lost Fleet of Kublai Khan," p. 636.

129 "Objects made of the hardest materials, such as stone, metal or porcelain," is from Mozai, "The Lost Fleet of Kublai Khan," p. 640.

130 *Bosatsu* is the Japanese term for an enlightened being that takes upon themself the suffering of all human beings.

130 "In less than two weeks our diving team recovered iron spearheads," is from Mozai, "The Lost Fleet of Kublai Khan," p. 644.

130 "... probably worn by a thirteenth century Mongol cavalry officer" and "no thought nor concern given to my age," is from Mozai, "The Lost Fleet of Kublai Khan," p. 644, and "The Mongol Invasion Fleet of 1281," p. 41.

130 "... revered by the Mongols as a protector for their armies" is from Mozai, "The Lost Fleet of Kublai Khan," p. 646.

131 "I immediately realized the seal was a national treasure," and "caused a great sensation in Japan" is from Mozai, "The Mongol Invasion Fleet of 1281," p. 36.

132 "... we still have not made the discovery of a Mongol ship itself" is from Mozai, "The Mongol Invasion Fleet of 1281," p. 36.

132 The discussion of the museum on Takashima is based on visits made in August 2002.

133 Kenzo Hayashida's biographical information is based on discussions with him in August 2002 and an interview with Randall Sasaki on October 13, 2006. The biographical information about George Bass is based on discussions with Dr. Bass throughout 2006, and in part on Bass, *Archaeology Beneath the Sea*.

135 "... one of the best archaeological documents for... the Mongolian armada," is from KOSUWA's Project Takashima report of 1996.

135 The discussion of the 1994–2002 excavations is drawn from KOSUWA's online, English summaries of their annual reports to the Takashima-cho Board of Education, from discussions with Kenzo Hayashida in August 2002 and Randall Sasaki in October 2006, and from Kimura's excellent overview article.

137 On the "last" field season in the summer of 2002, based on discussions with Kenzo Hayashida at Kozaki harbor, August 2002.

137 The discussion of the 2002 excavation season comes from observations made while visiting and diving at the site in August, thanks to the gracious permission of Kenzo Hayashida and KOSUWA, and as discussed in detail in KOSUWA, "Project Takashima" and Delgado, "Relics of the Kamikaze."

138 Sasaki's comment, "These pieces were put in a blender of sea and were mixed together," is from Takayama, "The Bay Was Packed With Ships," p. 52.

138 "It is possible there were many uses of this weapon—killing the enemy, blinding the enemy," is a quote from an interview with Kenzo Hayashida on August 15, 2002. KOSUWA and the Takashima Board of Education's press release on the *tetsuhau* was released on August 10, 2002. The story, in Japanese, did not reach the west until a year later. Delgado, "Relics of the Kamikaze," p. 41.

139 The discussion of the bones, armor and bowl with Wang's name and rank is based on observations of the site while diving on it before they were removed, on August 14, 2002, as well as a discussion with Kenzo Hayashida on August 15, 2002.

139 The ranking and commonality of the Wang surname is from a Beijing *People's Daily* article of July 30, 2002, which notes "After years of study, Yuan Yida, associate research fellow of Institute of Genetics and Development Biology, Chinese Academy of Sciences found that China's three largest surnames Li, Wang, Zhang account respectively for 7.9, 7.4 and 7.1 percent of the population. They feature a total number of 270 million, being the three large surnames of the world."

CHAPTER ELEVEN

140 Sasaki's quote is from "Where the Vessels Were Built," p. 22.

141 The discussion of Randall Sasaki is based on an interview with him at the

Institute of Nautical Archaeology offices at Texas A&M University on October 13, 2006.

142 I was the visiting scholar who gave the "brown bag" talk and then provided Randy Sasaki with Kenzo Hayashida's email address. While Randy, with his perseverance, would have doubtless tracked Kenzo down in short time, I am pleased and humbled that such a minor contribution brought them together and am impressed by the dedication and scholarship that Randy Sasaki has brought to KOSUWA and to the Takashima project.

142 "It is analogous to reconstructing 4,000 different jigsaw puzzles" is from Sasaki, "The Legend of Kamikaze," p. 5. "Those pieces were put into a blender of sea" is cited by Takayama in "The Bay Was Packed With Ships."

143 The discussion of the 2003 and 2004 excavations is from KOSUWA's online archaeological report summaries.

144 The attitude of the Japanese archaeological establishment is taken from my own observations, as well as from discussions with other scholars who have noted the curious lack of discussion of nautical or maritime archaeology in Japanese archaeological journals. Gina Barnes's excellent summary of Japanese (and Chinese and Korean) archaeology has few references to Japanese nautical archaeology, and no mention of KOSUWA's work—not because of Barnes's lack of interest, but no doubt because of the fact that the work at Takashima has been conducted in a veritable professional vacuum with the exception of scientific analysis of some of the discoveries.

144 "… nautical archaeology has yet to be developed in Japan" and "no funding from any Japanese institution was available," is from Sasaki, "The Legend of Kamikaze," p. 5.

145 The discussion of the timber analysis is from KOSUWA, Sasaki, "The Legend of Kamikaze," and "Where the Vessels Were Built."

146 Takano's reconstruction of probable storm strength is cited by Takayama in "The Bay Was Packed With Ships."

146 The Saffir-Simpson storm statistics are taken from an excellent online summary, *The Saffir-Simpson Hurricane Damage-Potential Scale* © 1999, by Keith C. Heidorn, PhD., available at http://www.islandnet.com/~see/weather/elements/safsimp.htm (accessed November 27, 2006).

146 The discussion of Typhoon Haitang is from a *China View* story of July 20, 2005, "Typhoon Haitang Causes Heavy Loss to Wenzhou," available online

at http://news.xinhuanet.com/english/2005-07/20/content_3243247.htm
(accessed November 27, 2006) and from NASA, which published images of
the storm at http://www.nasa.gov/mission_pages/hurricanes/archives/2005/
h2005_haitang.html.

147 The discussion on the nail holes and the mast step is from Sasaki, "The Legend of Kamikaze," p. 4 and pp. 6–7.

149 The discussion of the anchor is from discussions with Kenzo Hayashida
on August 13, 2002. I have also drawn from Kapitan, "Ancient Two-Armed
Stone-Stocked Wooden Anchors," and Yang, "South-Song Stone Anchors
in China, Korea and Japan."

150 "... the real cause for the failure of the invasion" and "if the ships were built
more carefully," is from Sasaki, "The Legend of Kamikaze," p. 5.

150 Turnbull's comment on the typhoon's limited effectiveness is from *The
Samurai and the Sacred*, p. 61.

152 The discussion of the final analysis and Sasaki's views on the nature of the
ships at Takashima and the reasons for the failure of the invasion are drawn
from an interview with him at College Station on October 13, 2006 and from
his article, "Where the Ships Were Built." I am deeply indebted to Randy
for his generous and gracious sharing of his thinking.

CHAPTER TWELVE

154 "... especially simple, with a single mast standing in the middle of the ship,"
is cited by Turnbull, "Fighting Ships of the Far East," p. 15.

155 "Korean vessels were strong, but small," is cited by Sasaki in "Where the
Vessels Were Built," p. 17. His observations on the relative lack of Korean
vessels (and artifacts) at Takashima is on p. 22. I have also utilized Turnbull,
Fighting Ships of the Far East (2).

156 The discussion of the history of Vietnam benefited from Tarling, *The Cambridge History of Southeast Asia*, and Stuart-Fox, *A Short History of China and
Southeast Asia*. On matters of maritime trade and the role of shipping, Tana,
"A View from the Sea: Perspectives on the Northern and Central Vietnamese Coast," was very helpful.

156 The discussion of Khubilai's invasion of Vietnam benefited from discussions in Vietnam at the Military History Museum, from Tarling, *The
Cambridge History of Southeast Asia*, pp. 148–149, 155, Stuart-Fox, *A Short*

History of China and Southeast Asia, pp. 58–61, and Rossabi, *Khubilai Khan*, pp. 216–218.

161 The discussion of the Battle of the Bach Đằng River benefitted, in addition to the other sources consulted for the Vietnam campaigns, from Lê Nẵng Hiên, *Three Victories on the Bach Dang River*, and a story by Nyugen Minh Huong, "Spears Offer Insight into early Military Strategy," *Vietnam News*, January 22, 2006.

163 "... since the past, the Bach Đằng has been red with blood," is from Lê Nẵng Hiên, *Three Victories on the Bach Dang River*, p. 137.

164 The discussion of Java's history benefited from Tarling, *The Cambridge History of Southeast Asia*, Stuart-Fox, *A Short History of China and Southeast Asia*, and Shaffer, *Maritime Southeast Asia to 1500*.

165 The discussion of the Mongol invasion of Java benefited, in addition to the other sources consulted for Java, from Groeneveldt, "The Expedition of the Mongols against Java in 1293, A D."

165 "... to send out a thousand ships and to equip them with provisions" is from the *Yüan-shi*, as cited by Groeneveldt, "The Expedition of the Mongols against Java," p. 246.

166 "... in order to prepare a new letter of submission" is from the *Yüan-shi*, as cited by Groeneveldt, "The Expedition of the Mongols against Java," p. 249.

EPILOGUE

168 "I sent my fleet against men, not against the wind and the waves," is cited by Martin and Parker in *The Spanish Armada*, p. 237.

169 The discussion of the Khan's failure benefited from a review of Rossabi, *Khubilai Khan*, pp. 212–213, Weatherford, *Genghis Khan*, pp. 210–212.

172 The "Great Khan is the mightiest man, whether in respect of subjects or of territory or of treasure," is from the Latham edition of *The Travels of Marco Polo*, p. 113.

172 "They have gold in the greatest abundance, its sources being inexhaustible," is from Latham, p. 244.

174 Electronic Arts released *Shogun Total War: Mongol Invasion* in August 2001. Details are available at http://www.totalwar.com (accessed November 19, 2006).

174 "… will the knowledge of science bring the God's power to an end?" is from Yamada, *Ghenkō*, p. ix.

175 Mozai's quote comes from an interview at Takashima conducted on August 14, 2002.

176 "I believe that further investigation will one day reveal the true nature of this event" is from Sasaki, "Where the Ships Were Built," p. 22.

177 The discussion of the present day circumstances of the site and funding comes from an interview with Randall Sasaki at College Station, Texas, on October 15, 2006.

177 The archaeological value of the site is based on personal observations, the interviews with Sasaki and Hayashida, and the excellent overview essay on Asian maritime and nautical archaeology by Geoff Wade, "The Pre-Modern East Asian Maritime Realm."

www.vintage-books.co.uk